AF600328

THE CATHOLIC UNIVERSITY OF AMERICA
CANON LAW STUDIES
No. 190

NATIONAL PARISHES IN THE UNITED STATES

by

JOSEPH E. CIESLUK, J.C.L.
Priest of the Diocese of Grand Rapids

A DISSERTATION

Submitted to the Faculty of the School of Canon Law of the Catholic University of America in Partial Fulfillment of the Requirements for the Degree of Doctor of Canon Law

THE CATHOLIC UNIVERSITY OF AMERICA PRESS
WASHINGTON, D. C.
1944

Nihil Obstat:

EDUARDUS G. ROELKER, S.T.D., J.C.D.,
Censor Deputatus.

Washingtonii, D. C., die 17 maii, 1944.

Imprimatur:

✠ FRANCISCUS J. HAAS, D.D., LL.D.,
Episcopus Grandormensis.

Grandormii, die 17, 1944.

Printed by
THE PAULIST PRESS
401 West 59th Street
New York 19, N. Y.

51

TABLE OF CONTENTS

FOREWORD

THE essential mission that Christ gave to Peter and to the Apostles was to teach the doctrine of salvation to all men regardless of race or color. This mission the Apostles and the disciples undertook with determined zeal and divine inspiration. Though they were cast among people of various nationalities and languages, they placed the foundation of an ecclesiastical structure that was destined to continue to the end of time. Since truth is eternal it is not to be constrained by differences of language or nationality, but is to find its way into the hearts of all men of good will, whether they are cast in the common mold of one nation, or whether, when separated from the ties of family and country, they work out their destiny in another land.

In the infant Church there is meager if any reference to national or language differences. The first Christian communities undoubtedly were those converted from Judaism, but the doctrine rapidly spread to the Gentiles, and was accepted so warmly that Peter was prompted to say, "now I really understand that God is not a respecter of persons, but in every nation he who fears him and does what is right is acceptable to him" (Acts x. 34-35). The success of the mission of the Apostles was based on the fact that they preached not themselves but Christ, that all might have life more abundantly.

Christ founded the Church, but the further organization and government of the Church was left to those who were to continue His mission here upon earth. In the early centuries, both Jew and Gentile worshiped in the common bond of faith, and a distinct parochial organization for each was not developed. Consequently in Apostolic times one can find no general legislation concerning parishes established for national or language groups within the political boundaries of another country. This legislation appeared only when parishes were comparatively well established.

During the last century, and also in the early decades of the twentieth century, many national parishes were established in this country. Their importance in safeguarding the faith of millions of

Catholic immigrants cannot be minimized. The present work outlines briefly some of the circumstances that necessitated the erection of national parishes, and analyzes their position before and after the Code. They have been the object of much controversy in the past, at times perhaps without a complete and sympathetic understanding of their position in the plan of faith. It is not the purpose of the writer to solve all the complex and controversial problems that may arise in individual instances, but rather to outline the position of national parishes according to the present law. The Church has condemned both exaggerated nationalism as well as the religious oppression of minority groups in another country. Its mind is that the common good of souls receive primary consideration, and in this it must be aided to a great extent by the prudence and the judgment of the ordinaries of dioceses.

Although parishes of rite are not considered strictly as national parishes, they are here considered by reason of their distinct character as personal parishes. In this connection it was thought advisable to add a brief outline showing their distinct organization in relation to the churches and the faithful of the Latin rite, and their time-honored customs and liturgy.

The writer wishes to express his gratitude to all who have made it possible for him to continue and complete advanced studies, and to those who have given him their direction and guidance, particularly the Faculty of the School of Canon Law of the Catholic University of America.

CHAPTER I

THE PAROCHIAL INSTITUTE IN GENERAL

ARTICLE I. THE ORIGIN AND GROWTH OF PARISHES

SINCE parishes are so intimately connected with the life of the Church in its members, and constitute a very important part of its external organization, it is first necessary to determine the nature of a parish. The term "parish" (*paroecia, parochia*) undoubtedly derives from the Greek παροικία ,[1] and has been accepted in various meanings since the earliest centuries of the Church. It was used much sooner than the word "parochus."[2]

Some understood παροικία to mean the neighboring district, or those who lived together in the vicinity of the same church, explaining that originally the word was used with respect to the country districts, and only later was applied to the cities. The reason for this, they said, was that the first meetings and assemblies of the Christians were outside of the cities.[3] Others took the word to mean rather a municipality or a territory, because the early Christian communities had understood by it also the country districts adjoining the city, which was under the jurisdiction of the local bishop.[4]

[1] Coronata, *Institutiones Iuris Canonici* (5 vols., Taurini-Romae: Marietti, 1933-1939. Vol. I, 2. ed., 1939; Vol. II, 2. ed., 1939; Vol. III, 1933; Vol. IV, 1935; Vol. V, 1936), I, n. 305, p. 365, in nota 1 (hereafter cited *Institutiones*); Wernz-Vidal, *Ius Canonicum ad Codicis Normam Exactum* (7 toms. in 8 vols., Romae: Apud Aedes Universitatis Gregorianae, 1927-1938. Tom. II, *De Personis*, 2. ed., 1928; Tom. V, *Ius Matrimoniale*, 2. ed., 1928), II, n. 719 (hereafter cited *Ius Canonicum*); Rossi, *De Paroecia* (Romae: Pustet, 1923), p. 1; Cocchi, *Commentarium in Codicem Iuris Canonici* (8 vols., Taurinorum Augustae: Marietti, 1931-1940; Vol. I, 5. ed., 1938; Vol. II, 4. ed., 1937), III, 7 (hereafter cited *Commentarium*); Schäfer, *Pfarrer und Pfarrvikare* (Münster, 1922), p. 6; Augustine, *The Canonical and Civil Status of Catholic Parishes* (St. Louis: Herder, 1926), p. 1 (hereafter cited *Status of Catholic Parishes*).

[2] Coronata, *Institutiones,* I, n. 305.

[3] Schäfer, *op. cit.,* p. 7.

[4] Wernz-Vidal, *op. cit.,* II, n. 719.

The word was further taken occasionally to mean a settlement or colony of strangers, because the Christian communities were believed to be composed of particular groups, mostly strangers in the country. Some even say that the word was used to denote the closed community of Jews residing in a heathen city, and that the Christians adopted the expression from them because they considered themselves merely as strangers and sojourners on this earth with heaven as their ultimate goal.[5] It is in this sense that the Apostle Paul speaks of the Church in several passages.[6]

It is important to note that parishes in the present acceptance of the word did not exist in the early centuries of the Church. The bishops alone conducted the sacred functions and administered the sacraments, and in their ministrations and the performance of their duties they were assisted by the priests and deacons. The bishop always celebrated the Holy Sacrifice of the Mass, and the priests of the city assisted in much the same manner as that observed by the priests of the Greek rite today in concelebration. The only remnant of this practice in the Latin church is found in the ordination of priests and the consecration of bishops.[7] If at times they were delegated to take the place of the bishops, their delegation was only *ad actum*. If their delegation was for a longer period of time it was still *ad nutum*, and was not a permanent office involving the care of souls in a definite locality. The reason for this was the position of the bishop as the supreme pastor of souls in the diocese.[8]

It is not surprising then that in the early ecclesiastical history

[5] Connolly, *The Canonical Erection of Parishes*, The Catholic University of America Canon Law Studies, n. 114 (Washington, D. C.: The Catholic University of America, 1938), p. 1; Stoltz, "Paroecia und Parochus"—*Theologische Quartalschrift* (Tübingen, 1819—), LXXXIX (1907), 424; XCV (1913), 193; CVII (1926), 1.

[6] Heb. xiii, 14; xi, 14; Phil. iii, 20; II Cor. v, 1.

[7] Rossi, *De Paroecia*, p. 9.

[8] Ferraris, "*Parochia,*" n. 7—*Prompta Bibliotheca, Canonica, Iuridica, Moralis, Theologica necnon Ascetica, Polemica, Rubristica, Historica* (9 vols., Romae, 1885-1899; hereafter cited *Bibliotheca*). A very strict law bound the faithful of the city and the surrounding districts to assist only at the functions conducted by the bishop. Cf. Bouix, *De Parocho* (3. ed., Parisiis, 1880), pars I, cap. III, par. 1.

one finds the word *paroecia* referring to a district under the jurisdiction of a bishop, now commonly called a diocese.[9] Beginning with the sixth century it was used to indicate the rural districts over which were placed the *presbyteri rurales*.[10] Gradually the term became accepted to indicate a certain determined territory, the people of which were spiritually cared for by one priest who was originally called the *presbyter, parochianus, parochitanus, parochialis, parochiensis, dioecesanus;* in the middle ages he was called the *plebanus, curatus, sacerdos parochialis,* and more commonly, after the Council of Trent, the *parochus*.[11]

A parish in the modern acceptance of the word is a minor territorial division resulting from ecclesiastical legislation. The Code of Canon Law refrains from directly defining the exact meaning of the word "parish," but an adequate notion can be gathered from the constituent elements that are mentioned in canon 216, § 1: "Territorium cuiuslibet dioecesis dividatur in *dictinctas partes territoriales;* unicuique autem parti sua *peculiaris ecclesia* cum *populo determinato* est assignanda, eiusque *peculiaris rector,* tanquam proprius eiusdem pastor, est praeficiendus pro necessaria animarum curia." These territorial divisions of the diocese are called parishes.[12]

There are four elements that enter into this more or less descriptive definition of a parish, and they are practically always the assigned features of a well established parish, namely, a definite territory, a specified congregation belonging to a particular church, and a resident priest who is called the pastor. These four elements are not inherent requisites, for a parish can be constituted also if one of them is missing. In the canonical sense, however, they should be included in every duly erected parish, and if a parish is estab-

[9] Cocchi, *Commentarium,* III, 7. According to Augustine the term was sometimes used to indicate a province. Cf. *A Commentary on the New Code of Canon Law* (8 vols., St. Louis: Herder, 1921-1938; Vol. II, 5. ed., 1928; Vol. VI, 2. ed., 1932), II, 202, in nota. Hereafter this work shall be cited as *"Commentary."*

[10] Chelodi, *Ius de Personis* (2. ed., Tridenti, 1927), p. 342; Coronata, *Institutiones,* I, n. 305.

[11] Coronata, *Institutiones,* I, n. 305; Wernz-Vidal, *Ius Canonicum,* II, n. 719.

[12] Canon 216, § 3. The italics as appearing in the quoted text of Canon 216 are those of the writer.

lished without one or the other of these elements, it should be considered more by way of an exception than according to the law.

Although it is easy to understand what is meant by this definition given in the Code, and the extent of its bearing on the present practice of determining parish boundaries, one will perhaps ask which of these elements is the most essential as a formal element in the founding of a parish. Considered from each of these four angles, a parish can be the territory itself, with definite boundaries which are not subject to change through legal prescription, and within which the faithful are under the jurisdiction of the pastor, who is bound *ex officio* to minister to their spiritual needs; or it can be the *coetus fidelium* living within a certain circumscribed territory, under the spiritual leadership of a pastor; or again it can be a definite church within the diocese, to which the faithful of a certain territory belong under their proper pastor; or it can also be the pastoral office with its responsibilities to the church and the people. In this last sense the parish constitutes a *beneficium curatum*.[13]

The first condition mentioned in the canon is the distinct territorial part of the diocese. Generally in the creation or division of parishes, the boundaries are, or should be, clearly defined, wherever such a division is possible or necessary. But many times this territorial delimitation is more or less arbitrary, because it depends on the number of the faithful residing in that particular locality, and requiring the ministrations of a priest. A territory without any faithful could not constitute a parish in any sense. Besides, there have existed in the past, and do exist at present, parishes that are not distinguished along purely territorial lines, which indicates that there must be a more adequately determining factor in the establishment of parishes.

As for the *coetus fidelium* it seems that, since the faithful [14] are the chief object of the Church in its efforts to save souls, they constitute the principal part of the parochial institute, together with the one who ministers to their spiritual needs. It has been said that

[13] Wernz-Vidal, *Ius Canonicum,* II, n. 719.

[14] Those who are not baptized, and the baptized non-Catholics are commended to the zeal of the pastor. Cf. canon 1350.

a parish can exist without actual parishioners, and is then a parish *in habitu* as distinguished from a parish *in exercitio*.[15] But such a distinction implies rather a temporary absence of people from the parochial district, e. g. in the time of war, flood, etc., with at least a moral possibility of their return. The case is more hypothetical than practical. One could in the same way understand the pastoral office, which is also a necessary element in the established parish. During the absence of the pastor through death or removal, the parish does not thereby cease to exist as such, nor does the pastoral office disappear, but rather continues *in habitu* until such time as another pastor is appointed to fill the office. But if a parish were not canonically established, neither the presence of the people nor that of the priest would *ipso facto* make it a parish.

Another element that is mentioned in canon 216, § 1 is the church. This is prescribed by law and is necessary as a means for the normal carrying out of the functions in a parish, although parishes can be canonically established before the church has been built.[16]

From what has been said so far it is easy to understand that the constitutive elements of territory, congregation, pastor and church are not of themselves sufficient, and can be considered merely as the material factors requisite for the establishment of a parish. What then, is the formal element that is required before a parish can be considered as canonically established? It seems that this formal element is the act of a competent ecclesiastical authority erecting the parish.[17]

Different persons can exercise their jurisdiction immediately and directly in the same territory and over the same people. Since the Roman pontiff exercises immediate power over each and every diocese and over all of the faithful, he has immediate and unrestricted competence for the erection and the suppression of any parishes that he chooses, and can at the same time restrict the power of a bishop with regard to certain parts of the diocesan territory, or certain

[15] Boehmer, *Jus Parochiale* (Halae, 1760), sec. III, cap. III, n. 17.

[16] Connolly, *op. cit.*, p. 5.

[17] "... *pastor est praeficiendus pro necessaria animarum cura.*"—canon 216, § 1.

groups of the faithful. This is actually the case as found in the present legislation with respect to consistorial benefices and personal parishes.[18] The local ordinary's competence, compared with that of the Roman Pontiff, is restricted; but he can erect non-consistorial benefices in his own territory,[19] and parishes are non-consistorial benefices, unless the appointment to them happens to be reserved to the Holy See. An act of a competent ecclesiastical authority is necessary, then, for the formal erection of a parish, although a formal decree of erection is not necessary in and of itself.[20]

To understand the growth and the development of the Church correctly, it is first necessary to comprehend its mission here on earth. Christ founded the Church in order to provide men with the necessary means of eternal salvation. For this purpose He chose the Apostles, and empowered them to preach the truths of faith, and to administer the sacraments in His name. It is through this medium of preaching and through the sacraments that the first Christian communities were organized.[21] The initial successes of the Apostles were limited to the cities, where the people were more easily accessible, and where greater numbers could simultaneously be brought to a knowledge of the true faith. In the New Testament are found evidences of the growth of the Christian communities, and with the conversion of St. Paul came the actual spreading of the Church to the Gentiles. It became more and more necessary to

[18] Canons 1414, § 1 and 216, § 4.

[19] Canon 1414, § 2.

[20] Cf. Letter of the Apostolic Delegate to the United States, November 10, 1922—Bouscaren, *Canon Law Digest* (2 vols., Milwaukee: Bruce, 1934-1943), I, 150 (hereafter cited Bouscaren). In a more recent reply of the Sacred Congregation of the Council it is noted that "a decree of erection, though it is the usual way of constituting a parish, does not seem to be necessary to its valid erection."—S. C. C., resolutio, 5 mart. 1932—*Acta Apostolicae Sedis, Commentarium Officiale* (Romae, 1909—), XXV (1932), 436 (hereafter cited *AAS*). This does not necessarily contradict the declaration of the Consistorial Congregation of August 1, 1919, which required a decree of erection, since this latter Congregation could be understood to recommend the usual procedure. Cf. *AAS*, XI (1919), 346; canons 1418; 687.

[21] Acts ii, 41-42.

provide for the spiritual welfare of the growing communities, and this was done by appointment of priests and bishops.[22] The bishops alone, however, celebrated mass and administered the sacraments.

During the Apostolic and post-Apostolic periods, there was an indiscriminate use of the words ἐπίσκοπος and πρεσβύτερος resulting in a somewhat obscure understanding of the relative functions of each. Some idea, however, may be formulated of the pastoral office of the bishop from the fact that, though frequently πρεσβύτερος was used to designate the bishop, ἐπίσκοπος, at least in the singular, was never used to denote the simple priest. The general practice of the Apostolic times, and during the centuries immediately succeeding, seems to have been according to the rule of St. Paul in his epistle to Titus, Bishop of Crete: "Ordain priests in every city, as I appointed thee." This practice is confirmed in the Acts of the Apostles as well as in the epistles of St. Paul.[23]

Because of this centralized government of the early Church, it is reasonable to believe that parishes, in the present sense, did not exist during the first three centuries, either in the rural districts or in the cities.[24] In the fourth century, however, there was a decided step forward in the diocesan organization. Freed from the oppressive persecutions of the preceding centuries by the Edict of Constantine in 313, the Church emerged with an ever increasing body of faithful whose spiritual needs called for attention. At first the bishops alone performed the parochial functions with the assistance of the priests and deacons, but as the need became more acute, the bishops had to provide for the people who were separated from the cathedral church in the city by greater distances.

The meeting of this need found expression in the East and in the West by a distinct development during the first half of the fourth century. In the East the *chorepiscopi*, or the "rural bishops," [25]

[22] Titus i, 5.

[23] Acts xiv, 22; xx, 28-30; I Tim. i, 3; I Thess. iii, 1-2; Coloss. i, 7; iv, 7.

[24] Thomassinus, *Vetus et Nova Ecclesiae Disciplina* (10 vols., Parisiis, 1724), pars I, lib. II, cap. XXI, n. 1 (hereafter cited *Ecclesiae Disciplina*).

[25] They are first mentioned in the Council of Ancyra (314), but they had existed already for some time. Cf. canon 12—Hardouin, *Acta Conciliorum et Epistolae Decretales ac Constitutiones Summorum Pontificum* (12 vols., Parisiis,

were appointed to take care of the country districts. They were not bishops in the full sense, since they could not ordain priests or deacons without the permission of the bishop of the city, even though they might have been previously consecrated. They were themselves ordained by, and dependent upon, the bishop of the adjoining city.[26] Although the *chorepiscopi* cannot be definitely said to have been the pastors in the modern sense, they show a definite trend of the Church toward the establishment of the individual parishes outside of the city.[27]

In the West the progress was somewhat slower. There were, however, "parishes" already established in Africa and in Spain in the fourth century,[28] and in Gaul during the fourth and fifth centuries.[29] In Italy about this time the baptismal church made its appearance, and may be regarded as the true predecessor of the present parish church. Already as early as the year 402, Innocent I had granted to the priests of Rome the privilege of baptizing,[30] and also the privilege of celebrating mass in the cemeteries and in the rural districts, for those who lived at too great a distance from the city.[31] In the beginning of the sixth century, however, the bishop reserved to himself the right of designating in which church there was to be public baptism, and consequently the baptismal churches determined

1715), I, 275. Hereafter cited Hardouin. Council of Neocaesarea (314), canon 13—Hardouin I, 286.

[26] Council of Ancyra, canon 12—Hardouin I, 275; Council of Antioch (341), canon 10—Hardouin I, 597; Mansi, *Sacrorum Conciliorum Nova et Amplissima Collectio* (53 vols. in 59, Paris, Arnhem, Leipzig, 1901-1927), II, 1311 (hereafter cited Mansi).

[27] Council of Chalcedon (451), canon 6—Hardouin II, 603.

[28] Council of Carthage (390), canon 9—Mansi III, 695; Council of Elvira (306), canon 21—Mansi II, 9.

[29] Council of Arles (314), canons 2, 21—Hardouin I, 263, 266; Council of Vaison (442), canon 3—Hardouin I, 1787.

[30] Synod of Rome (402), canon 7—Hardouin I, 1035; Mansi III, 1137.

[31] Innocentius I, *Ep. ad Decentium*, cap. 5—Mansi III, 1030. Note that according to the Roman Law, the cemeteries had to be outside of the city—C. (3.44) 12.

by him were few in number.[32] These churches henceforth became public churches under the charge of a priest. The people from the surrounding countryside attended mass there on Sundays and days of obligation throughout the year. From the fifth and sixth centuries these baptismal churches became more and more self-sufficient as parochial institutes.[33] Soon they became completely independent, in that all of the donations made by the faithful were to be expended on the parish itself, and for the support of the pastor.[34]

During the succeeding centuries, many chapels and oratories arose for the convenience of the increasing number of Christians in the various localities. Under the proprietary system during the eighth and ninth centuries many of the privately owned churches became parochial institutions separate and distinct from the baptismal churches.

The city parishes, with the exception of Rome and Alexandria,[35] underwent a much slower development, and it is not until the eleventh century,[36] that there are evidences of other baptismal churches in the city besides the cathedral church of the bishop.[37] Among the first indications of city parishes is a reference in the Council of Limoges (1031),[38] although the definite status of parishes within the city remains confused until the legislation of the Council of Trent.[39]

[32] Council of Auvergne (535), canon 15—Mansi VIII, 862; Council of Agde (506), canon 21—Mansi VIII, 328.

[33] Coronata, *Institutiones,* I, n.'305.

[34] Synod of Carpentras (527)—Hardouin II, 1095.

[35] Mario Lupi (+1789) finds abundant indications of parishes in these cities before the year 1000. Cf. Bouix, *De Parocho,* p. 33.

[36] Dr. Heinrich Schaeffer seems to have found sufficient evidence to show that there existed parishes in the ninth and tenth centuries. Cf. "Pfarrkirche und Stift im Deutschen Mittelalter"—*Kirchenrechtliche Abhandlungen,* hrsg. von U. Stutz, 2. Heft (Stuttgart, 1903), pp. 23-28.

[37] Wernz, *Ius Decretalium* (2. ed., 6 vols., Romae, 1908-1913; Vol. II, 2. ed., 1908), II, 821; Fanfani, *De Iure Parochorum* (Romae: Marietti, 1924), p. 4; Augustine, *Commentary,* II, 505-506.

[38] Sess. II—Mansi XIX, 536, 543.

[39] Hinschius, *System des katholischen Kirchenrechts* (4 vols., Berlin, 1869-1888), II, 281.

Article II. Principal Parish Forms

There were several different forms of parochial organization established in the course of the centuries, primarily with the view of providing for the need of the faithful under the pressure of circumstances, and sometimes merely for their greater convenience. These various forms may be reduced to two principal ones, namely the territorial and non-territorial.

1. *Territorial*

From what has already been said one can easily understand how this form of parochial organization would be selected as the ideal to be followed universally in the Church, and recommended, or even required by law, as the form to be adopted in a country or territory under its jurisdiction. In the very definition of a parish as a distinct part of a diocese, the idea of territory and of definite boundaries has a distinct place. A territorial parish may be defined as a part of a diocese having prescribed limits within which all who have a domicile or quasi-domicile are under the jurisdiction of a definite pastor, unless they happen to be exempt.[40] It is evident that the idea of territoriality conveys with it also the concept of a definite congregation assigned to a proper church in charge of a legitimately appointed pastor.

From the time of the *Decretum Gratiani* (ca. 1140) there was a gradual and marked development of city parishes. Their institution was not simultaneously accepted everywhere as a juridical fact, but depended upon the utility and necessity that were dictated by the circumstances.[41] A distinct territorial delimitation of the churches was promoted principally to safeguard the rights of the priests and the parishioners.

[40] Ferreres, *Institutiones Canonicae* (2. ed., 2 vols., Barcinone, 1920), I, n. 731 b; Fanfani, *De Iure Parochorum,* n. 3; Vermeersch-Creusen, *Epitome Iuris Canonici* (5. ed., 3 vols., Mechlinae: Dessain, 1934-1936), I, n. 329. Hereafter cited *Epitome.*

[41] Bargilliat, *Praelectiones Juris Canonici* (37. ed., 2 vols., Paris, 1923), II, n. 893.

In the sixteenth century there were still many parochial churches without definite territorial limits, both in the cities and in the rural districts.[42] In these places very frequently the sacraments were administered regardless of the church affiliation of the people. As a result this imperfect system of parochial care of souls did not meet with the approval of the Council of Trent (1545-1563). It was recognized as an inadequate organization, and provisions were made in the legislation of the Council for a healthy evolution of the parish as an institution of legal fact, by a pertinent decree.

> In iis quoque civitatibus ac locis, ubi paroeciales ecclesiae certos non habent fines, nec earum rectores proprium populum quem regant, sed promiscue petentibus sacramenta administrantur, mandat sancta synodus episcopis pro tutiori animarum eis commissarum salute, ut distincto populo in certas propriasque parochias unicuique suum perpetuum peculiaremque parochum assignent, qui eas cognoscere valeat, et a quo solo licite sacramenta suscipiant, aut alio utiliori modo, prout loci qualitas exegerit provideant. Idemque in iis civitatibus ac locis, ubi nullae sunt parochiales, quam primum fieri curent, non obstantibus quibuscumque privilegiis et consuetudinibus, etiam immemorabilibus.[43]

This decree of reformation, based on the principle of territoriality in the distinction of parish limits, and manifestly aimed at obviating the indiscriminate reception and administration of the sacraments, did not effect a complete change in the lax organization that had prevailed in many places. It was not immediately executed everywhere,[44] although in many places an attempt was made to adhere to its general principles.[45] Even as late as the seventeenth century there were several ancient and important cities in Italy which were not organized into parishes.[46] In the eighteenth century Innocent

[42] Wernz, *Ius Decretalium*, II, n. 821.

[43] Sess. XXIV, *de ref.*, c. 13; cf. sess. XIV, *de ref.*, c. 9.

[44] Wernz, *Ius Decretalium*, II, n. 821.

[45] Cf. *Acta Sanctae Sedis* (41 vols., Romae, 1865-1908), XV (1882), 309-326. Hereafter cited *ASS*.

[46] Cf. Rossi, *De Paroecia*, p. 13.

XIII (1721-1724) [47] and Benedict XIV (1740-1758) [48] found it necessary to remind the bishops that the law of the Council of Trent had not lost any of its force.

It is evident, then, that the Council of Trent adopted the fundamental principle of territorial distinction as regards parochial institutions. This principle, so frequently encouraged in the past, was taken up for the first time in a universal law of the Church, and was made mandatory for all of the bishops in their respective dioceses.

A provision similar to the one initiated in the Council of Trent was later made by the Sacred Congregation for the Propagation of the Faith for the territories under its jurisdiction. It decreed that in missionary countries parishes should be established as soon as possible, according to the principles of Canon Law, and that where this was not possible immediately, territorial districts should be established which were to be called "missions" or "stations" or "congregations," over which was to be placed a vicar or moderator.[49] This was the practice in the prefectures and vicariates apostolic,[50] and these territorial districts, instituted along identical lines with the territorial parish, were different from parishes principally because of the status of the hierarchical unit of which they were a part, and were called quasi-parishes. In the present Code of Canon law the same provision is retained with regard to the territorial delimitations of prefectures and vicariates apostolic,[51] and the

[47] Const. *"Apostolici ministerii,"* 23 maii 1723, n. 14—*Codicis Iuris Canonici Fontes* cura Emi Petri Card. Gasparri Editi (9 vols., Romae: Typis Polyglottis Vaticanis, 1923-1939. Vols. VII, VIII, IX ed. cura et studio Emi Iustiniani Card. Serédi), n. 280. Hereafter cited *Fontes.*

[48] Const. *"Ad militantis,"* 20 mart. 1742, nn. 11 and 16—*Fontes,* n. 326.

[49] S.C.C., 18 mart. 1881—*Collectanea S. Congregationis de Propaganda Fide* (2 vols., Romae, 1907), II, n. 1548 (hereafter cited *Coll.*); Benedictus XIV, ep. encycl. *"Cum semper oblatas,"* 19 aug. 1744—*Fontes,* n. 345; S. C. de Prop. Fide, litt. encycl. (ad Ep. Indiar.), 28 aug. 1893—*Coll.,* n. 1848.

[50] Clemens IX, bull. *"Speculatores,"* 13 sept. 1659—*Bullarium Pontificium S. Cong. de Prop. Fide* (7 vols., et index, Romae, 1839-1858), I, 172; S. C. Consist., declar., 1 aug. 1919, n. 1—*AAS,* XI (1919), 346.

[51] Canon 216, § 2.

quasi-pastors are practically equivalent to pastors as far as their rights and duties are concerned.[52] They differ in the stability of their office,[53] in their nomination and in their obligation of saying the official mass for the people.[54]

Even today there are many places in the world where the Catholic faith is little known, and has not sufficiently become a part of the fabric of the people to warrant the establishment of dioceses. These places are directly under the jurisdiction of the Holy See, which operates through the medium of vicars and prefects apostolic. These assign to individual priests certain territories over which they exercise the care of the faithful as it were in their own name, and are therefore called quasi-pastors. The Sacred Congregation for the Propagation of the Faith, with full understanding of the conditions that are likely to occur, urged that these territories be divided into quasi-parishes gradually as the opportunity presented itself. It is not necessary to divide the entire vicariate or prefecture into such territorial units at once.[55] For the erection of a quasi-parish, however, it insisted that a decree be issued by the Ordinary, clearly defining the boundaries, and when this was not practical, that at least certain communities be assigned to a definite quasi-parish.

An understanding of this territorial division of quasi-parishes is necessary for a clearer and better understanding of the position of parishes in the United States before the Code. Before the Constitution *"Sapienti consilio"* of June 29, 1908, this country was considered as a missionary country under the jurisdiction of the Sacred Congregation for the Propagation of the Faith.[56]

Since parishes are in the present Code of Canon Law principally indicated according to territorial lines, it is necessary that they have well defined boundaries, because it is within these limits that parishioners belonging to a particular parish will be found. Their affiliation with a definite church and a particular pastor will depend upon their place of residence. This is evidently the meaning of canon 216, § 1,

[52] Canons 461-470.

[53] Canon 454, § 4.

[54] Canons 457; 306.

[55] S. C. de Prop. Fide, instr., 25 iul. 1920—*AAS,* XII (1920), 332.

[56] Pius X, const. *"Sapienti consilio,"* 29 iun. 1908, I, 6°, n. 2—*Fontes,* n. 682.

although the canon seems to intimate that some who live within the territory may also belong to another church, according to the words *"cum populo determinato."* There should be a definitely assigned congregation within these territorial limits. The idea of territoriality however is stressed more clearly by the fact that a person has his pastor determined for him by means of his domicile or quasi-domicile.[57]

A domicile is acquired by the intention to remain in a particular locality permanently, or by actually remaining there for ten years.[58] A quasi-domicile, on the other hand, is acquired by an intention to remain in a place for the greater part of a year, or by actually remaining there for that length of time.[59] If the parish is strictly territorial, with definitely established boundaries, then the domicile or quasi-domicile determine the fact that one is a member of that particular church which happens to be assigned to the territory.

2. *Non-territorial*

It appears from canon 216, § 4, that there is another principle by which parishes are determined, besides the principle of territoriality. It is true that the most convenient basis of partition is that which is taken from the division of territory, because it is commonly accepted in human society that races and people be organized into political subdivisions by proper and distinct boundaries. Under circumstances in which the population was homogeneous, the faithful who lived within the limits of a certain country could, with comparatively little difficulty, be subdivided into distinct communities with definite territorial limits, constituted under the authority of a proper pastor.[60] But for various reasons it becomes evident that another principle must be taken into consideration, a principle that was basically acknowledged in the Decretals of Gregory IX,[61] and which later received acknowledgment also in the Council of Trent.

[57] Canon 94, § 1.
[58] Canon 92, § 1.
[59] Canon 92, § 2.
[60] Maroto, *Institutiones Iuris Canonici* (2 vols., Romae, 1921), II, n. 767.
[61] C. 14, X, *de officio iudicis ordinarii,* I, 31.

It is a principle whereby parishes are distinguished not according to the territory which they embrace, but by reason of certain people or families that happen to belong to them. Authors give them the generic term of personal or family parishes, as distinguished from local or territorial parishes.[62]

These parishes have been referred to here as non-territorial parishes, because the principle that determines their existence is non-territorial. It is true that in one sense it is practically impossible to divorce the idea of territory from a parish, because the people who belong to these parishes are not scattered throughout the whole world, but are presumed to live, and actually do reside, in a more or less determined locality. In the case of non-territorial parishes, however, the title which determines a person's affiliation with a given parish is a personal one, and not the domicile or quasi-domicile within a certain territory. This is the strict interpretation of the distinctive constituent element of personal parishes. This personal title by which one becomes affiliated with a certain parish may be the rite to which the person belongs (Greek, Mozarabic), and then the parish is called a parish of rite; or it may be the language or the nationality of the person (German, Polish), and then the parish is called a national parish; or it may be merely the family to which the person belongs (royal, noble), and then the parish is called a family parish; or again it may be a particular kind of work or a certain profession (soldiers) or a quality of the persons (lepers) which determines the parishioners for whom parishes have been established.

Although fundamentally a personal parish exists without respect to territory, it can also sometimes be understood in a broader sense as a mixed personal and territorial parish. Such is the case when a personal parish extends over one or more territorial parishes, but the jurisdiction of the pastor is limited to the people within certain

[62] Barbosa, *De Parocho* (Lugduni, 1665), pars I, cap. I, n. 23; Ferraris, *Bibliotheca*, s. v. "*Parochia,*" n. 17; Wernz, *Ius Decretalium*, II, n. 821 d; Wernz-Vidal, *Ius Canonicum*, II, n. 720; Schäfer, *Pfarrer und Pfarrvikare*, p. 8; Hilling, *Das Personenrecht des Codex Iuris Canonici* (Paderborn, 1924), p. 216; Coronata, *Institutiones*, I, n. 307;; Fanfani, *De Iure Parochorum*, n. 3; Ferreres, *Institutiones*, I, n. 731; Vermeersch-Creusen, *Epitome*, I, n. 329.

boundaries. Such a situation arises if two or more personal parishes exist in one city and certain limits are established within which the pastors of these parishes can exercise their jurisdiction.[63] It becomes evident in this case, that the territories of the national parishes become cumulative with those of the territorial parishes. This occurs simply by reason of the existing circumstances. It is a matter most difficult, if not practically impossible, to supervise and minister adequately to a community of people who differ greatly in their origin, language, customs or rite. These differences can pervade a city or a diocese to such an extent that if one considers the people and not the boundaries of a city, or of the diocese, there are in fact not one but two or more cities within the same limits.[64]

The fundamental principle underlying personal parishes was already recognized in a negative way by the Council of Trent. An analysis of that particular chapter of the decree which dealt with the establishment of territorial parishes [65] shows us that, in effect, it was intended only for those cities and places "ubi paroeciales ecclesiae certos non habent fines, nec eorum rectores proprium populum." In the case of personal parishes it is true that there were no definite boundaries, and probably a number of people did live within the limits of another parish. It could not be said, however, that the pastors did not have a "proprium populum," nor could they in that case be said to have administered the sacraments "promiscue petentibus." [66]

It should here be added that a positive approval of the principle was given in the same Council, for after imposing on the bishops the obligation of providing for the territorial division of their

[63] These parishes are called mixed personal parishes because of the personal and territorial elements. Thus Coronata, *Institutiones,* I, n. 307, and Vermeersch-Creusen, *Epitome,* I, n. 329. Beste in his work *Introductio in Codicem* (Collegeville: St. John's Abbey Press, 1938), p. 227, distinguishes between personal and mixed parishes, limiting the term "personal" to family parishes, and the term "mixed" to national parishes.

[64] Thomassinus, *Disciplina Ecclesiastica,* pars I, lib. I, cap. XXIX, nn. 1-3; cap. XXVI, n. 7.

[65] Sess. XXIV, *de ref.,* c. 13.

[66] Barbosa, *De Parocho,* pars I, cap. I, n. 23.

respective diocese, the Council left them free to use other means to be applied at their discretion, in the words "aut alio utiliori modo, prout loci qualitas exegerit, provideant." [67] The bishops were authorized to constitute parishes according to the necessity and utility of such a step. They could designate the boundaries, and determine the people who were to belong to the parish,[68] and thus it would appear that the temporal limits did not always necessarily imply also the extent of the spiritual jurisdiction. If the bishops saw that for some worthy reason it was necessary to establish a personal or family parish because of language, rite, privilege or some other circumstance, they could do so. This seems to have been the practice until the promulgation of the Code.

Authors generally conceded the actual existence of such personal parishes before and after the Council of Trent.[69] De Luca (1614-1683) echoed the general attitude expressed in his own day: ". . . si quis habet parochiam per capita hominum seu respectu certarum personarum seu familiarum, tale ius parochiale non cohaeret territorio, sed tamen illud est exercibile in quocumque loco illae personae moventur, et sic iure servitutis quam ita reliqui parochi in proprio territorio propriisque finibus pati coguntur." [70]

Family parishes existed already before the Council of Trent.[71] Their existence was confirmed after the Council of Trent in many instances, particularly through the Sacred Congregation of the Council, which was intended, according to the express desire of Pius V (1566-1572), to interpret the Tridentine decrees.[72] Barbosa (1589-

[67] Sess. XXIV, *de ref.*, c. 13.

[68] C. 11, C. XVI, q. 7; Barbosa, *De Parocho*, pars I, cap. I, n. 38.

[69] Thomassinus, *Ecclesiae Disciplina*, pars I, lib. II, cap. XXVI, n. 12; Barbosa, *De Parocho*, pars I, cap. I, n. 23; Leurenius, *Forum Beneficiale* (Venetiis, 1752), pars I, q. 160; De Luca, *Theatrum Veritatis et Iustitiae* (Coloniae Agrippinae, 1706), tom. VIII, disc. XX, n. 24; Bouix, *De Parocho*, pars II, cap. V, requisitum 4.

[70] *Loc. cit.*

[71] Ursaya, *Disceptationes Ecclesiasticae* (Venetiis, 1724), tom. III, pars I, discep. XXVII, nn. 1-4; cf. *Analecta Ecclesiastica*, X (1902), 159.

[72] Cf. Ayrinhac, *Constitution of the Church in the New Code of Canon Law* (New York: Longmans, Green & Company, 1930), n. 44. Hereafter cited *Constitution of the Church.*

1649) cited a particular instance current shortly after the Council was concluded. It is reflected in a report of the Bishop of Aquila to the Sacred Congregation of the Council in the year 1578. In this report the bishop explicitly mentioned the existence of such parishes, distinct not by material dwellings but rather by people or families.[73] The existence of similar parishes was subsequently mentioned in widespread localities, and the responses of the Sacred Congregation of the Council from the year 1587 to 1594 always maintained that parishes, distinct according to certain families and people, even though they did not have certain limits, were not affected by the dispositions of the Council of Trent.[74] This attitude was maintained throughout the seventeenth century, and is found again, confirmed more definitely, in the eighteenth and the nineteenth as well as the twentieth centuries, together with the reiteration of the Tridentine decree as found in the twenty-fourth session, chapter thirteen, *de reformatione*.[75]

In fact the existence of the family parishes became so firmly established that where such parishes existed the pastors could also accept new families *(familias exteras)* coming in from another city.[76] But once this parish had been chosen and definitely accepted by the newcomer, he was not permitted to change again to join another personal parish. He could, however, become affiliated with the territorial parish within whose limits he happened to reside. This had

[73] *De Parocho,* pars I, cap. I, n. 23.

[74] Pallottini, s. v. *Collectio Omnium Conclusionum et Resolutionum quae in causis propositis apud Sacram Congregationem Cardinalium S. Concilii Tridentini Interpretum prodierunt ab eius institutione anno MDLXIV ad MDCCCLX, distinctis titulis alphabetico ordine per materias digestas* (18 vols., Romae, 1868-1895), s. v. *Ecclesia Parochialis,* II, n. 12. Hereafter cited Pallottini.

[75] S. Cong. Concilii, *Mileten.,* 13 sept. 1721—*Thesaurus Resolutionum Sacrae Congregationis Concilii* (167 vols., Romae, 1718-1908), tom. II, 83 (hereafter cited *Thes. Resol.*); *Spoletana,* 18 iun. 1733—*Thes. Resol.,* VI, 111; *Toletana,* 11 maii 1748—*Thes. Resol.,* XIII, 99; *Toletana,* 11 aug. 1753—*Thes. Resol.,* XVII, 73; *Macerat.,* 14 mart. 1772—*Thes. Resol.,* XLVII, 65; *Cervien.,* 16 mart. 1782—*Thes. Resol.,* LI, 32; *Sancti Severini,* 25 ian. 1817—*Thes. Resol.,* LXXVII, 21. Cf. *Analecta Ecclesiastica,* X (1902), 157.

[76] S.C.C., *Maceraten.,* 14 mart. 1778—*Thes. Resol.,* XLVII, 65.

been the practice of the Sacred Congregation of the Council concerning similar cases.[77]

Special consideration was given to priests in charge of the spiritual welfare of military encampments. They were given jurisdiction over a particular class of people, that is, the soldiers, without regard to the territorial division of parishes. This could be done on the principle which was commonly accepted, according to De Luca, that jurisdiction can be given "in personas etiam sine territorio." [78] It was also for this reason that the establishment of parishes for lepers was called for under Alexander III (1159-1181) in the III General Council of the Lateran,[79] so that the bishops might find a suitable way to provide for their spiritual welfare.

As for national parishes in particular as distinguished from other kinds of personal parishes, the very fact of their existence today, particularly in the United States, furnishes a strong presumption for their existence in the past. But how precisely did the national parish first obtain juridical recognition? The entrance of the Church into the history of humanity brought a complete change in the political and social as well as the moral condition of mankind. The Church, a supernatural society, separate from the State, proclaimed a new doctrine that was above the plane of nationality, above all distinction of class and race, and was destined to unite all men in the service of the one true God. Its ideal was not human but divine, its end not material but supernatural. In the pursuit of this end,

[77] S.C.C., *Maceraten.*, 14 mart. 1778—*Thes. Resol.*, XLVII, 65; *Sancti Severini*, 8 febr. 1817—*Thes. Resol.*, LXXVII, 34. Note the similarity of this practice to that which later was urged in the case of national parishes in the United States by the decree of the Sacred Congregation for the Propagation of the Faith, April 26, 1897—*The American Ecclesiastical Review* (Philadelphia, 1889—), XVII (1897), 87. Hereafter cited *AER*. Cf. Bouscaren, II, 80.

[78] *Theatrum Veritatis et Iustitiae*, tom. VIII, disc. XX, n. 19; cf. Sacra Romana Rota in causa Faventina Iurium Parochialium coram Ansaldo, 21 iun. 1698—*Decisiones S.R.R. coram R.P.D. Ansaldo de Ansaldis* (8 vols., Romae, Vol. I, 1711; Vol. II, 1736; Vols. III-IV, 1739; Vols. V-VI, 1740; Vol. VII, 1743; Vol. VIII, 1777), I, Decis. LV, n. 22.

[79] Can. 23—Mansi XXII, 230; cf. c. 2, X, *de treuga et pace*, I, 34, and c. 10, X, *de censibus, exactionibus, et procurationibus*, III, 39; cf. Petra, *Commentaria ad Constitutiones Apostolicas* (5 vols., Venetiis, 1729), III, 238-239.

however, it was circumscribed in its choice by the exigencies of human nature which expressed themselves to some extent in the differences of language and custom. Although the Church embraced many nations in the great work of caring for souls, and drew them ever closer in the bond of spiritual union, relegating to the background their characteristic differences, it did not entirely uproot their diversifying elements. As a matter of fact she chose rather to adapt herself to their particular needs in those external things which reflected no direct relationship with laws of divine origin.

It was not the intention of Christ that the Church be limited to one nationality,[80] or that His doctrine be spread to all nations through the medium of one language. The manifestation of the Church's intention stood confirmed on the first Pentecost when the Apostles went forth endowed with the gift of tongues, in order that they might bring the truth to all nations.[81]

History does not refer to the difficulties of language that certainly must have confronted the Church as a result of wars and invasion, when peoples and nations were engulfed by the tide of military conquest. Outside of isolated legislation in the various councils, there was no general law which provided for the national minorities under the Church's jurisdiction until the thirteenth century. This lack of general legislation may have been partially due to the fact that, since the time of the Roman Empire, Latin was quite commonly understood throughout Europe until at least the ninth century.[82] From then on the vernacular development became more and more pronounced and accelerated, particularly on the continent. By the end of the twelfth century there must have been a number of cases called to the attention of the Holy See, in which different language groups within the cities and dioceses of another country were involved, because this matter was given consideration in the IV General Lateran Council (1215).[83]

[80] Matt. xxviii, 19; Mark xvi, 15.

[81] Acts ii, 4-11.

[82] Lot, "A quelle époque a-t-on cessé de parler latin?"—*Archivium Latinitatis Medii Aevii* (Paris, 1924—), VI (1931), 97-152.

[83] Canon 9—Mansi XXII, 998; c. 14, X, *de officio iudicis ordinarii,* I, 31.

The event that seems to have precipitated this more than any other, according to Gonzalez-Tellez (+ ca. 1674),[84] was the fall of Constantinople in 1204. Shortly after the conquest of this great metropolis of the East, Baldwin of Flanders was crowned the Emperor, and Innocent III (1198-1216) established a Latin Patriarchate under Archbishop Thomas Morosini.[85] Soon there were a number of Latin bishops in the cities of the Oriental rite where there were mixed Latin and Greek congregations. Since both the Latins and the Greeks wished to retain their own original religious affiliations, it was necessary to make some adequate provision so that, in the places where there were groups of different language and rite, there might be one bishop for both.

The wise and practical provision of Innocent III (1198-1216) was promptly absorbed into the Decretals of Gregory IX (1227-1241), and was confirmed as law[86] with their promulgation in 1234.[87] This law, providing for the peoples of different language and rite within the same city, expressed a con-

[84] *Commentaria Perpetua in Singulos Textus Quinque Librorum Decretalium Gregorii IX* (5 vols., Maceratae, 1761), I, tit. XXXI, cap. 14, n. 1. Hereafter cited *Commentaria.*

[85] Baronius, *Annales Ecclesiastici* (37 vols. Vols. I-XXVIII, Barri-Ducis, 1864-1875; Vols. XXIX-XXXVII, Parisiis, 1876-1883), XX, 160-166; Schaff, *History of the Christian Church* (7 vols., New York, 1904-1910), V, 276.

[86] Cf. Cicognani, *Canon Law* (2. ed., Philadelphia: The Dolphin Press, 1935), p. 299.

[87] "Quoniam in plerisque partibus infra eandem civitatem atque dioecesim permixti sunt populi diversarum linguarum, habentes sub una fide varios ritus et mores, districte praecipimus, ut pontifices huiusmodi civitatum sive dioecesum provideant viros idoneos, qui secundum diversitates rituum et linguarum divina illis officia celebrent et ecclesiastica sacramenta administrent, instruendo eos verbo pariter et exemplo. Prohibemus autem omnino, ne una eademque civitas sive dioecesis diversos pontifices habeat, tamquam unum corpus diversa capita, quasi monstrum. Sed si propter praedictas causas urgens necessitas postulaverit, pontifex loci catholicum praesulem nationibus illis conformem provida deliberatione constituat sibi vicarium in praedictis, qui ei per omnia sit obediens et subiectus. Unde si quis aliter se gesserit, excommunicationis se noverit mucrone percussum, et, si nec sic resipuerit, ab omni ministerio ecclesiastico deponendum, adhibito, si necesse fuerit, brachio saeculari, ad tantam insolentiam repellendam." —c. 14, X, *de officio iudicis ordinarii,* I, 31.

dition that already existed in many places *(plerisque partibus)*.[88] It was not possible perhaps to remedy this condition, but it could be provided for. The law made it the duty of the bishops of the cities and dioceses where these people resided to appoint suitable men, who knew their language, to take care of them.[89] If there was urgent need, the bishops could appoint a prelate *(praesul)* for some particular language. This prelate, however, was subject to the bishop, acting as his vicar in all things pertaining to the language.[90]

In vain does one seek any more definite general legislation concerning national and language parishes. The arguments in their favor are those adduced from reasons employed to show the status of personal parishes. The Council of Trent made it the obligation of the bishops to provide suitable pastors for the people, in order that they might explain the sacraments to them in the vernacular when-

[88] Abbas Panormitanus (Nicholaus de Tudeschis, d. 1453) in his *Commentaria in Quinque Libros Decretalium* (8 vols., Venetiis, 1588), II, tit. *de offi. iud. ord.*, ad v. *permixti*, mentions Constantinople, Calabria, Trent (where there were Germans and Italians), Metz (where there were French and Germans); Ioannes Andreae (+1348) had earlier mentioned Verona. Cf. *In Decretalium Libros Novella Commentaria* (5 vols., Venetiis, 1581), I, *de officio ordinarii*, cap. 14 (hereafter cited *Commentaria*); Barbosa, *Collectanea Decretorum* (6 vols., Lugduni, 1716), *de officio iud. ordin.*, cap. 14, n. 2.

[89] Gonzalez-Tellez, *Commentaria*, I, tit. XXXI, cap. 14; Barbosa, *Collectanea*, I, *de offi. iud. ordin.*, cap. 14, n. 2; Hostiensis (+1271), *In Quinque Decretalium Libros Commentaria* (5 vols. in 3, Venetiis, 1581), I, tit. *de offi. iud. ordin.*, cap. 14, n. 1 (hereafter cited *Commentaria*); Petra (1662-1747), *Commentaria in Constitutiones Apostolicas*, I, in proemio ad cap. III, n. 26; Riganti (1661-1735), *In Regulas Cancelleriae Commentaria* (2 vols., Coloniae Allobrogum, 1751), Reg. XX, nn. 1-2, 13.

[90] C. 9, X, *de renunciatione*, I, 9; Abbas Panormitanus, *Commentaria*, II, tit. *de offic. iud. ord.*, cap. XIV, ad v. *praesul;* Hostiensis, *Commentaria*, I, tit. *de offi. iud. ordi.*, cap. 14, ad v. *praesulem*; Ioannes Andreae, *Commentaria*, I, *de officio ordinarii*, cap. 14; in commenting on this point Ioannes Andreae (ad v. *praesulem*) understood a prelate or rector, and not a bishop, because the word *praesul*, he said was used as a general name. Hostiensis and Panormitanus interpreted the word as applying to a bishop also, for otherwise there was no one who could ordain. As bishop, they hastened to add, he could not be the ordinary of the place, but only a vicar, or an auxiliary in the modern sense. Gonzalez-Tellez seems also to favor this meaning. Cf. *Commentaria*, I, tit. XXXI, cap. 14, n. 13.

ever that was necessary.[91] These pastors had to be approved as fitted for their office "aetate, moribus, doctrina, prudentia et aliis rebus ad vacantem ecclesiam gubernandam opportunis." [92] In fact, it was left to the bishop entirely to choose and elect "quem caeteris magis idoneum iudicaverit." [93] Here one cannot doubt that the Council of Trent intended that the most suitable pastor be chosen for one particular parish, and not just for any parish in general.[94] The bishop in appointing a pastor had to look to his ability with regard to one particular parish, and unless he provided otherwise, the pastor was considered approved only for the parish for which he was elected, since the bishop could easily have reason to judge a priest suitable for one place and not for another.[95]

Since spiritual utility and necessity in the care of souls evidently was the principal juridical foundation for the establishment of parishes, it may also be said that it forms the basis for the establishment of language and national parishes. The Council of Trent recognized that instruction, preaching, and the administration of the sacraments were necessary means for the salvation of souls. It is easy to understand how a group of people, especially a large community of a distinct national or racial character, speaking the language of their native country, but living within the territorial limits of another nation, could constitute a unique problem as far as pastoral ministrations were concerned. This diversity of language could constitute a defect of service as far as that particular group was concerned.[96] The responsibility of appointing a suitable pastor for these people, who was capable of ministering to them in their own idiom, was left up to the ordinary in his prudent and sound

[91] Sess. V, *de ref.*, c. 2; sess. XXII, *de sacrif. missae*, c. 8; sess. XXIII, *de ref.*, c. 1; sess. XXIV, *de ref.*, c. 4, 7, 18.

[92] Sess. XXIV, *de ref.*, c. 18.

[93] *Loc. cit.*

[94] Schmalzgrueber, *Ius Ecclesiasticum Universum* (5 vols. in 12, Romae, 1843-1845), tom. II, pars III, tit. 14, nn. 32-36; D'Angelo, *Parroco e Parrocchia* (3. ed., Giarre, 1921), p. 139.

[95] Mühlbauer, *Decreta Authentica Congregationis Sacrorum Rituum et Instructio Clementina* (4 vols., Monachi, 1863-1867), ad v. *Parochus*, n. 2.

[96] Thomassinus, *Ecclesiae Disciplina*, pars I, lib. I, cap. XXVI, n. 7; cap. XXIX, nn. 1-3.

judgment,[97] since it remained a question more of fact than of law.[98] The necessary point to be determined was whether there existed a serious defect of service to souls. This seems to have been the basic factor of parochial distinction according to the Sacred Congregation of the Council, whereas distance and difficulty of travel were not always considered sufficient reasons for the establishing of separate parishes if this defect of service could not be proved.[99] The need for a priest who could speak the idiom of a particular language group could be so pressing that it could connote a definite hazard to souls. Such cases then, justified the existence of language and national parishes, particularly since family parishes, for which there was not a similarly urgent need, had been frequently recognized up to the time of the Code.

The Church has often recognized the need for ministering to the people in their own language, especially in missionary countries.[100] Even though these ministrations could perhaps be carried out to some extent by another priest appointed for that particular work,[101] they could not successfully be carried out for an indefinite period, particularly among groups large enough to constitute a parish. Besides, the Council of Trent insisted vehemently that pastors have their own people, *proprium populum,* assigned to them,[102] that they themselves preach to these people and instruct them,[103] and that they learn to understand their flock.[104] As pastors, then, they should

[97] Leurenius, *Forum Beneficiale,* pars I, q. 159.

[98] De Luca, *Theatrum Veritatis et Iustitiae,* tom. III, pars III, disc. XII, n. 6.

[99] *Recanaten.,* 26 febr. 1825, ad v. *deneganda*—Thes. Resol., LXXXV, 62.

[100] *Bullarium Pontificium S. C. de P. Fide,* tom. I, 168; S. C. de Prop. Fide (C.G.), 17 mart. 1760—*Coll.,* n. 427; S. C. de Prop. Fide (C.G.), 2 aug. 1726—*Coll.,* n. 444. Cf. *Fontes,* nn. 4531, 4540.

[101] Mühlbauer, *Decreta Authentica Cong. Sacrorum Rituum et Instructio Clementina,* ad v. *Parochus,* n. 2.

[102] Sess. XXIV, *de ref.,* c. 13; canons 216, § 1; 451, § 1.

[103] Sess. V, *de ref.,* c. 2; sess. XIII, *de ref.,* c. 1; sess. XXII, *de sacrif. missae,* c. 8; sess. XXIV, *de ref.,* cc. 4, 7; cf. canons 1329, 1332, 1344, 1347.

[104] Sess. XXIII, *de ref.,* c. 1; Zitelli-Natali (+1887), *Apparatus Iuris Ecclesiastici* (Romae, 1886), pp. 180-181.

habitually render this service themselves, and not through others.[105]

Although the Council of Trent legislated unmistakably concerning the territorial division of parishes, and this legislation was frequently insisted upon by the Church, personal parishes through indult or privilege or established custom continued to exist, even though they gave rise to controversies occasionally, as can be noted in the case of family parishes. Where they were established, their position was duly recognized, and is recognized today by the Code.[106]

In fact, the necessity and utility that were required by the Council of Trent for establishing parishes, began to be interpreted more mildly in the latter part of the nineteenth century. A new parish could be established as long as it was evidently for the good of the faithful, and as long as there was a reasonable assurance that there would be a sufficient income for the support of the church and the pastor.[107] Such being the case, the conclusion must be that the status of language or national parishes that sprang up particularly during the latter part of the nineteenth century and the first part of the twentieth century, was at least the same as that of the family parishes, and that they subsequently received the same recognition in the Code.

[105] Pallottini, ad v. *Ecclesia Parochialis,* II, nn. 64-65; Zitelli-Natali, *op. cit.,* p. 171; cf. canon 1344, § 2.

[106] Canon 216, § 4.

[107] *ASS,* X (1877), 271-272; *S.R.R., in causa Bobien., dismembrationis,* 14 mart. 1911, coram R.P.D. Michaele Lega, Dec. XI, nn. 2, 9, 10—*Sacrae Romanae Rotae Decisiones seu Sententiae* (Romae, 1912—), III (1911), 105, 109, 110 (hereafter cited *S.R.R. Decisiones*). The case is also found in the *AAS,* III (1911), 456-466.

CHAPTER II

CATHOLIC INCREASE IN THE UNITED STATES

It is an evident fact that national parishes have already existed in this country for some time, and that there must have been a sufficient reason for their origin and development. In order to understand this reason better it is first necessary to study the various racial and national influences merging in the physical growth of this nation. There was such an increased influx into the United States from foreign countries, particularly during the nineteenth century and the first decade of the twentieth century, that it may prove useful to give a brief description of the rôle that immigration played in our national development, particularly from the Catholic standpoint.

Article I. The Catholic Population

1. *Catholic Growth to 1820*

One cannot attempt to trace the various causes that contributed to the emigration of Catholics from other countries in a work of this kind. Suffice it to say that they were mostly political, religious, military and economic. In the early part of the sixteenth century there were predominantly three European nations which claimed the different portions of our territory, and influenced them respectively; France in the north, England along the eastern coast, and Spain in the south, particularly in Florida.[1] After the treaty of 1763, Florida fell under a violent British domination, and the Spanish Catholic population emigrated in a body, while the rest of the territory also fell under British political influence with the defeat of the French.[2]

[1] Shea, *History of the Catholic Church in the United States* (4 vols., Akron, 1886-1892), I, 13. Hereafter cited *History*.

[2] Shea, *History*, II, 89.

In the American colonies under British domination, with the exception of Maryland and Pennsylvania, the Catholic Church was ostracized. Three forms of Protestantism predominated, the Congregational Church, the Church of England, and the Reformed Church.[3] A Federal Church was not practicable due to the fact that many of the Fathers of the Republic were strongly opposed to an established State Church. These circumstances eventually necessitated a provision for religious liberty which is found in the form of the First Amendment to the Federal Constitution.[4]

Early history does not record large voluntary migrations of individual Catholic groups. Those who came maintained their religious practices in their adopted country to the best of their ability, or eventually lost the faith entirely. In Virginia about the middle of the seventeenth century there were at least 300 Irish immigrants.[5] A gradual influx of Catholics into this country continued, however, and there were many French Catholics in New York, and in the Québec province, and in Maryland there were about 2000 in 1674.[6] In Pennsylvania in the latter part of the seventeenth century there were found a number of German Catholic settlers. The English constituted the majority of the population of the country, and only a very small portion of it was composed of Catholics.[7] In the year 1790, of the entire population of the United States (3,172,006), the census showed approximately 275,000 persons of Catholic descent, and actually only about 35,000 Catholics.[8] By 1820, principally through territorial acquisitions (Louisiana and Florida), immigration and national increase, the Catholic population rose to 195,000.[9]

[3] Zwierlein, "New Netherlands Intolerance"—*The Catholic Historical Review* (Washington, D. C.: The Catholic University of America, 1915—), IV (1918), 200. Hereafter cited *CHR*. Cf. Zollman, *American Church Law* (St. Paul: West Publ. Co., 1933), p. 3.

[4] Martin, "The American Judiciary and Religious Liberty"—*CHR*, VIII (1928), 13-27.

[5] O'Brien, *A Hidden Phase of American History* (New York, 1919), p. 325.

[6] Shea, *History,* I, 82.

[7] Shaughnessy, *Has the Immigrant Kept the Faith?* (New York, 1925), p. 51.

[8] Shaughnessy, *op. cit.,* p. 73.

[9] *Loc. cit.*

2. *Catholic Growth from 1820 to 1920*

From this time on the statistics of immigration are more accurate in view of the immigration law of 1819. During this century the Catholic growth in the United States mounted by leaps and bounds. In 1850 the Catholic population increased to 1,606,000, due principally to immigration from Catholic countries, especially Ireland, Germany and France, with sizable contributions from Spain and Canada.[10] During the next decade, the principle Catholic immigrants continued to come from Germany and Ireland, but other nationalities soon began to arrive in larger numbers, until in 1880 there was a marked increase in Italian, Mexican and Polish immigrants. By 1900 Italian Catholic immigrants were the most numerous, followed closely by the Polish Catholics.[11] The Catholic population of the States rose to 12,000,000.

The next decade showed an increase of the Catholic population by over 4,000,000 with large groups from most of the European countries, especially Italy, Poland and Austria-Hungary. By 1920 the Catholics numbered 19,828,000, showing a sharp decrease in the immigration figures of the previous decade, due principally to the World War. The immigration laws of 1921 and 1924, plus the provision of 1927, successively reduced the number of immigrants by limiting the quota for each country, thus controlling the influx of foreign peoples.

Article II. The Founding of National Parishes

During the early period of its development this country was considered as a missionary country, and actually depended for its jurisdiction upon Europe, until the appointment of the Rev. John Carroll as Prefect Apostolic on June 9, 1784. The priests who came to this country usually came with a particular group of settlers to minister to their needs, or to work among the Indian tribes. These priests were few in number, and entirely insufficient for the population and the territory that they had to cover.[12]

[10] Shaughnessy, *op. cit.*, p. 134.

[11] Cf. Shaughnessy, *op. cit.*, p. 169.

[12] Shea, *History*, II, 257.

In 1634 the first church in Maryland was founded. In Pennsylvania there was later a large number of German Catholics. In Philadelphia in 1757 under Father Schneider they outnumbered the English-speaking Catholics and built for themselves a separate church about the year 1764.[13] In 1788 a group of German Catholics wrote to the Very Rev. John Carroll for permission to erect a new church, one for their own people. He was reluctant to grant the permission, but did so "for the preservation of charity, and in the hope of its being hereafter conducive to the interests of religion. . . ."[14] This group then erected the church of the Holy Trinity which was opened November 20, 1789, and was considered the first exclusively national church organized in this country. Later, due to national difficulties, a schism arose that lasted from 1796 to 1802. After its successful termination, Father Britt was made pastor in 1807, and the people had become so completely Americanized that many of the congregation could no longer confess in German.[15]

After this experience in Philadelphia, Bishop Carroll declined to permit a separate parish in Baltimore a decade later. The problem, however, was simply one of administration. In August, 1841, when the Very Rev. Prost, the superior of the Redemptorist Order visited Baltimore, Archbishop Eccleston prevailed upon him to accept the care of the German Catholics in Baltimore. They numbered about 5,000 souls at that time, and soon a new church was built for them.[16] In New York by 1834 the German Catholics had increased to such an extent that a church dedicated to St. Nicholas was built for them and was dedicated on Easter Sunday, 1836. The first pastor was Father John Raffeiner who later became the Vicar General for the Germans of the diocese.[17]

In Boston the German Catholics, who long had been without a priest of their own, erected in 1841 a church with the encourage-

[13] Shea, *History*, II, 64.

[14] Very Rev. John Carroll to the German Catholics of Philadelphia, March 31, 1788—Shea, *History*, II, 320.

[15] Shea, *History*, II, 422.

[16] Salzbacher, *Meine Reise nach Nord-America im Jahre 1842* (Vienna, 1855), II, 130.

[17] Shea, *History*, III, 508.

ment of the bishop who gave them Father Roloff as pastor.[18] In Ohio by 1820 there were so many Catholic families of German descent that Cincinnati was made a diocesan seat,[19] and in Pittsburgh the church of St. Philomena for the Germans was first organized in 1839. Similar conditions existed in Chicago (1844) and in St. Louis (1850) where there were also German congregations.[20]

What has been said of the German parishes may be applied also to the French language congregations which, though not as numerous perhaps during this period, were nevertheless distinct. In New York the French Catholics were organized through the zealous efforts of Msgr. da Forbin Janson, who gave a mission for them in February, 1841. The Rt. Rev. John Hughes, Bishop of the Diocese, encouraged further organization. In consequence the church of St. Vincent de Paul was built and placed in charge of the priests of the Society of Mercy. There was a French priest in Boston for the members of the French congregation as early as 1788. In the south, besides the Spaniards, there were also a number of French-speaking people, especially the Acadians, and parishes were founded for them by 1779. A number of French priests had arrived in Baltimore in 1792, and some of these were immediately sent out by Bishop Carroll to the Great Lakes mission where the French language was quite widespread.[21]

During the latter part of the nineteenth century, when the Poles began to immigrate in greater numbers, an identical situation arose. In 1868, at the request of the Bishop of Detroit, Bishop Lefevre, the Polish settlement of Parisville received it first resident pastor.[22] In Detroit itself there were many Polish families, and the church of St. Albertus was built and dedicated July 13, 1872, by Bishop Borgess, and St. Josephat's received its first resident pastor in

[18] Shea, *History*, III, 400.

[19] Pius VII, bull. *"Inter multiplices,"* 19 iun. 1821—*Bull. Pont. S. C. de Prop. Fide*, IV, 385.

[20] Shea, *History*, IV, 222, 230.

[21] Shea, *History*, III, 314, 407, 538, 549.

[22] Kruszka, *Historya Polska w Ameryce* (13 vols., Milwaukee: Kuryer, 1905-1908), XI, 149.

1891.[23] Thus during this period, and particularly during the first part of the twentieth century, many other parishes for language groups came into existence in different parts of the country with apparently fruitful results.

These were the general conditions under which the language parishes arose and thrived. They had received their initial sanction from the Very Rev. John Carroll, as Prefect Apostolic. After his consecration as the first bishop of the United States, in one of his pastoral letters he expressed the thought uppermost in his mind. Exhorting the faithful, whose numbers had increased rapidly through immigration, he reminded them that, existing as a congregation gathered in any district, their duty was to erect a church suited to their needs and to maintain a resident pastor if possible. This obligation had not been generally recognized, and he showed its binding force.[24]

Legislation, however, concerning language parishes is meager, and the first reference that indicates a sanction in favor of these institutions is the direction of the Synod of Baltimore (1791) that the congregation should recite the Lord's Prayer, the Hail Mary, the Apostles Creed, the Acts of Faith, Hope, and Charity in the vernacular tongue after mass, and that the priest should give instructions and read the gospel in the vernacular.[25] In 1862 Bishop Alemany held a synod in San Francisco and promulgated the decrees of the I Plenary Baltimore Council (1852) defining the limits of the missions. He determined, however, that the French, Spanish, and Germans were to be under the jurisdiction of their respective pastors wherever the language parishes had been established.[26]

In 1847 a division of parishes was made for the German people in Philadelphia, where those in the north were to attend St. Peter's Church, while the others were to be taken care of by the clergy of

[23] Kruszka, *op. cit.*, XI, 177, 200.

[24] Shea, *History*, II, 400.

[25] Synod of Baltimore (1791), n. 18—*Acta et Decreta Sacrorum Conciliorum Recentiorum, Collectio Lacensis* (7 vols., Friburgi Brisgoviae: Herder, 1870-1890), III, 5. Hereafter cited *Coll. Lac.* Cf. Conc. Plen. Balt. II (1866), n. 181—*Coll. Lac.*, III, 452.

[26] Shea, *History*, IV, 708.

Holy Trinity.[27] This evidently was an effort to carry out the provisions of the Council of Trent with regard to the assigning of definite territorial limits to each parish.[28] In such cases, and they were multiplied when they were several parishes of the same language in one city, there was evidently fulfilled the condition required by the Council of Trent as to the proper people and boundaries.

In the I Plenary Council of Baltimore (1852) it was enjoined upon the bishops to designate the limits of parishes, but they were given the power to change these, and to determine the jurisdiction of the pastors.[29] In the pastoral letter of the Fathers of the II Provincial Council of Cincinnati (1858) explicit provisions were made for the distinct nationalities existing in the province, particularly for the Germans, and the French, but applying also to all others.[30] The Fathers of the II Plenary Council of Baltimore (1866) themselves adverted to the fact that the existence of parishes along strict territorial lines in this country was not yet possible.[31]

Article III. Immigrant Clergy

In the early period of American colonization, the priests who came to provide spiritual solace to the early settlers were mostly voluntary laborers for the missions.[32] After the Church in the United States became a distinct body in 1784, under the jurisdictional care of the Very Rev. John Carroll, he sent urgent appeals to Rome for priests to take care of the increasing flock which was composed of divers foreign elements.[33] In the Synod of Baltimore (1791), the clergy who met with the Americans, English, Irish, Germans, French, Belgians, and Hollanders.[34]

Although the Sulpicians had founded the seminary at Baltimore

[27] III Synod of Philadelphia (1847), n. 5—*Statuta Provincialia et Dioecesana* (Philadelphia: Catholic Standard and Times Print, sine anno), p. 19.

[28] Sess. XXIV, *de ref.*, c. 13.

[29] I Conc. Plen. Balt. (1852), n. X—*Coll. Lac.*, III, 146.

[30] Litterae Past. II Conc. Prov. Cincinnat. (1858)—*Coll. Lac.*, III, 1230 b.

[31] II Conc. Plen. Balt. (1866), n. 123—*Coll. Lac.*, III, 432.

[32] Shea, *History*, II, 80, 145, 205.

[33] Cf. Shea, *History*, II, 263.

[34] Shea, *History*, II, 395; cf. Syn. Dioec. Balt. (1791)—*Coll. Lac.*, III, 1.

in 1791, it could not supply the increased demand for priests, and many Catholics were lost to the faith because of the lack of clergy who could speak their language and who were familiar with their national customs. An attempt was made to provide for these language groups by having priests knowing these languages stationed at the church of the territory in which they were found. In 1808 at St. Peter's parish in New York services in English, French and German were conducted every Sunday.[35] In 1837 the Fathers of the III Provincial Council of Baltimore wrote to Gregory XVI (1831-1846), and indicated to him the urgent need for more priests to meet the spiritual requirements of the people.[36]

Bishop Carroll had already observed that it was necessary to impress upon the minds of the priests who were volunteering to come to the United States that they must be filled with zeal and high motives, and be prepared to endure the greatest hardships, and not be drawn to come by any visions of quick gain. The I Plenary Council of Baltimore (1852) stressed this point further, by requiring letters from the European Ordinaries before priests could be admitted to the dioceses in America,[37] and the next Plenary Council (1866) warned against the priests who came "more for material gain than for the zeal of souls."[38] The Sacred Congregation for the Propagation of the Faith in a special instruction of January 24, 1868, in article 3, informed the bishops that if, in view of being hard pressed, they had to resort to the services of the *vagi sacerdotes*, they first had to receive secure testimony of their probity and doctrine.[39] It was apparently the wish of the Holy See to care for the immigrants by erecting separate churches with their respective pastors. This seems to have been implied in the letter of Pope Leo XIII, who spoke of the need of Italian priests, and hoped that the

[35] Shea, *History*, III, 196.

[36] III Conc. Prov. Balt. (1837), Epistola Patrum Concilii ad Summum Pontificem—*Coll. Lac.*, III, 53.

[37] I Plen. Conc. Balt. (1852), n. IX—*Coll. Lac.*, III, 146.

[38] II Plen. Conc. Balt. (1866), n. 120—*Coll. Lac.*, III, 432.

[39] Cf. II Conc. Plen. Balt., n. 122—*Coll. Lac.*, III, 432.

new Apostolic College established at Piacenza for the training of missionary priests would help solve the problem.[40]

Beginning in 1890, the Sacred Congregation of the Council issued a series of instructions and letters concerning immigrant priests. Treating first of the Italian clergy, it provided for arrangements to be made directly between the Italian and American ordinaries, with the approval of the Sacred Congregation.[41] The Sacred Congregation for the Propagation of the Faith further required that before immigrant priests were accepted in a diocese, they had to show letters granting them permission to leave their own diocese, and testimony of their own freedom from censures, as well as of their good character. Since there were many Polish priests leaving for the United States at this time, a special provision was made for them and they were obliged to have letters from this same Congregation, showing their legitimate departure, and their immunity from censures.[42]

When the abuses continued, due to the great number of priests migrating from Europe, the Sacred Congregation of the Council extended its requirements to all priests. The European ordinary had to obtain the consent of the ordinary in America, and give secret assurances concerning the age, morals and ability of the priest before granting discessorial letters. In this procedure it required for the validity of these letters that a set form furnished by the said Congregation be used.[43]

Pius X (1903-1914) took a particular interest in the Italian emigrants and by decree established a college in Rome for the preparation of secular priests who would be able to care for the Italians abroad.[44] In the same year the Sacred Consistorial Congre-

[40] Litt. ap. *"Quam aerumnosa,"* 10 dec. 1887—*ASS*, XXI (1888), 258; *AER*, I (1889), 45.

[41] S.C.C., litt. encycl. (ad Epp. Ital. et Americ.), 27 iul. 1890—*Coll.*, n. 1734; *Fontes*, n. 4280.

[42] S. C. de Prop. Fide, instr. (ad Ep. Stat. Foeder. Americae), 25 febr. 1896 —*Coll.*, n. 1918; *Fontes*, n. 4933.

[43] S.C.C., 14 nov. 1903—*Coll.*, n. 2180; *Fontes*, n. 4315; *AER*, XLI (1909), 619.

[44] Pius X, motu propr. *"Iam pridem,"* 19 mart. 1914—*AAS*, VI (1914), 173-176; *AER*, L (1914), 719.

gation issued a decree reiterating the provisions made previously for immigrant priests, and outlined in detail the conditions under which priests of the Latin rite could emigrate to America and the Philippines, even though for a short visit. Those who wilfully disregarded these laws were *ipso facto* suspended.[45]

The same Sacred Congregation issued another decree describing in detail the conditions under which clergy emigrating from Europe to these regions, either permanently or temporarily, were to travel, and be accepted.[46] Having summarized the previous legislation, it went on to say that only bishops could grant discessorial letters to priests going to America or to the Philippines, and then only on the condition that these be secular priests with a canonical title of their own, who had given some years of service in their own dioceses after ordination, during which they gave evidence of good morals and sufficient learning. It required a just reason for making the journey, as for example, the spiritual assistance of the faithful of their own nation, or the necessary care of their health. It specified that the dismissing bishop was to communicate in advance with the bishop *ad quem*, informing him of the name of the priest and the reason for his migrating, and asking him if he be willing to accept him and give him ecclesiastical work consisting of more than merely saying mass. It provided that the bishop *ad quem* was not to receive the priest unless his services were necessary or advisable for the good of the diocese, or there was some other good reason justifying it. The dismissing bishop further could not give the permission or discessorial letters to the emigrating priest until he had received an affirmative answer to these questions. Both bishops were under grave obligation in conscience to abide by the indicated ruling.

As for the discessorial letters, the decree enacted that they had to be made out in a special form, expressing the perpetual, temporary or revocable consent of the bishop *a quo*, describing the priest's qualities and characteristics for his unmistakable identification, and

[45] S. C. Consist., decr., 25 mart. 1914—*Fontes*, n. 2088; *AAS*, VI (1914), 182-186.

[46] S. C. Consist., decr. 30 dec. 1918—*AAS*, XI (1919), 39-43.

adding mention of the acceptance of the bishop *ad quem.* Without these the letters were null and void.

Italian bishops were bound to make the preliminary preparations and then to refer the matter to the Sacred Consistorial Congregation, which then issued the permission and made the necessary communications itself.[47] A similar restriction applied to the bishops of Spain and Portugal, but in their case the Apostolic Delegate in those countries granted the permission. Without discessorial letters the priests were not to be admitted to the exercise of the sacred ministry. Only under these conditions, and in conformity with the provisions of the law,[48] the consent of both ordinaries having been obtained, could priests from Europe be incardinated in America. The receiving bishop was to notify the bishop *a quo* of the arrival of the priest in the diocese, or his whereabouts.

Regarding religious, their superior could send them to religious houses of their society in America under the obligation that they send only men of good character, sound vocation and sufficient learning.[49] Exclaustrated and secularized religious[50] were under the same regulations as the secular clergy.

These rules applied also to priests who dwelled in foreign countries and there ministered to immigrants, whether they did this of their own initiative or whether they had been sent by some organization for that purpose. Those who rashly or arrogantly emigrated without following these regulations were *ipso facto* suspended, and if they attempted to perform sacred functions they incurred an irregularity from which they could be absolved only by the Sacred Consistorial Congregation.[51]

Thus the Holy See tried seriously to aid the established and growing Church in the United States, encumbered though it was with numerous difficulties of divergent language and national cus-

[47] S. C. Consist., decr. 25 mart. 1914—*AAS,* VI (1914), 182; *Fontes,* n. 2088.

[48] Canons 111-117.

[49] S. C. Consist., decr. 30 dec. 1918, cap. I, n. 9—*AAS,* XI (1919), 41.

[50] Cf. canons 638-640.

[51] There were special regulations for secular and religious clerics who wished to leave Europe for America or the Philippines for a time not exceeding six months. *Ibid.,* cap. II—*AAS,* XI (1919), 42.

toms. The need of priests able to minister to the congregations in their own idiom was an imperative one, but also one fraught with many dangers to souls from unscrupulous persons who seized the opportunity to benefit themselves. These dangers were obviated in a large measure by the vigilance of the Church in providing good priests to the best of its ability for the salvation of souls and the glory of God.

CHAPTER III

PARISHES IN THE UNITED STATES

THE Church in the early period of its history in this country was confronted with many difficulties. Because of the vastness of the territory, to a great extent unexplored, and because of the sparse number of Catholics in many localities, this country was considered as a missionary dependency. The French and Spanish explorers, through the missionaries who came with them, had made definite but for the most part unsuccessful attempts to establish an enduring Church discipline in the lands that they opened through conquest and colonization.[1]

In that early period the Church in the Americas required aid and help from the established Church in Europe. The assistance given was material as well as spiritual, material in that Europe furnished the necessary financial means for founding missions and churches as well as charitable institutions, and spiritual in the sense that Europe provided priests and religious to administer the churches, to instruct the faithful and to spread the gospel of Christ. Since the territory could not be divided into dioceses, it was first placed formally under the jurisdiction of the Sacred Congregation for the Propagation of Faith when, on June 9, 1784, Father John Carroll was made the "head of the missions in the provinces of the new Republic of the United States of North America" as a Prefect Apostolic.

Even with the successive establishment of the Catholic hierarchy in the United States this dependence continued for more than a century. Particularly due to the small number of priests, and the widely scattered congregations, it was necessary to make provisions according to the existing circumstances. As a result there was not always a strict adherence to the ideal methods as prescribed by the common law of the Church for strict parochial organization.

[1] Guilday, *A History of the Councils of Baltimore* (New York, 1932), pp. 20-49.

Article I. Status Before and After the Code

The practice of the Church in missionary countries with regard to the disciplinary organization of dioceses naturally takes the form of progressive development. First a Prefect Apostolic is appointed for such a country by the Sacred Congregation for the Propagation of Faith. Then, when the country is sufficiently organized along diocesan lines, it is given a Vicar Apostolic and eventually a resident bishop. In the United States this gradual plan was accelerated and at an early date the priests were given the rare privilege of selecting their own bishop, and the Very Rev. John Carroll was elected the first bishop of this country in May, 1789.[2] The choice of the clergy was confirmed by Pius VI (1775-1799) when the new See of Baltimore, with John Carroll as the ordinary was erected on November 6, 1789. When the diocesan organization had progressed still further other bishops with residental sees were appointed. In the United States this progress was rapid, and in 1808 Sees were created at Boston, New York, Philadelphia and Bardstown. Despite this rapid growth the bishops and their dioceses remained under the direct jurisdiction of the Sacred Congregation for the Propagation of the Faith and retained their missionary character until they reached such a degree of development that they were in full conformity with the sacred canons and came under the jurisdiction of the common law of the Church.

As for the parochial organization in the missionary countries, it undergoes the same gradual change. At first simple missionaries bring the faith from place to place, and gather the small and scattered congregations together in the missions for their spiritual nourishment. With the growth of these missions and congregations they assume the character of quasi-parishes with fixed boundaries, especially in the well populated districts, and the priest becomes the resident rector of the quasi-parish. The final and complete step comes when the quasi-parish is recognized as having acquired a stable existence, so that being possessed of a sufficient income for the maintenance of the church properties and the rector it is raised to the dignity of a parish in the canonical sense of the term, and the

[2] Guilday, *op. cit.*, p. 59.

rector becomes the canonical pastor. When the diocese and its parishes have arrived at this final stage of development, they are generally transferred from the direct control of the Sacred Congregation for the Propagation of the Faith and are placed under the general disciplinary law of the Church.[3]

In the United States this development was initiated with the missionary endeavors of the early priests and bishops. Because of the vast extent of the territory, the initial efforts of the clergy were not strictly limited by territorial boundaries, but priests were sent out with a sort of general care of the people in a certain district. This was particularly noticeable in the practice sanctioned by the bishops in 1810, permitting a priest who had faculties in one diocese to exercise them in a neighboring diocese.[4] These faculties were revoked in the II Provincial Council of Baltimore (1833) both because of certain abuses that arose, and also because of the abuses that could arise from the practice of unknown and unscrupulous priests.[5] From this time on the priests were required to have the authorization of the ordinary of the diocese in which they happened to be.

The question proposed is whether there existed any canonical parishes in the United States. At the time of the I Provincial Council of Baltimore (1829) it seems to have been the opinion of the bishops that there existed only one such parochial benefice in the provinces, and that was in New Orleans.[6] This same observation was made in the II Plenary Council of Baltimore (1866) in exactly the same words,[7] although in the Synod of New Orleans (1844)

[3] Const. *"Sapienti consilio,"* 29 iun. 1908—*Fontes,* n. 682.

[4] Cf. articles of ecclesiastical discipline approved by the common consent of the American bishops in 1810—*Concilia Provincialia Baltimorensia* (Baltimori: Joannes Murphy et Soc., 1851), p. 25.

[5] *Concilia Provincialia Baltimorensia,* n. X, p. 105.

[6] "Hac autem declaratione nihil innovare volumus quoad illos qui parochialia obtinerent beneficia, quorum unum tantum scilicet in civitate Neo-Aurelia adhuc noscitur in hisce provinciis."—I Conc. Prov. Balt., n. I—*Conc. Prov. Balt.,* p. 73.

[7] Cap. IV, n. 108—*Concilii Plenarii Baltimorensis II Acta et Decreta* (Baltimorae: Joannes Murphy, 1868), p. 75. Hereafter cited *Acta et Decreta.*

there was no mention according to Shea, of such a benefice in that diocese.[8] It is no longer mentioned in the III Plenary Council of Baltimore (1884).

On the west coast there seem to have been canonical parishes established also.[9] From the words of the I Synod of San Francisco (1862) on the mutual duties of pastors and people it seems clear that there existed at least some canonically established parishes in that province.[10] As a matter of fact these parishes existed prior to the Synod and are called "paroeciae proprie dictae." In Canon Law *paroeciae proprie dictae* means parishes in the strict sense of the word,[11] so there is some reason to believe that canonical parishes did exist in some parts of the United States, though they were not commonly referred to as such. Undoubtedly, if one considered the concept of an ecclesiastical benefice with regard to the perpetuity and the stability of funds and property, one would discover many cases in which these institutions measured up to the requirements of canonical parishes. The fact remains, however, that since this country was under the jurisdiction of the Sacred Congregation for the Propagation of Faith, the status of bishops, even though they had fixed sees, was that of delegates and representatives of the Holy See. As such therefore they did not, as long as this country was considered a missionary dependency, exercise the faculty of erecting canonical parishes,[12] even though they had the power *ex potestate ordinaria.* The II Plenary Council of Baltimore (1866) sought to establish parishes as far as possible according to the decrees of the Council of Trent, with definite parochial limits, but insisted that, because of the conditions existing in this country, it was not yet possible to have parishes considered as such in the true sense of the word.[13] In spite of the use of the words "parochial rights," "the parish" and "the pastor," the

[8] *History,* IV, 269.

[9] Shea, *History,* IV, 352.

[10] Cf. Smith, *Elements,* I, n. 654.

[11] Smith, *Counter-points in Canon Law* (Newark, 1879), p. 33. Hereafter cited *Counter-points.*

[12] Smith, *Counter-points,* p. 40.

[13] "Verum ea sunt nostra rerum tempora, quae id fieri nondum patiantur." —II Conc. Plen. Balt., n. 123—*Acta et Decreta,* p. 79.

decree of the Council insisted emphatically that it did not intend by that to confer the right of irremovability. Even in larger cities where there were a number of churches with distinct boundaries they were not to be considered canonically as parishes, but merely as quasi-parishes,[14] and their rectors were to act merely in the name of the bishops, and not with the ordinary jurisdiction of canonical pastors.

The Fathers of the III Plenary Council of Baltimore (1884) adopted the same decrees with the added recommendation that irremovable rectors be appointed for certain missions which seemed most suited to be regarded as *paroeciarum instar,* and that these quasi-parishes have a church, school, priest's house, and a sufficient income for the maintenance of all needs.[15] According to the Council, then, there were two kinds of missions or quasi-parishes, those which had irremovable rectors and others with removable rectors. This was the condition of the Church in the United States until the time of the Constitution *"Sapienti consilio"* of June 29, 1908, when the dioceses were withdrawn from the jurisdiction of the Congregation for the Propagation of the Faith and placed under the common law of the Church.[16]

After this country was brought under the common law, where there were only quasi-parishes before, the strict parochial system was thenceforth to prevail.[17] Although the necessary permanence and organization had undoubtedly been reached in many dioceses with regard to parochial institutions, there existed no direct evidence to show that, by the very fact of the withdrawal of the Church in this country from the jurisdiction of the Sacred Congregation for the Propagation of the Faith the parishes were thereby made canonical parishes in the strict sense and ceased to be quasi-parishes. Nor was it clear that at least those parishes which were erected after 1908 were to be considered as canonically established. If these parishes had the

[14] The parochial districts were designated by the words *"paroeciae instar."* —II Conc. Plen. Balt., nn. 124-125—*Acta et Decreta,* p. 79.

[15] Conc. Plen. Balt. III (1884), n. 33—*Acta et Decreta Concilii Plenarii Baltimorensis Tertii* (Baltimorae: John Murphy, 1886). Hereafter cited *Acta et Decreta.*

[16] Cf. *Fontes,* n. 682.

[17] Ayrinhac, *Constitution of the Church,* n. 5.

necessary requirements there seems to be no reason why they could not have been considered as parishes in the strict canonical sense under the general law of the Church. This situation was not clarified by the decree *"Maxima cura"* of the Sacred Consistorial Congregation of August 20, 1910, dealing with the administrative removal of incumbents from offices and benefices having the care of souls.[18] This decree was also applied to the United States in 1911 [19] but still left some doubt as to whether it referred only to the irremovable rectors or also to those who were irremovable.[20] In a later reply the Sacred Consistorial Congregation definitely clarified this response in applying the decree *"Maxima cura"* only to the irremovable rectors in the United States.[21]

This doubt was carried over after the promulgation of the present Code of Canon Law, and it did not appear whether or not the quasi-parishes become *ipso facto* parishes, or whether a certain formality had to be followed in determining their status. It was the opinion of the majority of American canonists that, since the parishes in this country conformed to the requirements of canonical parishes as described in canon 216, § 1, of the Code, no special decree of erection was necessary.[22] The very recognition by the Code of these parishes authorized their existence.

A more definite position was taken with the declaration of the Sacred Consistorial Congregation concerning the nature of quasi-parishes or missions in some dioceses after the promulgation of the Code. Doubts had been proposed to the Sacred Congregation by some dioceses which had been under the jurisdiction of the Sacred Congre-

[18] *AAS,* II (1910), 636; *Fontes,* n. 2074.

[19] S. C. Consist., 13 mart. 1911—*AAS,* III (1911), 133.

[20] S. C. Consist., decr. *"Maxima cura,"* 20 aug. 1910, can. 30—*Fontes,* n. 2074.

[21] S. C. Consist., *Statuum Foederatorum Americae Septentrionalis,* de amotione parochorum, 28 iun. 1915: "Sed rectores missionum seu paroeciarum qui in Foederatis Americae Statibus inter inamovibiles recensiti non sunt ex taxativa Concilii Plenarii Baltimor. II et III lege, ab Apostolica Sede confirmata, iuri antiquo adhuc subsunt, et habentur qua Ordinariorum vicarii ad eorum nutum amovibiles."—*AAS,* VII (1915), 378-382, and in particular p. 381: *Fontes,* n. 2090.

[22] Cf. Ayrinhac, *Constitution of the Church,* n. 5; *AER,* LX (1919), 544.

gation for the Propagation of the Faith before the Constitution "*Sapienti consilio,*" and which later were placed under the common law of the Church. These doubts concerned the nature of the parishes and the missions into which the dioceses had been divided, and the rights and duties of their rectors. The answer was that in the diocese in question the territorial divisions that had a distinct rector had to be regarded as real parishes in name and in fact, the appellation quasi-parishes or missions being reserved to portions of vicariates or prefectures apostolic. It further went on to say that to constitute parishes a decree of the ordinary was needed, fixing the limits and seat of the parish and the income necessary for the support of the clergy and church.[23]

There was still some uncertainty with regard to the real status of parishes in the United States, however, and this was resolved in a reply of the prefect of the Commission for the Authentic Interpretation of the Code of Canon Law, Cardinal Gasparri, to the doubts proposed by His Excellency the Apostolic Delegate to the United States. This reply, which was communicated to the bishops under the date of November 10, 1922, states that it is not necessary for the ordinary to issue a special decree for the erection of a parish, and that it was sufficient to define the territorial limits, and to assign the rector to the people and the church within the said limits. A parish was further an ecclesiastical benefice according to canon 1411, § 5, whether it had the proper endowment according to canon 1410, or was erected according to the provision of canon 1415, § 3. Furthermore, no special decree of the ordinary was necessary to constitute as canonical parishes those which before the promulgation of the Code, had been established in the manner mentioned, and such parishes became canonical parishes *ipso facto* after the promulgation of the Code.[24]

From the context of this reply, the Apostolic Delegate concluded that the parishes in the United States, inasmuch as they had the three necessary qualifications of resident pastor, revenue, and boundaries, were not only parishes in the strict canonical sense, but were also ecclesiastical benefices, and their pastors had the duties and

[23] S. C. Consist., resp., 1 aug. 1919—*AAS*, XI (1919), 346.

[24] For the full text of this letter cf. Bouscaren, I, 149.

obligations of canonical pastors.[25] This position was later confirmed in the resolution of a case submitted to the Sacred Congregation of the Council, which resolution indicated that the canonical erection of a parish may appear not only from a formal decree of erection, but also from various other elements that go to make up a parish, namely, a certain definite territory, a definite population, a certain rector having the care of souls, and finally the authority of the bishop maintaining and approving this juridical condition.[26]

Article II. Status of National Parishes

So far the general status of parishes in the United States from the time when they were merely missions until their eventual recognition as canonical parishes has been considered. The question that next proposes itself is, whether national parishes are included in the category of parishes thus recognized. A thorough examination of the III Plenary Council of Baltimore reveals no provision for the establishment of churches for individual language groups. Its reference is strictly to territorial parishes along the lines of the Tridentine legislation.[27] It did, however, recognize and acknowledge the presence of an immigration problem that existed at that time, and urged the spiritual and temporal care of these Catholic immigrants.[28] It recommended that particularly in the metropolitan seaboard area prudent priests be stationed who knew the language of these people, and whose principal duty it would be to act as leaders and advisers of these incoming Catholic foreigners.[29] In further recognizing the need of providing for the spiritual welfare of these foreign elements, the Fathers of the Council ruled that besides English, students studying for the priesthood should acquire a knowledge of at least one other modern language, either German, French, Polish (or one of the other Slav languages), Italian, or Spanish, according to the need

[25] Canons 466; 339.

[26] S.C.C., resol., 5 mart. 1932—*AAS,* XXV (1932), 436; S.C.C., litt., 18 mart. 1881—*Coll.,* n. 1548.

[27] III Conc. Plen Balt., n. 32 ff.—*Acta et Decreta.*

[28] *Acta et Decreta,* nn. 232-233.

[29] *Acta et Decreta,* n. 234.

of the diocese, as directed by the bishop.[30] In ordaining that a uniform catechism be prepared for the instruction of Catholic children, it recommended that this be translated also in other languages for the use of the faithful.[31] If the parents were foreign-born and the children spoke both languages, they were to learn their catechism also in English, especially if they lived among English-speaking people.

Since outside of these few instances in the Baltimore Councils there is no further mention of needs arising from foreign language or foreign elements, it is to be presumed that the Fathers considered the problem a diocesan one at the time, leaving it to the individual ordinaries to erect parishes according to the need as it arose in their particular dioceses. The bishop was the supreme head of the diocese and, though he could not legislate contrary to the general law, or without grave reason dispense from the general observance, he was in a position to judge the immediate conditions which made possible such observance, and could interpret the law in its application to the actual conditions over which he was guardian.

That the bishops had the power to erect churches and constitute quasi-parishes or parishes, as the case might be, cannot be denied. It is evident from the Council of Trent as well as the III Plenary Council of Baltimore. The Council of Trent authorized the bishops to appoint assistants, or to erect new parishes in places where the people would otherwise have been deprived of the sacraments in consequence of their overflowing numbers in any one parish, or also in view of their great distance from an existing parish church, or for any similar serious inconvenience for approaching it.[32] In the III Plenary Council of Baltimore (1884) the wise decrees of the Council of Trent (1545-1563) were recognized with full acknowledgment, and the written permission of the bishop was required to build a church.[33]

The power of the bishops also extended to the national groups

[30] *Acta et Decreta,* n. 147; cf. n. 216.

[31] ". . . valde in votis habemus, ut a fidelibus aliarum quoque linguarum in eorum idioma conversus adhibeatur."—*Acta et Decreta,* n. 219.

[32] Sess., XXI, *de ref.,* c. 4; cf. c. 3, X, *de ecclesiis aedificandis vel reparandis,* III, 48.

[33] *Acta et Decreta,* nn. 33, 279.

within their jurisdiction, and before the Code they could grant permission to erect churches and establish national parishes if they saw that it was necessary.[34] This may well be concluded from the silence of the Baltimore Councils on this particular phase of parochial organization, as well as from the actual procedure of the ordinaries in a matter of such great spiritual importance. They actually did establish national parishes, and appointed men who knew the language of the people to act as rectors. In some cases they even appealed to foreign countries to provide priests for their particular congregations. Conditions in this country were different from those in other countries and there were districts, particularly in the large cities where foreign languages were (and still are today) in common usage. Faith and zeal for souls, and not any alien patriotism, was the dominant motive for this solicitude of the bishops in their respective dioceses.[35]

Real and alleged abuses arose, but they cannot all be taken into consideration. The fact remains that the bishops had the power to found such parishes before the Code. They had a right to make them purely personal parishes independent of any boundaries, intended only for the people of a certain language or nationality; or they could make them mixed territorial parishes, that is, for the people of a certain language or nationality within definite limits. In either case they were considered before the Code as quasi-parishes or missions for their particular nationality, and not simply as chapels of ease, precisely because of the parochial nature of the elements that contributed to their formation, namely, a definite congregation, a rector duly appointed for the care of souls, and in the case of mixed territorial parishes, even territorial delimitations.[36]

There was also the revenue sufficient to maintain these institutions. If the bishops before the Code did not have the power to establish parishes, national as well as territorial, this lack of authority would have appeared, by contrast, in the present law, and the possession of it under the present law would have been noted as a change from the old law. The fact that they now possess the power of erecting parishes, but not as a new power, indicates that they had it also be-

[34] Beste, *Introductio,* p. 227.

[35] Cf. *Acta et Decreta,* n. 232.

[36] Cf. Wernz-Vidal, *Ius Canonicum,* II, n. 719.

fore the Code. For in the case of national parishes, it is worth noting that the power is not taken away from them, but rather a condition is placed according to which that power is to be exercised.[37]

As in the case of territorial parishes in the United States before the Code, the national parishes were not considered strictly as parishes but as quasi-parishes erected for distinct language and national groups. With the promulgation of the Code, quasi-parishes in this country became parishes *ipso facto* if they had the required qualities. According to the letter of the Apostolic Delegate and his interpretation of the response of the Holy See, all of the parishes in the United States having the three necessary qualifications are not only parishes in the strict canonical sense but are also ecclesiastical benefices.[38]

Since these three conditions are explicitly mentioned as necessary for a canonical parish, some authors concluded that this reply did not include national parishes.[39] It is true that this reply did not explicitly include national parishes, but it would be wrong to conclude that national parishes therefore remained quasi-parishes, for the simple reason that they did not have strict boundaries. The reason is that boundary lines, though very desirable as already noted, do not form the essential part in the constitution of every parish. Furthermore, it would be wrong to say that a national parish has no boundaries, because there are very many mixed parishes that have limits in common with one or more parishes. They are then said to be cumulative with a strictly territorial parish, or even with another national parish. If national parishes were not parishes under the present Code it would be difficult to classify them. They would be neither quasi-parishes, since this country was withdrawn from the jurisdiction of the Sacred Congregation of the Propagation of the Faith, nor missions, nor chapels of ease.

The essential elements constituting a parish are: a definite congregation, and a duly appointed pastor for a particular church with sufficient revenue, constituted under a legitimate authority. It follows then that if, prior to the Code, a parish was constituted on the basis of these three elements for a distinct group of the faithful, and

[37] Canon 216, § 4.

[38] Bouscaren, I, 150.

[39] Cf. Ayrinhac, *Constitution of the Church*, n. 6.

if the same conditions prevailed after the Code, it was to be considered a canonical parish, and the pastor, a canonical pastor, removable or irremovable as the case might be. The fact remains that he had assigned to his care, a definite portion of the faithful of the diocese over whom he exercised jurisdiction. Since territorial lines are not in themselves essential, they cannot be considered absolutely exclusive of the right of a parish to be regarded as such. Thus pastors of national parishes exercised their jurisdiction over a distinct body of the faithful in a territory held in common with one or more pastors. It was sufficient that the parish was distinct in some way to obviate all possible basis in law of a mutual clash of rights, so that the pastor could administer the sacraments to his people without confusion or uncertainty regarding jurisdiction. It was principally because of this confusion that the Council of Trent insisted on the distinct territorial distribution of parishes wherever this was possible, that is, to avoid the indiscriminate administration of the sacraments, and to limit the mutual rights and obligations of priests and people in relation to a definite priest and a definite people.[40]

But even as to the existence of territorial boundaries the following considerations seem to indicate that they are not wanting, at least in a great number of national parishes. Aside from the fact that national parishes have a definite congregation, they may also have a more or less determined territory, in which case they are mixed personal and territorial parishes. As in the case of territorial parishes, these limits may not have been defined by the ordinary at the time of the founding of the parishes, but rather by custom and the lapse of time. This custom does not necessarily set canonical boundaries, but in many instances can, through legitimate prescription, obtain the force of a law, which is of equal import with a law whereby boundaries have been set. Custom has the force of law if vested with the proper qualities.[41]

Though certain and indubitable parish lines are not subject to formation or change through the agency of legal prescription,[42] there is nothing in law which precludes the certification of existing doubt-

[40] Sess., XXIV, *de ref.*, c. 13.
[41] Canon 28.
[42] Canon 1509, 4°.

ful boundaries through the operation of legal prescription. Moreover, even before doubtful boundaries are legally prescribed they can be determined by the local ordinary, if not explicitly by a formal decree, at least implicitly by acknowledging certain parochial limits in the administration of the diocese. The general extent of this territory does not matter as far as a personal parish is concerned. It may comprise but a few city blocks, or the entire city, or an entire county. Thus a national parish may include the people of a particular language group in a certain portion of a city, in the entire city or in the surrounding district. A national parish in the city where there are one or more territorial or national parishes may be cumulative with them.[43]

To say, then, that national parishes have no territory would not be absolutely correct, because besides the primary characteristic that they exist as personal parishes for a definite language group, their secondary characteristic is that the latter group is composed of a particular people in a certain locality within reasonable distance of the church that is erected for them, and that the parish is therefore also territorial. Though sometimes not outlined by clear and distinct boundaries, a certain district could be called the territory of the national parish, with the approval or the understanding of the ordinary. It would be ridiculous and unreasonable to say that one particular national church was for all the people of that nationality in the country or in the State, or even in the diocese, because of the practical impossibility of mutual co-operation of the pastor and of the people. In some of the larger cities where two or more parishes exist for the same language groups, their boundaries are usually more clearly defined, so that even from the standpoint of territoriality it is easy to understand that they do not lack the condition necessary for a canonical parish. Since the other elements are not wanting, namely, a distinct portion of the faithful, a proper church and proper pastor, there seems to be no element lacking to prevent national parishes from enjoying the status of parishes.[44]

One must conclude, then, that the status of national parishes in

[43] Wernz-Vidal, *Ius Canonicum,* V, n. 535.

[44] Augustine, *Status of Catholic Parishes,* p. 67.

the United States is that of true canonical parishes if they were established with the necessary qualities by a legitimate authority for a particular portion of the faithful who spoke a common language. Their position is duly recognized by the law of the Church in canon 216, § 4, which requires that no changes be made regarding parishes established along personal lines. The Code does not make any revolutionary statements in this respect, but merely crystallizes the past provisions for national groups as made by their respective bishops. At the same time it does not suggest coercion in its method, but rather gives the respective bishops of dioceses where such need may arise in the future the credit for sufficient zeal and interest to petition the Holy See for the required apostolic indult whenever necessary or useful.

CHAPTER IV

NATIONAL PARISHES IN THE UNITED STATES

It has already been noted that, because of the vast number of Catholic immigrants in this country, a condition that is peculiar to the Catholic Church in the United States has developed. It is peculiar not in the sense that it has never existed before, or that it does not even now exist in countries outside of the United States,[1] but its peculiarity consists in the fact that it is in this country that the necessity and utility of national parishes was first recognized on a large scale. It is easy to understand how the need for these parishes became imperative with the influx of numerous foreign elements. When these people first came to the shores of this friendly country they possessed little if any knowledge of its language. They were practically cut off from any communication with their native country because of the vast distance that separated them, and because of the meager education that very many of them had.

They may have been prompted to leave their native land because of despotism, or they may have been enticed to come to the land of opportunity because of the flaunted hope of coming into their own, and of providing for a comfortable existence. They not only left their native soil, but many of them parted with their family and friends. It is only natural, then, that they sought out, or were directed to, certain localities in this country where they knew they would be among those of their own nationality. Here they could at least make themselves understood through the medium of a common language. Since the mother tongue is the ordinary means of acquiring knowledge and instruction, it was also the logical means to be employed in the religious instruction of the faithful, to preserve them in their faith, and to exhort them to persevere in their religious practices. If they were sufficiently numerous, they soon made generous contributions toward the building of magnificent churches and

[1] Similar conditions have been found to prevail in certain European countries, and also in Canada. Cf. Schäfer, *Pfarrer und Pfarrvikare*, p. 9.

co-operated in maintaining them. They learned to love this country, and most of them decided to remain here.

The national churches are a testimony of their faith and devotion during a time when they were very much exposed to the danger of losing their faith, as did many who came to this country. A rapid transition from an environment possessing one form of culture and tradition to an environment possessing a completely different one invariably has the tendency of demoralizing fixed standards of life and conduct for the greater number of persons, or at least of upsetting their normal practices to some extent, especially if that change is to an environment marked by a more liberal attitude toward the world and its institutions.[2] Since the immigrants were not educated and reared according to the traditions of freedom on which this country was founded, they could have in this transformation instinctively learned to despise the moral and religious principles that formed a part of their ancestral heritage. Since the population of this country professed many religious beliefs, and in great part none whatever, the danger of aberration with respect to the profession of distinctive dogmatic truths was great. The fact that these people found friends in bishops and priests who provided for their religious and spiritual needs is a credit to the great institution which is the Catholic Church. Churches were built and parishes were organized exclusively for them. These parishes became known as national parishes.

Article I. General Notions

Although the purpose of national parishes in the United States was to provide for the spiritual needs of the immigrants who did not understand English, the common language of this country, it would not be absolutely correct to say that according to the law the status of these parishes was precarious or subsidiary.[3] In the Code these parishes have been given a special recognition wherever they happen

[2] Creusen, "L'Eglise Catholique aux Etats-Unis,"—*Nouvelle Revue Theologique* (Tournai, 1869—), LIV (1927), 663.

[3] Cf. Augustine, *Status of Catholic Parishes*, p. 67; Ayrinhac, *Constitution of the Church*, n. 7.

to exist, and their existence had been determined to such an extent that, in the future, nothing is to be done with regard to their status unless the Holy See is first consulted.

> Non possunt sine speciali apostolico indulto constitui paroeciae pro diversitate sermonis, seu nationis fidelium in eadem civitate vel territorio degentium, nec paroeciae mere familiares aut personales; ad constitutas autem quod attinet, nihil innovandum, inconsulta apostolica sede.[4]

Canon 216, § 4 may-be divided into two distinct parts. The first is concerned with the future, and clearly states that parishes for distinct national and language groups, living in the same city or territory, are not to be established without a special apostolic indult. This also applies to purely personal and family parishes. The second part refers to the parishes which have already been constituted along national, personal and family lines, and states that these are in no way to be changed without a previous consultation with the Holy See. The law is evident and clear on this point, stating the position of the Church. There is no revolutionary statement in the canon. It does not absolutely prohibit the erection of national parishes should the need arise in the future, nor does it abrogate or abolish parishes that have been so established before the Code. In fact they are designated definitely as parishes.[5]

1. *Definition*

The Code refrains from defining exactly what it means by a parish "pro diversitate sermonis seu nationis fidelium," as it refrains also from the exact definition of a parish. It calls a certain territorial division of a diocese a parish if it has its own pastor, church and a definitely assigned people.[6] But it also recognizes another principle for the determination of parishes when it speaks of parishes for

[4] Canon 216, § 4.

[5] Cf. Studies and Conferences, "Canonical Parishes Territorial"—*AER*, LIX (1918), 537; "National Parishes in America"—*AER*, LXXVII (1927), 523.

[6] Canon 216, § 1.

diverse languages and nationalities as well as families and persons.[7] This principle points primarily to a non-territorial element, which element is also called personal. Although the Code recognizes both the personal and the territorial principles, it gives preference to the territorial when it urges that the territory of every diocese be divided into distinct territorial parts. This is the generally constituted rule for the Church universal and the rule by which ordinarily jurisdiction is circumscribed. Wherever possible these limits should be certain, perpetual and unchangeable, not arbitrarily modified by private individuals or by the civil authorities, but regulated solely by the ecclesiastical superiors.[8]

It is for this reason that some authors conclude that all personal parishes, whether by reason of language, nationality or family, are considered rather as an exception to the law.[9] They draw their reasons for this opinion from the practice before the Code as well as from the present ruling contained in canon 216, where, because of this secondary position in the law, a special apostolic indult is required for their erection. Maroto (1875-1937) seems to include the personal principle of parochial distinction in the general diocesan division into parishes, stating that, although regularly the distribution of a diocese into parishes is according to territorial division and co-ordination, a principle independent of territory is to be adopted, and this primary principle is personal.[10] Because of the position that the Code takes in requiring a special apostolic indult for the erection of personal parishes in the future, it is reasonable to assume that such parishes are to be regarded more by way of exception to the law than according to it. The law clearly states that dioceses should be divided into distinct territorial parts, and this is to be done presumably to simplify the administration of the diocese and the component

[7] Canon 216, § 4.

[8] Cf. Canon 1509, 4°.

[9] Chelodi, *Ius de Personis*, n. 220; Cocchi, *Commentarium*, III, 8; Augustine, *Status of Catholic Parishes*, p. 77; Coronata, *Institutiones*, I, n. 307; Beste, *Introductio*, p. 227; Ayrinhac, *Constitution of the Church*, *n.* 7.

[10] ". . . per se latius patet et aliunde quoque, independenter a territorio potest adhiberi."—*Institutiones*, II, n. 766, p. 109; also in n. 740, p. 13, of the same volume the author explains this principle in length.

parts. Any condition of things that does not conform to such a division, even though it be recognized by the law as a distinct parochial unit, is abnormal and must be provided for separately.

A personal parish can be described as a group of faithful determined by reason of rite, language, nationality, family or other qualities, whose spiritual care, together with the corresponding parochial rights and duties, is committed to a priest who is their pastor.[11] Since the primary determinant of a personal parish is the quality of the persons who belong to it, it will be admissible to make a further distinction between personal parishes in the strict sense and personal parishes in the broad sense. In the strict sense a personal parish is said to include persons without any regard to the territory in which they live. In the broad sense a personal parish may include persons of a distinct quality or characteristic living within certain limits, and then it is known as a mixed personal parish. In adapting this definition to a national parish one may define such a parish as a particular portion of the faithful, distinct by reason of language or nationality (national origin), whose spiritual care is committed to a proper pastor by a legitimate authority.[12]

2. *Meaning of "National"*

In the first place the term "national" in connection with these parishes seems to be inappropriately chosen because of its political implication. The word "nation" in English, like the word "natio" among the old Romans, expresses the political idea as differing from the "people," or "peuple" in French, which conveys rather the idea of a definite civilization and culture.[13] In speaking of parishes as national, one adopts a natural and inadvertent association with cer-

[11] Coronata, *Institutiones,* I, n. 467.

[12] Augustine describes a national parish as one in which a "priest was or is exclusively appointed for a particular portion of the faithful who were or are united precisely by reason of speaking the same language, provided it was and is recognized as such by the authorities."—*Status of Catholic Parishes,* p. 75.

[13] Bluntschli, *The Theory of the State* (Oxford, 1892), p. 86.

tain political ideologies that in some cases might even be detrimental to the best interests of faith and religion. This is perhaps a little better illustrated in the case of National Churches, which usually are understood to be limited primarily to the political boundaries of one particular country, and are brought under its sphere of influence, sometimes even under State interference in ecclesiastical matters. They may be spoken of as National Churches also because of the political as well as the religious adherence of its members. In the case of national parishes it could even so happen that they are mistakenly thought to be the schismatic branches that have established themselves in some communities. Such could be the case with regard to the Polish National Church in the United States which has separated itself from the authority of the Holy See, and now numbers some 60,000 members.[14]

Aside from the political implication, the term "national" does not correctly express the unity of faith that is the heritage of all Catholics throughout the world, regardless of national or racial origin. It seems to convey with it the odious inference of a church within the Church, somewhat like a State within a State.[15] This is obviously not true, for Catholics the world over acknowledge the same God as their Father, profess the same doctrines, and submit themselves to the same authority of the visible head of the Church here on earth, the Vicar of Christ. This they do regardless of the language they happen to speak, or of the racial characteristics they inherited from their forefathers. In the United States it may so happen that these people, though originally from another country, and still using the vernacular to a great extent if not exclusively, have become citizens in the land of their adoption, and are even politically united with it. Since the expression "national parish" has been so widely used and commonly accepted in reference to personal parishes distinct by reason of language or national origin, the writer will continue to refer to them throughout this study in the same way.

[14] Studies and Conferences, "The Validity of the Orders of the Polish National Church,"—*AER,* CVIII (1943), 452-454; *The National Catholic Almanac* (Paterson, N. J.: St. Anthony's Guild, 1943), p. 643.

[15] Augustine, *Status of Catholic Parishes,* p. 77.

3. *Component Elements*

A parish essentially consists of a definite people under the spiritual jurisdiction of a legitimately appointed pastor. This jurisdiction is principally in the internal forum.[16] In order to be valid therefore it can be exercised only over baptized persons, because only by baptism does a person become a member of the Church, and subject to its law.[17] In a national parish, therefore, as in a territorial parish, the members can only be a definite group of persons baptized in the Catholic faith.

Since before the Code the local ordinary was the only one besides the Holy See who could canonically establish a national parish with full parochial rights,[18] it was his obligation to determine whether the parish was to be purely personal, that is, for the people of a certain language or nationality, or whether it was to be a mixed personal parish, that is, for the people of a certain language or nationality within definite or approximate limits. The bishop of the diocese was the legitimate authority who established and provided for the spiritual care of national parishes, since he was the one who was directly responsible for those Catholics who were of another language and lived within the territorial limits of the diocese.

What these provisions were in particular cases according to the dispositions of individual bishops in their respective dioceses it is practically impossible to determine, as such documents of erection, if they exist, are ordinarily kept in the archives of the diocese. The same may be said concerning the synodal and statutory legislation, where certain laws were made for national parishes in the diocese. As for the particular legislation in synodal and statutory law it appears that the general law of the Church, as contained in canon 216, § 4, conforms to the general principles of the Code, and does not intend to abrogate or derogate from the existing particular statutes, as long as it does not explicitly state so.[19] The fact that canon 216, § 4, explicitly states that nothing is to be changed is certainly suffici-

[16] Vermeersch-Creusen, *Epitome,* I, n. 534.
[17] Canon 87.
[18] Augustine, *Status of Catholic Parishes,* p. 77.
[19] Canons 3 and 22.

ent indication of the fact that no abrogation or derogation has occurred.

a. Language

In the definition of a national parish there is necessarily included an element that formally distinguishes it from all other parishes. That element is indicated in canon 216, § 4, as the element of language and nationality. It appears from the context of the canon, and from a subsequent response of the Pontifical Commission for the Interpretation of the Code,[20] that the words "pro diversitate sermonis, seu nationis" are to be taken disjunctively.[21]

It can easily happen, and such conditions actually exist, that people who express themselves through the medium of different languages reside within the borders of the same country, and are its nationals, either by birth or through the process of naturalization. In such a case the difference of language does not connote a difference of nationality. It can also happen that people of another nationality, whether they speak a different language or not, live within the territorial limits of a country without being its citizens. In the first case the parish established would be primarily "pro diversitate sermonis," and in the second, primarily "pro diversitate nationis." It ordinarily happens that those of another nationality speak a different language, but the fact that the disjunctive conjunction *seu* is used indicates that either of the two reasons adduced (language or nationality) may have to be taken into consideration. The choice is different in the respective cases, even though it may coincide in some, or even in the majority of instances.

Generally taken, the national parishes which have been founded in this country are for the people of a certain language. These are distinct language parishes, because they are for a particular portion of the faithful who were or are united by reason of speaking the same language. In such parishes there is usually one language involved, and one pastor who speaks that language, and who is in charge of their spiritual needs. What is to be said of two or more languages in the same city or locality? If, for example, a priest spoke several languages

[20] *AAS,* XVI (1924), 113.

[21] Cf. Vermeersch-Creusen, *Epitome,* I, n. 330.

and could satisfy the demands of several different language groups, would such a parish be classified as a national parish? Augustine says that such a congregation under one spiritual head could not be called a national parish.[22] Would the fact that one particular language group predominates numerically in a given locality justify its being called a national parish?

This question is difficult to answer with any degree of certainty because of the absence of any definite legislation on the matter, as well as because of the uncertainty of the norms followed and the variant practice in similar cases. The only rule that one can apply is the one already intimated concerning personal parishes. The status of these parishes was determined by the ordinary at the time of their erection before the Code, for since the promulgation of the Code the power of the bishops, or at least the exercise of that power, has been restricted as regards the erection of personal parishes. If a national parish was established for one particular language group it is still a distinct national parish for that particular language group today. In the case of various language groups, there seems to be no reason why the bishop could not have established a national parish for the prevailing language or nationality, and, if the same priest could understand the idiom of another group, make it at the same time a personal parish for the other language group. In the same way if there existed a minority language group in the particular city or locality where English was used predominantly, he could have established a territorial parish, at the same time directing that a certain language or national group be under the jurisdiction of that particular pastor, even though they lived outside of the territorial limits of his parish. In this case, however, the parish would not be considered a national parish. Whatever remains to be said for or against the advisability of such procedure, the fact is that in his diocese the bishop had the authority to establish such parishes, and as far as the present Code is concerned "nihil innovandum inconsulta Apostolica Sede."

The fact that people of a certain language or nationality began attending one particular church was not enough to constitute such a church as a national parish church. It would have had to be

[22] Cf. *Status of Catholic Parishes*, p. 75.

canonically established by the ordinary to have full parochial rights. In regions which were settled practically by the people of one nationality or language, so that the resulting parishes were from the beginning exclusively for those people, there is no reason to suppose that they were national parishes if they also had exclusive territory.[23]

It could easily happen that two or even three different nationalities could belong legally to one parish which was established as a "language" parish. Thus, with very slight differences, Spanish could be the common language of Spaniards, Cubans and Mexicans. This does not mean that a parish established for one language group necessarily included people of related languages which are by no means mere dialects. In places where there were several related languages or nationalities, but nominally only one parish, it seems that the mind of the ordinary would have had to be made clear as to whether a pastor was entrusted also with the care of these people who were related by language.

b. Nationality

As regards the words "*seu nationis fidelium,*" it has already been indicated that a difference of language does not necessarily mean a difference of nationality, thought it generally does denote different national origin. It may happen that together with a territorial parish a parish was founded for a distinct national group in the same city or territory. It might even be possible that this particular national group spoke and understood the language of the country in which it resided. In large cities where there were colonies of people from other countries, particularly in cases where these people had no intention of changing their citizenship, but resided there merely because of the nature of their occupation, there could have been some utility in establishing churches exclusively or partially for their convenience. In Rome there are many such churches for national groups, and they are found also in other large cities, particularly in the capitals.[24]

[23] Cf. Augustine, *Status of Catholic Parishes*, p. 77.

[24] Cf. Maroto, *Institutiones*, II, n, 776, p. 115.

ARTICLE II. NATIONAL PARISHES AS BENEFICES

A national parish, to be a parish in the true sense, must have its own pastor to whom is given the parish with the care of the faithful.[25] It has already been mentioned that the parishes in this country are to be considered as such in the strict sense if they have the required elements. They had to have: (a) definite boundaries fixed by the local ordinary or by legitimate custom; (b) sufficient means of support from some source, not necessarily from an endowment; (c) a parish priest or pastor appointed by a legitimate authority for the care of the faithful, and possessing all of the ordinary powers attaching to that office. Every parish with the above outlined qualities became a canonical parish *ipso facto* with the Code, and no formal decree was necessary on the part of the bishop, even if in the past such parishes did not have a decree of canonical erection, but had *de facto* been constituted.[26]

The letter of the Apostolic Delegate sent to the ordinaries of the United States on November 10, 1922, containing the reply of the Pontifical Commission for the Interpretation of the Code, further added that a parish is always an ecclesiastical benefice according to canon 1411, 5; whether it had the proper endowment (resources or revenue) as described in canon 1410, or even when lacking such endowment, it had been erected according to the provisions of canon 1415, § 3.[27]

It follows that every canonical parish is *ipso facto* a parochial benefice, and if it is not a canonical parish it cannot be a benefice. In fact the ideas of parish and benefice are so correlated that they mutually supplement each other in the various canons of the Code that treat of parishes and benefices. As an example of this one may mention that the Code maintains a significant silence with regard to the formalities required for the valid and licit erection of parishes, with the exception of a few canons.[28] There can be no doubt that it

[25] Canon 451.

[26] S.C.C., *Principis Alberten. et Saskatoonen.* (*Missae pro populo*), 5 mart. 1932—*AAS*, XXV (1932), 436-438.

[27] Cf. Bouscaren, I, 150.

[28] Cf. canons 216; 451; 454; 455.

intended the laws governing benefices to be applied also to parishes. This becomes more manifest when one considers that parishes are mentioned expressly in some of these canons.[29] There can be no question of the character of a benefice on the part of parishes, but it will be useful to consider the nature of benefices in order to conclude that parishes have all of the requirements of a benefice.

In defining a benefice the Code says that it is a juridical entity erected in perpetuity by a competent ecclesiastical authority, and consisting of a sacred office along with the right of receiving such revenues as accrue from the endowment attached to the office.[30] In this definition it is necessary to distinguish first of all two elements, a spiritual and a temporal one, namely the sacred function and the right to support. These are the general constituents of any benefice.[31] The sacred office however is the principal element of these two, because it is the fundamental reason for the right of acquiring the temporal element according to the principle: *beneficium propter officium.*[32]

A benefice is a sacred office in the strict sense so that it cannot be conferred upon any person other than a cleric. It is evident that a benefice must be erected by a legitimate ecclesiastical authority, because a juridic personality receives its existence from a competent authority which, in the Church, is the supreme ecclesiastical authority; or by another person, either physical or moral, to whom that power has been given by the supreme authority of the Church.[33] This precludes any interference on the part of any civil authority even in cases in which, by some arrangement, the permission of the State is acknowledged as necessary for the erection of a particular parish.[34] The competent authorities for erecting ecclesiastical benefices are

[29] Cf. canons 1423; 1425; 1426; 1427.

[30] Canon 1409.

[31] Cf. Coronata, *Institutiones,* II, n. 972; Ayrinhac, *Administrative Legislation* (New York: Longmans, Green and Co., 1930), n. 257.

[32] Reiffenstuel, *Ius Canonicum Universum* (7 vols., Venetiis, 1735), lib. III, tit. V, cap. I, n. 10. Hereafter cited Reiffenstuel.

[33] Coronata, *Institutiones,* II, n. 972.

[34] Bouuaert-Simenon, *Manuale Juris Canonici* (3 vols., vols. I and III, 3 ed., 1930; vol. II, 1931, Gandae et Leodii: Dessain), III, n. 222. Hereafter cited *Manuale.*

the ecclesiastical superiors, who have full and exclusive right in the Church. The Pope alone has the authority to erect consistorial benefices, such as dioceses.[35] Although he may erect non-consistorial benefices in any part of the world, he does not usually exercise that power. Local ordinaries in their respective territories can erect non-consistorial benefices,[36] but not the vicar general except with a special mandate.[37] A Cardinal can also erect benefices which do not entail the care of souls, unless the church belongs to exempt religious, but only in his own title or *diaconia*.[38]

Briefly, the four conditions required for the erection of an ecclesiastical benefice are: (1) A sacred office, imposing some obligation and implying some participation in ecclesiastical power, either of orders, of jurisdiction, or of administration governed by Church law and reserved to clerics.[39] (2) Erection by a competent ecclesiastical authority. Any provision made by private persons or by civil authority must further receive the sanction of the ecclesiastical authorities. (3) Perpetuity, at least objectively. Objective perpetuity means that the benefice once erected must not cease to exist of itself.[40] Subjective perpetuity consists in the irremovability of the incumbent except through legally sanctioned methods. The present law does not demand subjective perpetuity, at least not for benefices in the broader sense,[41] and the ordinary does not have to establish irremovability in the decree of erection, particularly with regard to parishes.[42] This perpetuity does not necessarily imply continuity. (4) A right to a portion of the endowment, or to the income accuring from the office. The office is something spiritual, the right to the income is annexed to the spiritual, and the income itself is temporal. Formerly the endowment consisted of land or other real estate. The

[35] Canon 1414, § 1.

[36] Cf. Coronata, *Institutiones,* II, n. 977.

[37] Canons 152; 455, § 3; 1414, § 3.

[38] Canon 1414, § 4.

[39] Cf. canons 145, § 1, 197, § 1.

[40] Coronata, *Institutiones,* II, n. 972.

[41] Ayrinhac, *Administrative Legislation,* n. 257; Hilling, *Das Personenrecht,* p. 85.

[42] S. C. Consist., 1 aug. 1919 ad II—*AAS,* XI (1919), 346; cf. canon 454, §§ 3-4.

present law extended the character of the endowment to include definite contributions, and reliable voluntary offerings of the faithful, as well as stole fees fixed by diocesan taxation or legitimate custom. The ordinary can erect parishes and quasi-parishes even if he can merely prudently foresee that the necessary maintenance will be forthcoming from some other source.[43]

In applying these conditions to parishes there can arise no question for concluding that parishes, whether removable or irremovable, are benefices if they have been erected by the proper authorities.[44]

It seems, since national parishes, if they have been lawfully established, have all the parochial rights of territorial parishes with regard to their subjects, restricted only according to the principle of personal parishes, that there can be no reason why they should not be considered as benefices. The distinction that is advanced concerning national parishes with boundaries, and those that are strictly personal does not seem to be valid, for even in cases in which boundaries are given to national parishes these boundaries usually are cumulative with those of other parishes, and so cannot be called strictly territorial, since their sphere of jurisdiction is still drawn according to the difference of language or nationality within a certain district. The sense of canon 216, § 1, evidently is that there should be only one parish within a certain territorial part of the diocese. This does not obtain in the case of national parishes with boundaries, because they generally extend over one or more territorial parishes, and enjoy jurisdiction cumulatively with them. The Code recognizes national, personal and family parishes, even though it limits their erection in the future. Such personal parishes, then, can be benefices, since nothing in the conditions mentioned for benefices made reference to strict territorial limitation.

It could be objected that the condition demanding sufficient resources or revenue is not fulfilled in the case of national parishes. A study of canon 1410 shows that besides an endowment, which is a kind of trust of goods or money for the future support of the church

[43] Canon 1415, § 3.

[44] Coady, *The Appointment of Pastors,* the Catholic University of America Canon Law Studies, n. 52 (Washington, D. C.: The Catholic University of America, 1929), p. 71.

and its property, the reliable and certain contributions of the faithful are to be considered as an adequate guarantee of that support. If a parish can be reasonably certain of an income from the voluntary contributions of the faithful, it can be considered as having a sufficient patrimony.[45] These prospective offerings should be substantially assured even though the amount is indefinite. In the United States, pew rent, seat money, offertory and envelope collections, form the main support of the churches, and can be classified as the voluntary offerings of the faithful which may be deemed equivalent to an endowment as a source of church support.[46] The reason for considering these contributions as sufficiently reliable is the moral obligation of all Catholics to give to the support of their church and pastor.[47] This obligation, if sufficiently stressed, is adequately realized by present day Catholics in the fulfillment of their duty, even though there is no sanction applied for the non-fulfillment of it. Under the Council of Trent there was particular emphasis placed on this obligation.[48]

Although the following plan is not commonly adopted in this country, stole fees can also be employed for this purpose as a part of the revenue necessary for the support of the parish and the priests.[49] Ordinarily the pastor has a right to the stole fees according to the common law, as his own personal property,[50] inasmuch as these offerings are considered as a remuneration for a special service to individuals on particular occasions, and therefore not essentially connected with the fulfillment of an obligation arising from the benefice, or from the administration of the parish property. These levies and

[45] Cf. Vermeersch-Creusen, *Epitome,* II, n. 743; Wernz, *Ius Decretalium,* III, n. 182; SCC., *Sabinen.,* 17 iun. 1807—*Thes. Resol.,* LXXIII, 130.

[46] Kremer, *Church Support in the United States,* The Catholic University of America Canon Law Studies, n. 61 (Washington, D. C.: The Catholic University of America, 1930), pp. 38-54.

[47] Cf. Hannan, "The Obligation of Church Support"—*The Jurist,* I (1941), 343.

[48] Sess. XXI, de ref., c. 4.

[49] Canon 1410; S.C.C., *Quebecen.,* 1 iul. 1917—*AAS,* X (1918), 198; *Canarien.,* 16 iul. 1927—*AAS,* XX (1928), 391, n. 3.

[50] Canon 463, § 1.

fees should not be exacted above the amounts approved by the Holy See for the diocese.[51]

As to the assurance of parish support by the faithful, there can be no question as far as national parishes are concerned. They have been built by the generous and consistent contributions of the faithful, and continue to be supported in the same way. Certainly, if the voluntary offerings of the faithful in territorial parishes suffice to constitute those parishes as benefices, then they are also sufficient in the case of national parishes.

A more serious objection may arise in connection with the condition of perpetuity. National parishes have been considered by some to be merely of a subsidiary and fluctuating nature, and therefore as only temporary in their establishment pending the cessation of the specific need which called them into existence.[52] In speaking of perpetuity one must distinguish between objective and subjective perpetuity. Objective perpetuity is generally recognized as necessary for a benefice.[53] Canon 216, § 4, explicitly uses the word "parish" in reference to parishes distinct by reason of language or nationality. In the law they must consequently be considered as parishes, and as moral persons, only insofar as they constitute an office and parochial benefice, because the people are the ones for whom the parochial benefice is primarily instituted. National parishes, then, as moral person, must have at least objective perpetuity, because moral persons are by nature perpetual.[54] The fact that there was and at present is a possibility that such parishes may one day cease to exist, does not conflict with the fundamental notion of benefices. Perpetuity does not mean that the benefice, or parish, at its erection, is guaranteed to last forever. It means simply, that such a parish or benefice is so

[51] Canon 1507, § 1. When the stole fees are determined by the ordinary as constituting an endowment, then the pastor is obliged to surrender only the amount assigned to the benefice within the limits of diocesan assessment or legitimate custom. Cf. Ferry, *Stole Fees,* The Catholic University of America Canon Law Studies, n. 21 (Washington, D. C.: The Catholic University of America, 1924), p. 61.

[52] Cf. Augustine, *Commentary,* VI, 495.

[53] Ayrinhac, *Administrative Legislation,* n. 257.

[54] Canon 102.

established that it will not of itself cease to exist.[55] In other words, it can possibly happen that at some future time, such a parish or benefice, which now is permanently established, may become unnecessary for various reasons. This may occur when people no longer live in the vicinity of the church in sufficient numbers to constitute a parish, or in view of certain economic, political or social reasons. Such conditions cannot always be foreseen, and can happen regardless of the nature of the parish, whether it be territorial or non-territorial. Canon Law makes provisions for just such instances in permitting the suppression of benefices either completely or partially.[56] If it should so happen that the people of a national parish have all acquired the idiom of this country, and no longer need the ministrations of a priest in their own language, the parish still would not have to be suppressed. Suitable arrangements might perhaps be made along territorial lines, or by applying the personal principle with regard to parish affiliation. The members of national parishes are no more fluctuating in the matter of acquiring domicile or quasi-domicile than are the members of the territorial parishes.[57]

From what has been said there appear to be sufficiently convincing reasons for considering national parishes as benefices in the same way that territorial parishes are. The conditions mentioned for benefices have been applied also to national parishes, and unless there happen to be special provisions in particular cases made by the proper superior, one must conclude that these parishes can also be considered as benefices in the proper sense.

Article III. Erection of National Parishes

It is to be noted that there are ordinarily only two ways in which parishes are canonically erected, namely, by creation and by division. A parish is erected by way of creation when a new parish is established in a territory hitherto unassigned to any parish, and for a people not previously affiliated with a particular church.[58] The

[55] Coronata, *Institutiones,* II, n. 972.

[56] Canons 1421, 1422.

[57] Coady, *The Appointment of Pastors,* p. 74.

[58] Wernz, *Ius Decretalium,* III, n. 822.

diocesan organization into distinct territorial parts was already made mandatory in the Council of Trent.[59] Today in countries where the Church has been organized for some time it is not likely that there exist unassigned territories or groups of people so as to necessitate the erection of parishes by creation. The Code stresses the obligation of dividing the diocese into distinct territorial parts,[60] and therefore, if any part of the diocesan territory exists independently, it should be determined with regard to parochial organization. As for missionary countries, there is a similar provision made to determine the territorial limits of quasi-parishes.[61] A relatively recent instruction of the Sacred Congregation for The Propagation of the Faith gave specific norms to insure uniformity of action in vicariates and prefectures apostolic.[62]

The erection of a parish by division implies the formation of two or more new parishes from one previously established parish in a certain territory. The Code makes a distinction between division and dismemberment, and the two are not to be used indiscriminately.[63] Dismemberment does not give rise to a new moral person, but rather signifies the transferring of part of the territory or goods of one parish to another. It pertains to the union of parishes and, hence, does not call for consideration in a matter dealing with the erection of new parishes, since it rather presupposes already existing parishes or benefices.

For the creation of a parish certain conditions are required. The territory must be a territory which is independent of any existing parish, for otherwise the new parish would be erected by division. The boundaries must be accurately determined; there must be a sufficient number of people, that is, at least ten families according to the common interpretation of canonists; [64] there must be a sufficiently

[59] Sess. XXIV, *de ref.*, c. 13; Benedictus XIV, const. *"Ad militantis,"* 30 mart. 1742, n. 16—*Fontes*, n. 326.

[60] Canon 216, § 1.

[61] Canon 216 § 2.

[62] S. C. de Prop. Fide, instr. 25 iul. 1920—*AAS*, XII (1920), 331-333.

[63] Canon 1421.

[64] In the Decree of Gratian, a canon (c. 3, c. X, q. 3) taken from the XVI Council of Toledo (693), used the words *decem mancipia*. Some of the earlier

certain revenue to provide for the maintenance of the parish and the pastor; the erection must be effected by a legal document or decree of the ordinary indicating the exact boundaries, endowment and other necessary conditions,[65] although it is not stated in canon 1418 that this is for the validity of the act; the newly erected parish must have an irremovable incumbent, according to the Code, unless in the prudent judgment of the ordinary, after hearing the consultors, and taking into account the circumstances of place and persons, it appears more advisable to make him removable.[66]

Since the more common method employed in the erection of parishes is that of division, it is necessary to mention the requisite conditions for erecting parishes by that process. According to canon 1427, § 1, the ordinary can divide any parishes in the diocese, without the consent of the people, or against the will of the pastor, but not without consulting him.[67] He cannot divide them, however, without a just and canonical cause.[68] The canonical cause adduced by the Code is twofold, namely, the difficulty for parishioners to attend the parish church, and an excessive number of parishioners, so that even one or more assistants are not able to help the pastor to provide for the spiritual needs.[69]

It is important to note that the words of canon 1427, § 2, mention great difficulty *(magna difficultas)* in attending the church as the condition for division. In the Council of Trent the wording was *"sine magno incommodo,"*[70] and in the Constitution *Ad audientiam* of

canonists interpreted *mancipia* to mean single persons, and the gloss seemed to favor that interpretation, but later canonists held that a population of less than ten Catholic families was hardly sufficient for the establishment of a new parish. Cf. Barbosa, *Ius Ecclesiasticum Universum,* lib. I, cap. 20, n. 16; Pirhing, *Jus Canonicum Nova Methodo Explicatum* (5 vols., Dilingae, 1674-1678), lib. III, tit. XXIX, n. 1; De Luca, *Theatrum Veritatis et Institiae,* XXIII (De Parochis), n. 17; Leurenius, *Forum Beneficiale,* pars I, q. 160.

[65] Canon 1418.

[66] Canon 454, § 3.

[67] Canon 1428, § 1.

[68] Canons 1427; 1428, § 2.

[69] Canon 1427, § 2.

[70] Sess. XXI, *de ref.,* c. 4.

Alexander III (1159-1181), the words *"sine magna difficultate"* had been used. A strict interpretation of the disposition of the Council of Trent was applied for about two centuries, and the practice of the Roman Rota was against the division of parishes in cases in which the need could be supplied by additional priests. In the eighteenth century, however, there seems to have been adopted a broader interpretation of the degree of inconvenience that was required, especially in the practice of the Sacred Congregation of the Council. The reason for this was the spiritual necessity of the faithful and the consideration of the primary law of the salvation of souls. Therefore, if there was great utility resulting from the division of parishes it was held that it could be permitted.[71] This evident utility and moral necessity could be the just and canonical cause of which the canon speaks.[72]

Since the difficulty mentioned is more a matter of fact than of law, the ordinary must evaluate the relative difficulty which may inconvenience the people in attending the parish church. In formulating this judgment he cannot forego the opinion of those who experience this difficulty. Today the modern methods of transportation have reduced greatly the inconvenience of travel, and, consequently, the canonical cause of distance would not be as urgent as formerly. There can easily arise circumstances, however, under which such means of transportation are not available, or are too expensive, or cannot be used without great hardships for the persons concerned. The law in its application has been reasonable, however, and the practice of the Roman tribunals has been to uphold divisions made by the bishop when a notable portion of the people was farther removed than two miles from the church.[73]

[71] S.C.C., *Hipporegien.*, 20 aug., 20 sept. 1879—*ASS*, XIII (1880), 293-307; also in *Fontes*, n. 4245; S.C.C. *Concordien.* 19 ian. 1889—*ASS*, XXII (1889), 74; *S.R.R. in causa Sedunen., Dismembrationis Paroeciae*, 2 apr. 1912, *coram R.P.D. Antonio Perathoner*, Dec. XIII, n. 4—*S.R.R. Decisiones*, IV (1912), 153; also in *AAS*, IV (1912), 450-461.

[72] Cf. Sebastianelli, *Praelectiones Iuris Canonici, De Rebus Romae* (1905), p. 326.

[73] S.R.R. *Decisiones*, IV (1912), 152, n. 3; S.C.C., *Placentina*, 28 maii 1791—*Thes. Resol.*, LX (1791), 136; *Aquen.*, 13 iul. 1720—*Fontes*, n. 3212—*Thes. Resol.* I, 346-348; *Aquen.*, 31 maii 1721—*Fontes*, n. 3225, *Thes. Resol.*, II, 32; *Aquen.*, 2 aug. 1721—*Fontes*, n. 3225, *Thes. Resol.*, II, 56.

The other canonical cause posited by the Code for the erection of a parish by division is an excessive number of parishioners.[74] There is a condition attached to this cause, however, which makes it depend upon the possibility of providing for the parishioners by means of added help through one or more assistant priests.[75] This was the usual method, according to the Council of Trent, of providing for the necessary spiritual help in more thickly populated communities, where the congregations had become so numerous that the pastors themselves were no longer able to administer to them effectively.[76] Consequently, inasmuch as this need could be supplied by adding more priests to the parish to assist the pastor, it was not considered as a canonical cause for the division of a parish in the old law.[77] Today the Code, based partly on the Tridentine law, stipulates that if the spiritual welfare of the people cannot be adequately provided for even with assistant priests, the bishop can divide the parish.[78] What constitutes an excessive number of parishioners is difficult to say because of the absence of any set norm.[79] There may be such a sudden growth in the number of people belonging to a particular parish as to exceed the physical capacity of the church even with extra masses. This would not happen necessarily through natural increase, but could easily happen by reason of immigration, or migration of people from one parish to another by reason of industrial opportunity. The ordinary can best determine the existence of the canonical cause by personal investigation and inspection of the parish, and through inquiry from the pastor as well as the consultors. He can thus best ascertain whether it is necessary to divide the parish, and whether there is a sufficient number of people to form a new parish that they might be able to support conveniently.[80]

The authority to erect parishes, whether by creation or by division, is primarily vested in the Holy See. The ordinary, however,

[74] Canon 1427, § 2.

[75] Canon 476, § 1.

[76] Sess. XXI, *de ref.*, c. 4.

[77] Rossi, *De Paroecia*, p. 27.

[78] Canon 476, § 8.

[79] Connolly, *The Canonical Erection of Parishes*, p. 57.

[80] Canons 1428, § 1; 1427, §§ 1 and 3.

within the limits if his jurisdiction can also erect parishes.[81] The reason, in cases where the territory of the diocese has not been divided completely so that parts of it have not been ascribed to any particular church, is that the bishop has the spiritual care of the entire diocese, and since he cannot minister to all personally, he is bound by his office and by the law to use those means which are prescribed for the care of souls. In the case of territorial parishes, where the people are not affiliated with any other parish, he can erect a parish by creation. As for the erection of parishes by division, the bishops have ordinary power by virtue of canon 1427, § 1, if there is a just and canonical cause. This power they had in the old law from the Constitution *Ad audientiam* of Alexander III and especially from the Council of Trent.[82]

In this general legislation on the erection of parishes there is nothing to indicate that this power was to extend to the erection of national parishes. The provision in the IV Lateran Council (1215)[83] required that suitable priests be provided to minister to people in their own language and rite. It did not clearly state that their priests were to be pastors in charge of parishes established for the people of these different languages and rites, but the nature of their work involving the care of souls indicated their parochial office. Nor was there any general legislation requiring the establishment of national parishes. It seems that the bishops were to adopt the most practical means at their disposal in providing for the spiritual needs of the national or language minorities under their particular jurisdiction, according to the latitude that was given them in the IV Lateran Council, and in the Council of Trent, which allowed them to employ that useful method which was more adaptable to the local situation.[84] If a particular situation necessitated the erection of parishes for a certain national or language group in the prudent judgment of the ordinary, such a parish was duly established according to the general principles of the ninth canon of the IV Lateran Council, which re-

[81] Canon 1414, § 2.

[82] Sess. XXI, *de ref.*, c. 4.

[83] Can. 9—Mansi, XXII, 998; c. 14, X, *de officio indicis ordinarii,* I, 31.

[84] Sess. XXIV, *de ref.*, c. 13.

mained substantially the same until the codification of the present law.

The basis of this law was the Church's traditional practice and teaching concerning minority language groups in another country, and its insistance upon the use of the diverse idiom for these people, both in missionary and parochial activity. The problem of training missionaries in various languages for missionary work was already seriously taken up by the popes of the late middle ages, and heartily encouraged.[85] German Catholics in Italy maintained their distinct identity through the Confraternities, which were later given their own churches. Thus the "Anima" received papal approbation in 1399. In Poland the German Confraternity founded in 1632, built its own church of St. Bono, which remained in use until 1808 when it was closed by Napoleon. The fact that the Church permitted the establishment of parishes for national and language groups shows that it considered the spiritual welfare of those people of sufficient importance to necessitate ministering to them in their own language.[86]

Man living in society is liable to be cast into a way of life that is not in conformity with the traditional practices of his race, and may thus form a part of a national minority of a country that is not his own. The Catholic Church in its true mission and interest is far above any political or national aims of any one country. Its purpose is more than international, it is supranational, and consequently it must provide justly for the spiritual needs of all the faithful, whether they form the majority or the minority group. If it compelled a group to accept the language of another country in the spiritual ministrations to be bestowed upon the faithful, it could perhaps be accused of political or national favoritism. Such is the practice of totalitarian states which have adopted the false idea that the State is the end for which man exists, and that all rights and all duties reside in the

[85] Schmidlin, *Catholic Mission History* (Techny: Mission Press, 1933, p. 223; Braun, "Missionary Problems in the Thirteenth Century: A Study in Missionary Preparation"—*CHR,* XXV (1939), 146.

[86] Grentrup, *Nationale Minderheiten und Katholische Kirche,* p. 55, quoted by Eppstein, *The Catholic Tradition of the Law of Nations* (London: Burns, Oates and Washbourne, Ltd., 1935), p. 389.

majority without due consideration for the minority.[87] This doctrine was strenuously opposed by Pius XI in his Encyclical *"Non abbiamo bisogno."* [88]

In some parts of the world there is such an intermingling of language groups which retain their own national culture and characteristics, that it is practically impossible to find a single parish that is composed of the same racial elements. In such cases the Church recognizes that fact, and does everything possible to provide religious and spiritual guidance in the several languages of the inhabitants. Every possible measure consistent with the essential unity of the diocese is allowed and enjoined upon the priests to enable them to minister to the faithful in their own tongue. In this the Church does not follow the logic of books that enunciate the theory that cities and States should consist of people of the same race. The Church's position is just and reasonable since, if the State has not the right to infringe upon the sacred traditions of family life, such as the customs and the language of the home, the Church, which is a supernatural society founded by God, must the more vigorously safeguard and seek to promote the religious liberties of national and language minorities extant in a strange country. The State has a providential mission to fulfill in providing for the well-being of all of its citizens. The Church has a divine mission to fulfill in securing the salvation of all of its members.[89]

In countries where there are two or more nationalities it is necessary for adminstrative, political and economic reasons to have a common language that can be understood and used by the people. Such a common language was Latin during the entire period of the development of western civilization until the middle ages. The knowledge of another language besides the maternal tongue in such a case should not be regarded as a hardship, but as an added cultural development for those whose opportunity it is to study that language in school. It enables them to be versed in the language of their national origin,

[87] Eppstein, *op. cit.*, p. 381.

[88] June 29, 1931—*AAS,* XXIII (1931), 285.

[89] Leo XIII, encycl. litt. *"Immortale Dei,"* 1 nov. 1885—*ASS,* XVIII (1885), 161.

and at the same time will open to them opportunities afforded by the knowledge of the official administrative language.[90]

But the presence of two or more national groups in a country can also be the cause of strife and discord even in matters of ecclesiastical administration and discipline. It became the dolorous duty of Benedict XV to exhort the bishops and the clergy of Canada to cease their contentions arising from questions of race and language, and to have, above all, the need of the faithful at heart.[91] It is this same principle of spiritual unity "in the bond of peace" that is found in the Church's insistence upon freedom of language in the practice of religion in the Concordats made with other countries.[92]

[90] Such language combinations may be found in Wales (English and Welsh), in Belgium (Flemish and French), in Malta (Maltese and English), in Switzerland (French, German and Italian) and in Canada (French and English).

[91] "In our Apostolic Letter *'Commissio divinitus'* which we sent you on September 8, 1916, we earnestly exhorted the clergy and the Catholic people of your country that they should lay aside all contentions and quarrels which have arisen either by reason of race or from diversity of languages. . . . Now the time has come to address our words to all our brethren, the Bishops of the Dominion of Canada, and to repeat to them from the depths of our soul the exhortation which we gave two years since: That they 'be of one heart and of one mind,' and that there be no division among them by reason either of racial origin or of speech. For one and the same spirit 'set them to rule the Church of God,' the Spirit of Unity and of Peace (I Peter v, 3). Thus will it be right for you with greater authority and efficacy, Venerable Brethren, to order your priests (and we enjoin that this order be strictly given), both to observe spiritual concord amongst themselves and strive by word and example to have it so preserved by the faithful. To which end we desire again and again to recommend what in earlier Apostolic letters we have recommended, that all the priests should seek to acquire the habit of speaking competently each of the two languages, English and French, and casting all prejudice aside, should use, now one now the other, to meet the needs of the faithful."—Apostolic Letter to Cardinal Begin, Archbishop of Quebec, and the other Archbishops and Bishops of Canada—*AAS,* X (1918), 440. Cf. Eppstein, *op. cit.,* p. 388.

[92] Concordat between the Holy See and Lithuania, September 27, 1927, Article 21: "Ordinaries shall see to it that all the faithful receive religious assistance in their mother tongue according to the rules of the Church."—*AAS,* XIX (1927), 431. Concordat between the Holy See and Poland, February 10, 1925, Article 23: "No change in the language used in dioceses of the Latin Rite shall be made without special permission granted by the conference of Bishops of the Latin Rite in the case of sermons, supplementary prayers and lectures, other than the lectures on sacred sciences in seminaries."—*AAS,* XVII (1925), 281.

As in other countries the Church has sought to defend the religious instruction of the faithful,[93] so also in the United States the provisions of the III Plenary Baltimore Council (1884) urged that, wherever necessary, catechisms be translated into different languages for the use of the people who spoke an idiom other than that of the country.[94]

Because of the facility with which any action of the clergy could be misinterpreted with regard to national differences, the Church has prudently restricted the participation of the clergy in civil administration and particularly in controversies that could be related to national questions.[95]

In the United States, where many national parishes exist, there has never been general legislation providing for their erection. This does not mean that such parishes came into existence without ecclesiastical approbation. The Fathers of the III Plenary Council of Baltimore already recognized the tremendous problem that faced them in the great numbers of immigrants who were almost daily arriving in this country. They anxiously urged that prudent priests be appointed, particularly in the East, to meet these Catholic strangers and assist them to the best of their ability.[96] But they provided no general parochial organization for them. Perhaps they considered this situation as a diocesan problem that had to be provided for in particular cases as it developed.

Under the old law, by virtue of the ordinary power that the bishops had, they could erect parishes by creation where the people and territory had not yet been assigned to any parish.[97] Because of the numerous immigrants it happened that many people of the same national origin settled in a particular locality never before affiliated

[93] In connection with the language question in Alsace-Lorraine in 1926, where an effort was made to teach the catechism in the maternal tongue, and in Italy in the Diocese of Trent the same year, where the Italian had been imposed upon foreign elements even in religious instruction, cf. Eppstein, *op. cit.*, p. 392.

[94] *Acta et Decreta*, n. 219.

[95] Canons 139; 121. Cf. Benedictus XV, ep. ad Ludovicum S.R.E. Card. Begin—*AAS*, X (1918), 440-442.

[96] *Acta et Decreta*, n. 234.

[97] Smith, *Elements*, I, n. 254.

with any parish. If they comprised a sufficiently large number they were organized into a parish. The question is whether such a parish was to be considered as a national or a territorial parish. The fact that a certain language or national group settled in a certain locality did not necesarily make the parish founded for them a national parish. It is evident that, before a national parish could be established canonically, it had to be established precisely *as such* by the local ordinary if it was to be a national rather than a territorial parish.

It is of course difficult to determine if this was the case in individual instances. Augustine mentions that in Osage County, Missouri, several parishes were classified as German parishes merely because of the German element that settled there to the exclusion of practically all other nationalities, and because that particular language was predominant.[98] Undoubtedly in the erection of parishes during the period of growth of this country such cases were multiplied. If they were not specifically determined in the decree of erection as parishes for that particular language group, they cannot be considered as national parishes, for the presumption then as now was in favor of a territorial parish. With the creation of territorial parishes later on their status could have been changed to, or recognized by competent authorities before May 19, 1918, as that of national parishes. The same applied to the many instances of Spanish predominance in the south-western part of the United States. The fact that one particular language predominated within the limits of a parish did not necessarily make it a national parish for that language.[99] This would have had to be determined at the time of the erection of the parish, or subsequently with the erection of another parish which was of a territorial character.

In the erection of parishes by division, the ordinaries had to follow the prescriptions of the Council of Trent.[100] The just and reasonable cause, which had to be expressly stated,[101] was the residence of the parishioners at too great a distance from, and great inconvenience for them in attending the parish church. Evidently these two reasons

[98] *Status of Catholic Parishes,* p. 77.

[99] Augustine, *Status of Catholic Parishes,* p. 78.

[100] Sess. XXI, *de ref.,* c. 4.

[101] Smith, *Elements,* I, n. 263.

were not always present physically in the erection of national parishes. The bishops had to follow another norm for the erection of such parishes, and this norm could be no other than the grave spiritual need of the foreign-born Catholics, and the provisions of the old law as first stated in the IV Lateran Council,[102] and later repeated in the Decretals of Gregory IX.[103]

It is necessary to note that in many cases national parishes had their origin by division from another national parish, or from a territorial parish. People of one particular language or national group affiliated themselves first with local or national parishes, and, when they were sufficiently numerous, usually petitioned the bishop for a church of their own. This request was either refused or granted. If it was granted, the bishop erected either a succursal chapel or a parish for that particular language group. This was done in the case of parishes, either by a decree defining the limits of the parish, if necessary, and the people who were to belong to it, and also making other recommendations; or by an act indicating the intention of the bishop to establish the parish for a particular national group. Such an act could be reflected in the appointment of a priest who knew the idiom of the people to act as their pastor and organize them into a parish. A special indult or permission from the Holy See was not required for the erection of such parishes before the Code, and consequently they must be considered as validly erected, even though no formal decree of erection was issued, or special permission from the Holy See obtained.

Article IV. The Apostolic Indult

The legislation in the Code of Canon Law for the first time makes definite reference to national and language parishes as such. Before parishes of this kind can be erected, a special apostolic indult must be obtained . . . "non possunt sine speciali apostolico indulto constitui paroeciae pro diversitate sermonis seu nationis fidelium in eadem civitate vel territorio degentium. . . "[104] The departure from the old

[102] Canon 9—Mansi, XXII, 998.

[103] C. 14, X, *de officio iudicis ordinarii,* I, 31.

[104] Canon 216, § 4.

law in the matter of erecting parishes for a particular nationality or language seems to be a restriction not in the power of the bishops to erect such parishes, but rather in the exercise of that power. The bishop still has the power, but may not exercise it without a special indult from the Holy See,[105] and therefore, if, in the prudent judgment of the ordinary, a situation should exist requiring the establishment of a parish exclusively for the people of a certain language or national group within the same city or part of the diocese, he should refer the matter to the Holy See.

Indults proceed from the favor of a superior and are granted contrary to or outside of the law.[106] They differ from privileges strictly so-called in that they are not necessarily perpetual, but are faculties or favors that the legislator grants for a time. Since the law distinctly states that dioceses are to be divided into definite territorial parts which are to be called parishes, any parish that deviates in its integral characteristics from this provision is to be considered as exceptional in the law.[107] This special indult then must be considered as a kind of dispensation from the general law requiring the establishment of only territorial parishes, because a dispensation is nothing else than a relaxation of the law in particular cases for a sufficient reason and by a competent authority.[108] A dispensation, therefore, does not abrogate or in any way change the law, but merely suspends it in a particular case. The law still is in force though it may be relaxed in particular cases by a competent authority. Such a dispensation does not necessarily have to be in favor of a single individual, but can also be in favor of a whole community or a moral person, such as a parish.[109] But since the existence of national parishes is acknowledged in the law, the indult must be considered as merely activating the provision made in the law for national parishes.

[105] Cf. *AER*, LX (1918), 691.

[106] Cicognani, *Canon Law*, p. 477.

[107] Michiels, *Principia Generalia de Personis in Ecclesia* (Lublin: Universitas Catholica, 1932), p. 175. Hereafter cited *De Personis*.

[108] Canons 80 and 84. Cf. Wernz, *Ius Decretalium*, I, n. 120; Maroto, *Institutiones*, I, n. 302.

[109] O'Neill, *Papal Rescripts of Favor*, The Catholic University of America Canon Law Studies, n. 57 (Washington, D. C.: The Catholic University of America, 1930), p. 28.

In other words, national parishes that had been established before the Code are to continue to exist without any change in their status, whereas new ones are not to be erected without permission of the Holy See.

In considering the nature of the required indult, one must first necessarily determine the force of the words "non possunt." Are these words to be taken in the sense of merely prohibiting the erection of national parishes, or do they have to be regarded as actually rendering the contrary act of erecting such a parish without an indult as null and void? Toso says that the indult is necessary for the validity of the act, and cites canon 11, which states that those laws only are to be considered invalidating which explicitly or equivalently state that an act done in violation of them is null and void.[110] Connolly speaks of this part of canon 216, § 4 as using "invalidating phraseology," [111] but does not consider the question at length. Other authors fail to mention whether the indult is necessary for validity or merely for liceity.

Concerning invalidating laws, there has been considerable controversy among canonists, and many questions have been raised concerning their force and application.[112] The authors generally agree in defining the meaning of an express invalidating law.[113] The difficulty arises in determining the meaning and the extent of the equivalent clause, which is also given the force of invalidating an act contrary to the law, whether or not it is to include such expressions as *non potest* or *nequit*. It is not difficult in itself to grasp the wish of the lawmaker, that the equivalent clause as described in canon 11, is intended to have the same force that the expressly invalidating clause has. It does not, therefore, include implicit invalidation, since this implies a process of reasoning, and is consequently a deduction from the law.[114] It would be more correct to refer to the

[110] Toso, *Ad Codicem Iuris Canonici Commentaria Minora* (Vol. II, Romae, 1922), 557. Hereafter cited *Commentaria*.

[111] *The Canonical Erection of Parishes*, p. 106.

[112] Cf. Cicognani, *Canon Law*, p. 557.

[113] Cf. Coronata, *Institutiones*, I, n. 21.

[114] Reiffenstuel spoke of implicit invalidation in connection with certain formality that was prescribed by the law. Cf. *Ius Canonicum Universum*, lib.

operation of these two clauses as *direct* in the case of an expressly invalidating clause, and *indirect* in the case of an equivalently invalidating clause, even if it merely requires certain formalites in the absence of which an act is to be regarded as null.[115] But with regard to the actual nature of the equivalent clause described in canon 11, there is no definite agreement among the authors. Some teach that an implicit invalidation is comprehended by the canon,[116] and others insist that only that clause can be considered an equivalent clause which has the same force as the express invalidating clause.[117] Coronata considers an equivalently invalidating law as one which defines what essentially constitutes the act, or which states the conditions and solemnities required by the sacred canons under the pain of nullity.[118] Such conditions according to him would be introduced by the particles *si, dummodo,* etc.; [119] or such laws should contain a prescribed formula determining the nature of the act.[120]

The problem becomes no simpler when one tries to determine the force of the words *"non posse."* Van Hove admits that there is a doubt concerning the force of these words.[121] The Romanists interpreted them as having invalidating effect, since they considered every prohibitory law as an invalidating one. Of themselves the words, Van Hove says, have only the effect of prohibiting, and therefore not of invalidating the act. Beste [122] admits that the matter is simplified if the words are modified by *"licite"* or *"valide,"* [123] but that, unqualified, they remain ambiguous, and recourse must be had to the con-

I, tit. II, cap. XI, n. 243. This does not seem to correspond with the expression that the Code uses in speaking of an equivalent clause. Cf. Wernz-Vidal, *Ius Canonicum,* I, n. 163, nota 145.

115 Roelker, "The Interpretation of Invalidating Laws"—*The Jurist* (Washington, D. C.: The Catholic University of America, 1941—), III (1943), 391.

116 Coronata (*Institutiones,* I, n. 21) cites Maroto, Blat, Cocchi, and Ojetti.

117 Van Hove, *De Legibus Ecclesiasticis* (Mechlinae: Dessain, 1930), n. 161 cites Toso, Leitner, Cicognani, Vermeersch-Creusen.

118 *Institutiones,* I, n. 21; cf. canon 1680, § 1.

119 Canon 39.

120 Cf. canon 148, § 1.

121 *De Legibus Ecclesiasticis,* n. 161.

122 *Introductio,* p. 68.

123 Cf. canons 964, n. 2; 1151, § 1; 147, § 1; 170.

text and circumstances of the law. If the doubt persists, Beste says that they imply rather illicitness than invalidity. Of themselves, then, the words *non posse* have merely the force of a prohibiting law.[124] A prohibitory law of itself, however, does not invalidate a contrary act, but merely renders an act unlawful as against the will of the legislator.[125] If the prohibitory law is also to have an invalidating effect, then this must be clearly indicated, for these two effects are separable.[126] The invalidation of an act must not be assumed, but must be unmistakably indicated by the legislator. It is to be supposed that, if the legislator wanted to make the prohibitory law also an invalidating one, he would have indicated that intention.[127] In the case of the erection of national parishes it could have been sufficiently indicated that their erection without an apostolic indult would be invalid by simply adding the word *"valide"* to the words *"non possunt . . . constitui."*[128] Since the absence of such an express statement creates a doubt, it seems right to assume that the minimum effect of the prohibition is to be admitted rather than the maximum, which would invalidate the contrary law.[129]

Furthermore, in the case of doubt whether some provision of the canons differs from the old law, the old law must be followed.[130] According to the old law the erection of national or language parishes was left to the prudent judgment of the ordinary, and such parishes were validly and licitly erected.[131] The exercise of this power is evidently prohibited by the present law,[132] but, because of the element

[124] Wernz-Vidal, *Ius Canonicum,* I, n. 163.

[125] Suarez, *Opera Omnia, Tractatus de Legibus ac Deo Legislatore* (Parisiis, 1856), Tom. V, lib. v, cap XXV, n. 13.

[126] Roelker,—*The Jurist,* III (1943), 390.

[127] Reg. 57, R.J., in VI°: "Contra eum, qui legem dicere potuit apertius, est interpretatio facienda."

[128] Among other numerous examples in which this was actually done in the Code, the following might be cited: canons 157; 693, § 1; 1417, § 2; 1434; 1436; 1487. In canon.721 practically the same words are used as in canon 216, § 4, with the exception that *valide* is inserted.

[129] Reg. 30, R.J., in VI°: "In obscuris minimum est sequendum."

[130] Canon 6, n. 4.

[131] Blat, *Commentarium Textus Codicis Iuris Canonici,* II (Romae, 1921), n. 170 (hereafter cited *Commentarium*); Bouuaert-Simenon, *Manuale,* I, n. 372.

[132] Blat, *Commentarium,* II, n. 170.

of doubt arising from the force of the words "non possunt." a national parish erected for a just cause may be considered validly but not licitly erected if there is no special apostolic indult according to the provision of the law.[133]

The departure from the old law on this point cannot be said to be substantial because the old law is not abrogated, nor is there anything in the new law directly contrary to the former law, nor does the new law readjust the entire subject matter of the former law.[134] The new law merely adds somethng to the already existing law and therefore substantially the old law is to be followed because any correction of the law is odious.[135] If the text and the context of canon 216 are considered, and the purpose of the law,[136] it appears that territorial parishes are intended to be the ordinary and required form of parochial organization, and that national and personal parishes in general are to be regarded as exceptional. But are they not to be regarded as an exception provided by the law? It is true that any exceptions established even by the law are odious and to be interpreted strictly,[137] but those laws that favor religion are to be considered favorable rather than odious laws, even though they may establish exceptions, and therefore are in no way to be interpreted strictly.[138] The purpose of the law seems to be rather to prevent the abuse of erecting national and personal as well as family parishes in places where such need does not actually exist, or where it may operate to the disparagement of ecclesiastical discipline as well as the spiritual detriment of the faithful. For this reason it seems that the prudent provision in the law is made, so that in each particular case the bishop have recourse to the Holy See for the apostolic indult in erecting a parish that is exclusively intended for people of a particular language or nationality. To obviate the necessity of recurring to the Holy See in each case

[133] Canons 216, § 4; 6, n. 4; 15; 23.

[134] Canon 22.

[135] Cicognani, *Canon Law*, p. 633.

[136] Canon 18.

[137] Canon 19.

[138] Cicognani, *Canon Law*, p. 68. "Laws made in favor of religion are to be considered favorable laws, and consequently are, subject to a wider interpretation."—S. C. de Prop. Fide (C. P. pro Sin.—Vic. Ap. Concinc.), 2 iul. 1827—*Coll.*, n. 1732.

it appears that an indult might be granted for a certain length of time or for a certain number of cases, especially when the ordinary foresees that it will become necessary to erect more than one national parish.

In the report that the ordinaries have to make to the Holy See, there is a question that expresses the solicitude of the Church with regard to the spiritual welfare of special groups of faithful. It is: "An adsint paroeciae per linguas seu nationes distinctae, et an per familias et non territorio divisae, et quo iure."[139] In this question the words "quo iure" do not seem to be prohibitive but rather explanatory in the sense that an accurate description of the circumstances necessitating such parishes is required to be given, and also whether they were established before or after the Code with or without an apostolic indult.

That there is the requirement of an apostolic indult for the erection of a national parish is sufficiently clear in instances that involve the use of a language that can in no way be considered the official language of the country, or which is not used commonly by the other inhabitants of that country. Since, according to the wording of the law, a national or language parish is not to be erected in the same city, the law seems to indicate that, if there already exist one or more territorial parishes in a city, a parish exclusively for one national or language group is not to be erected without a special apostolic indult. This applies not only to a city but also to the whole territory included by an established parish. Since canon 216, § 1, refers to the area under the jurisdiction of a bishop as the territory of a diocese, it is reasonable to suppose that also in this case the territory mentioned disjunctively with city in canon 216, § 4, refers to the diocese, or at least to a sizeable portion of the diocese. Therefore, if a certain national or language group resides within the territorial limits of the diocese, the bishop cannot erect a parish exclusively for them, or divide the already existing national parish, without a special apostolic indult. All the more would he require such an indult if the diocese extended over a territory that belonged politically to different states, because of the politico-ecclesiastical considerations that might be involved.[140]

[139] Cap. I, n. 3 f—*AAS,* X (1918), 489.

[140] "Responsio"—*Jus Pontificium,* IV (1924), 3.

In a territory which is under one political government, and is subject to a single State, the circumstances may be quite different. It sometimes happens that two or more languages are the so-called official languages of the State. Would a parish for one of these language groups require an apostolic indult? The answer to a question proposed to the Pontifical Commission for the Interpretation of the Code is of help in solving this problem.[141] The Code Commission was asked: "Whether, in regions of mixed tongue which politically constitute a single State, but where various so-called official languages are used, canon 216, § 4, requires an apostolic indult for the erection of a parish which is destined exclusively for the faithful of a certain language, even if that language be one of the official ones, and even if the parish to be so erected have its own distinct part of the territory of the diocese." The reply of the Pontifical Commission May 20, 1923, was in the affirmative, namely, that an apostolic indult was required.

Besides clarifying the significance of the words *"pro diversitate sermonis seu nationis,"* [142] this response shows how the canon is to be applied in particular instances. It is important to note that, in the question as it was formulated, the words used are: "parish . . . destined exclusively for the faithful of a certain language . . ." It makes no difference, then, whether the language is the one that is predominantly or even exclusively used in that particular region, or whether it is an official or semi-official language of a country; it makes no difference, as long as the parish is meant to serve the needs of the faithful of a certain language to the exclusion of all other Catholic residents in the territory, whether the parish is to be erected as a territorial parish, distinct or cumulative with other parishes; it makes no difference whether it is for the people of the same nationality as that which is represented by one of the official languages of the country: in all of these cases, if such a parish is to be erected exclusively for the faithful of a certain language, then an apostolic indult is necessary, according to the given response.

[141] Cf. *AAS,* XVI (1924), 113; Bouscaren, I, 151.

[142] Creusen, "Responses"—*NRT,* LI (1924), 301; *Il Monitore Ecclesiastico* (Romae, 1876—),—XXXVI (1924), 77 (hereafter cited *ME*); *Periodica,* XIII (1924), 83.

This does not mean that without an indult the bishop can never erect a parish which is to be used by the people of a certain language group. From what has been said so far it, is easy to see that the canon is concerned primarily with the formal erection of parishes for the *exclusive* use of a definite language group, so that if members of another language group happen to come within the territorial influence of such a parish, and establish a domicile or a quasi-domicile there, they would be, as it were, without a parish. This is a condition that the law wishes to avoid,[143] for the social end of man requires that Christian charity unite all men regardless of their differences of language. If a language parish is established *exclusively* for a group of people, even if such a parish is territorial, it is very probable that in the course of time people using a different idiom will establish their domicile or quasi-domicile within the limits of that parish, and thereby will be automatically excluded from that parish by reason of the personal principle of language on which its existence is based.[144]

It may happen that in some parts of the United States, in cities as well as in certain districts, languages that are different from the common language of the country are used to a great extent. Such places may be likened by comparison to places where two or more languages are the semi-official languages of that particular district, and the same rules of the reply of the Pontifical Code Commission would call for application.[145]

To clarify the implications of the requirement of the apostolic indult for the erection of a parish by creation or division, as well as by union with another existing parish, the following principles may be stated: (1) if a parish is to be erected *exclusively* for the use of the people of a certain language in a *city* where parishes already exist, an indult should be obtained; (2) if a parish destined for the exclusive use of one language group is to be erected within the territory of an already existing parish, an indult should be obtained; (3) if a parish for the *exclusive* use of a language group is to be erected in a community or district where previously there was no parish, even if that parish is to be territorial, then there is needed

[143] "Annotationes"—*Periodica,* XIII (1924), 82.
[144] *Jus Pontificium,* IV (1924), 3.
[145] *AAS,* XVI (1924), 113.

a special indult. The reason for this last conclusion, besides the political significance, is that, even though a language different from that of the country is used exclusively in a certain locality, there is a possibility of another language group moving in and being excluded from the jurisdiction of the pastor. Some authors suggest that an apostolic indult is not necessary for the erection of a parish for a definite language exclusively, even though it happens to be different from the language of the country, because then it is not a question of erecting a parish for the faithful of a different language living together in the same city, according to the requirements of canon 216, § 4.[146] If this statement is to be considered in the sense of a strictly territorial parish for the people of a certain language group in a given community, then it can be regarded as true, since there is nothing to prevent the erection of such parishes. This is true, even though the canon is more inclusive than the authors cited imply, in that it excludes national parishes without an apostolic indult, not only in the same city, but also in the same territory. It would, therefore, be more correct to say that such an indult is not required in erecting a national parish in a territory (rather than in a city) that had never been assigned to any other parish.

In opposition to this view, there has been an opinion expressed that an apostolic indult would be required to erect a strictly territorial parish for a group of people in a district where an idiom different from that of the country is used.[147] The reason adduced is that such a parish would become a personal parish for that particular group indirectly, and *ipso facto,* when a person of another language took up his residence there. This does not appear to be true, because if a parish is erected as a territorial parish in the strict sense of the word, the boundaries determine the parish affiliation, and anyone residing within the territorial limits of such a parish automatically becomes a member of it.

Practically viewed, with the general distribution of the population in the United States today, it is not likely that any one language group would be found the sole inhabitants of a community, to the

[146] Cf. Coronata, *Institutiones,* I, n. 367, nota 3; Connolly, *The Canonical Erection of Parishes,* p. 106.

[147] Cf. *Jus Pontificium,* IV (1924), 3.

exclusion of groups speaking any other language. Such a group, however, may constitute the majority in some places, and then there is nothing to prevent the bishop from erecting a territorial parish (not cumulative in this sense) for the good of all of the faithful in that community, including the minority. The fact that the majority of the people use a particular idiom does not necessarily make such a parish a national parish. As for cities and regions where other parishes already exist, when there arises a need to care for the faithful of a particular language group, canon 216, § 4 does not prohibit the erection of chapels or missions under the jurisdiction of the pastor of the territorial parish.

It is easy to conceive a case in which a territorial parish had been erected for all of the people of a certain community in which a foreign idiom was predominantly used, and in which, later, a large English-speaking element had settled, so that it becomes necessary to establish another parish. This can be done in two ways: by dividing the territory, the procedure that is favored by law, or by erecting a territorial parish for the English-speaking congregation coextensive with the original parish. In the latter case, since the former parish was territorial, and the idiom of the country is English, it would be necessary to obtain an indult to change the former territorial parish into a parish for the foreign language group.[148]

If the former parish existed as a national parish, the bishop could, without further formality, establish a territorial parish for the faithful of the English-speaking population. In erecting church edifices for either national or territorial parishes, the ordinary should, with prudent forethought, bear in mind the possibility of future developments, and seek to obtain a location that is reasonably distant from the other church or churches, so that, if it becomes necessary to convert the national parish into a territorial parish, it will not be difficult to effect an equitable distribution of territory.

Since national parishes are not to be erected except by special apostolic indult, there is involved a process of petitioning the Holy See for his indult. The bishop, because of the office that he holds,

[148] Studies and Conferences, "Territorial or National Parish?"—*AER,* LXI (1920), 97.

is the logical person to petition for the indult.[149] But since the canon does not specify the actual petitioner, stating merely that such parishes are not to be constituted, it seems that other persons are not excluded from submitting the petition for this indult.[150] Such a petition, however, should always be accompanied by a recommendation from the ordinary.

The correct and requisite form of the petition should be adhered to, that is, it should be written in one of the official languages of the Roman Curia. These languages are Latin, Italian and French.[151] It is to be addressed to the Sacred Congregation of the Council, but should be directed to the Holy Father, e.g. *Beatissime Pater.* After the indication of the name of the diocese and of the petitioner, the customary formula can be appropriately used: "Ad pedes Sanctitatis Vestrae humillime provolutus," or a similar expression of submission to the authority of the Holy See.[152] The body of the petition should be clear and concise, drawn up according to the style of the Curia in the three corresponding parts of the papal rescript: the narrative, the motive and the dispositive.[153] Therefore, a brief outline of the circumstances existing in the city or the diocese could be inserted at the beginning of the petition. This outline could include the number and quality of persons of a certain language group involved: how they have been provided for in the past, the number of churches in the city or district, the number of Catholics in the same community, etc. This could be followed by a description of the need or the reason which affords the immediate occasion of the petition, and the setting forth of the request. Finally, the ordinary should state briefly his reasons for considering the granting of the indult as necessary and expedient.[154] The petition can conclude with the customary formula of "Et Deus . . . ," or "Pro qua gratia . . . ," indicating gratitude in anticipation of the expected concession of the indult. It should be

149 O'Neill, *Papal Rescripts of Favor,* p. 93.

150 Cf. *AAS,* I (1909), 53.

151 S. C. de Prop. Fide, litt. encycl., 29 sept. 1868—*Coll.,* n. 1335; S. C. de Prop. Fide, litt. encycl. (ad Superiores Mission.), 18 maii 1896—*Coll.,* n. 1929.

152 Hilling, *Procedure of the Roman Curia* (New York, 1907), p. 148.

153 Cicognani, *Canon Law,* p. 699.

154 O'Neill, *Papal Rescripts of Favor,* p. 97.

addressed to the Cardinal Prefect of the Sacred Congregation of the Council,[155] since this is the Roman Congregation that has particular competence in the matter.[156]

ARTICLE V. PERMISSION INVOLVING CHANGE

Since the Code recognizes the canonical existence of national parishes, it is reasonable to conclude that they were lawfully erected before the Code. This is more apparent in the light of the letter of the Sacred Congregation of the Council of March 18, 1881,[157] which stated that a formal decree of erection was not required for the canonical erection of a parish, but that such an erection could be determined from other elements, such as the appointment of a certain rector for the care of souls, a definite congregation, and the authority of the bishop maintaining and approving this juridical condition. If national parishes were regarded as such before the Code, their status remains unchanged now, because in general the Code is not retroactive.[158] More than this, the prescriptions of canon 216, § 4 provide that in the future nothing is to be changed without a prior consultation with the Holy See. There are three elements to be considered in this provision, namely, the parishes themselves, the consultation with the Holy See, and the contemplated change.

It is evident from the wording of the canon that the law forbidding the change of status affects only those parishes that have been established and recognized as national parishes with their own proper pastor. Churches that had been erected rather as succursal chapels dependent upon a neighboring parish and within its boundaries, are not considered as parishes. In such cases the bishop could make necessary changes without previously consulting the Holy See, not to the extent, however, of establishing a national parish. If, in the

[155] All' Eminentissimo Cardinale Prefetto, S. Congregazione del Concilio, Palazzo della Cancelleria, Piazza della Cancelleria, Roma.

[156] Pius X, const. "Sapienti Consilio"—*AAS,* I (1909), 11; canon 250. This competence would also extend to religious parishes. Cf. S. C. Consist., 5 iulii 1915—*AAS,* VII (1915), 327.

[157] S.C.C., litt., 18 mart. 1881—*Coll.,* n. 1548; S.C.C., Principis Alberten. et Saskatoonen., Missae pro populo, 5 mart. 1932—*AAS,* XXV (1933), 436-438.

[158] Canon 10.

course of time, the subsidiary chapel has acquired a sufficient number of people of a particular language group so that it requires a priest of its own to provide adequately for its spiritual needs, the bishop would have to petition the Holy See for an indult to erect a national parish, if he deemed it advisable, or he would have to plan a division of the parish.

The words "without consulting the Apostolic See" indicate the procedure to be followed in changing the *status* of national parishes. It is evident that to change the juridical status of a national parish lawfully, the bishop must first consult the Holy See. A doubt arises with regard to the invalidity of an act without such consultation. The canon requiring the counsel of others for the validity of an act [159] is not in itself sufficiently clear, and authors are divided among themselves. Those who claim that for the validity of an act the seeking of the counsel is required follow the strict interpretation of the canon according to the text and context.[160] The authors who maintain that the seeking and obtaining of counsel is not required for validity argue that the words in themselves are not clear, and that what is sufficient, i.e., the consultation, is not necessarily required for validity. Furthermore, the requirement for validity could entail serious consequences in cases in which the superior neglected to consult the necessary persons, as for example, in the appointment of the *vicarius cooperator*.[161] Since there has been no response from the Pontifical Commission for the Interpretation of the Code, to which Commission the question was submitted, and since there are considerable authorities for both sides, the practical conclusion must be that, because of

[159] Canon 105, 1°.

[160] Canon 18. Thus Maroto, *Institutiones*, I, n. 471; Ferreres, *Institutiones*, I, n. 229; Ojetti, *Commentarium in Codicem Iuris Canonici* (4 vols., Romae: Apud Aedes Universitatis Gregorianae, 1927-1931), II, 186; and more recently Beste, *Introductio*, p. 162. Coronata (*Institutiones*, I, n. 153, p. 187, nota 8) considers this the more probable opinion.

[161] Canon 476, § 3. Cf. Vermeersch-Creusen, *Epitome*, I, n. 229; Bouuaert-Simenon, *Manuale*, I, n. 259; Michiels, *De Personis*, p. 418; Boudinhon—*Jus Pontificium*, VIII (1928), 29-35; Vromant, "De Actibus Personae Moralis Collegialis ac Superioris,"—*Ephemerides Theologicae Lovanienses* (Lovanii-Brugis, 1924—), VII (1930), 681. Vermeersch also cites Van Hove, Vidal and Triebs as holding the same opinion.

the doubt, the invalidity of the act cannot be insisted upon,[162] at least in every instance, because canon 105, 1° seems to refer only to those cases in which the law requires the consent or counsel for a valid act.

It is important to note, however, that in canon 216, § 4, the text does not refer to consultation with an inferior, but with a superior, in that the Holy See is an authority above the bishop, and the words could even be construed as requiring consent.[163] It would seem that the consultation with the superior is in a favored position as compared with the consultation of inferiors, and that, even if the neglect of the latter under canon 105, 1° would not render an act invalid, neglect of consultation with the Holy See would. Consultation with a superior, however, is different from the consent of the superior, and does not necessarily imply that an act performed without consultation would be invalid. In fact a number of canons requiring consultation with the ordinary,[164] and even his permission,[165] seem to indicate this.

As for the Holy See, it seems that when the law reserves to it exclusive power there is a definitely more restrictive terminology employed.[166] An act performed against such prescriptions would be invalid. At other times the invalidity or the illiceity of the act performed without the permission of the Holy See is expressly stated in the law.[167] There are also a number of canons that require consultation with the Holy See.[168] The authors generally agree that the consultation in canon 492, § 1 is not necessary for validity.[169] The removal of the procurator general mentioned in canon 517, § 2, if made without the consultation of the Holy See, is also considered valid.[170] According to canon 880, § 3, the ordinary can also validly,

[162] Coronata, *Institutiones,* I, n. 153, p. 187, nota 8.

[163] Reiffenstuel, *Ius Canonicum Universum,* lib. III, tit. X, n. 4.

[164] Canons 137; 767; 919; 1023, § 3; 1063, § 2; 1065, § 2; 1066; 1240, § 2.

[165] Canon 1091.

[166] Canons 215, § 1; 331, § 3; 494, § 1; 638; 782, § 2; 913, 1°; 1141; 1257; 1414, § 1; 1422; 1517; 1520, § 2; 1551, § 1; 1999.

[167] Canons 534, § 1; 955, § 2; 978, § 3; 1073; 1147, § 1, § 3; 1281, § 1.

[168] Canons 217, § 2; 492, § 1; 517, § 2; 880, § 3.

[169] Coronata, *Institutiones,* I, n. 511, p. 626, nota 3; Vermeersch-Creusen, *Epitome,* I, n. 598, p. 432.

[170] Coronata, *Institutiones,* I, n. 543, p. 673; Vermeersch-Creusen, *Epitome,* I, n. 636, p. 457.

though illicitly, deprive all the confessors of a religious house of their jurisdiction.[171] If the ordinary can act validly, though not licitly, when consultation with the Holy See is required in matters in which he has ordinary power, it would be logical to conclude that the consultation is not required for the validity of an act involving any change in the status of national parishes.[172] If, however, there did not appear to be sufficient reason for such a change, recourse to the Holy See could be made.[173] The action of the ordinary could be rescinded by the Holy See with which the consultation should ordinarily be made. Until otherwise decided, then, the consultation is not to be considered as necessary for the validity of the act involving any change in the status of national parishes.

Since it is likely that particular difficulties will always attend not only the erection of national parishes, but also their suppression and division or conversion into territorial parishes, the law has summarily stated that nothing is to be changed without a prior consultation with the Holy See. A national parish does not over night become a parish of people speaking the idiom of the country in which they happen to live. It is for this reason that the Holy See has required that it be consulted when a change is deemed necessary. The gradual compenetration of people of different racial strains, the advent of a modern and rapid system of communication, the intervening predominance of a different particular nationality, and the prevalent use of a different language, may be circumstances that gradually bring about a factual change and cause the use of one language to yield to or to supersede the use of another, not only in public relations, but even in the home. If this is the result of a series of voluntary acts, and in accordance with the practice and the inclinations of the individual groups, there can be no objection to a corresponding juridical change either on the grounds of reason or religion. The new generation which then develops has a native language and culture that has become by degrees different from that of the parents or grandparents, no less a nationality, though different from the older one, or from each of the several older ones from which it was derived.

[171] Cf. Vermeersch-Creusen, *Epitome,* II, n. 150, p. 102.

[172] Cf. Connolly, *The Canonical Erection of Parishes,* p. 106.

[173] Cf. Canon 1428, § 3.

The "American nationality" is as real and as closely related to the enjoyment of natural rights as the British, Irish, German, Polish or Italian nationality of the forefathers of those who are now American citizens.[174] When such a development occurs, there exists no longer a difference of language or nationality, and it then can become advisable in the prudent judgment of the ordinary, for administrative reasons, to seek, if not the suppression of a national parish, at least its conversion into a territorial one. In order to do this he should first consult the Holy See.[175]

Such consultation would also be necessary when the division of a national parish is involved, whether it be for the purpose of erecting a territorial parish, or another national parish. In the latter case, however, the petition for the indult of erection could be considered sufficient if it included the circumstances of the erection of the new parish. In erecting a new parish by a division of this kind, it is advisable to establish definite boundaries affecting persons belonging to each parish, not only for adminstrative reasons, but also from the standpoint of civil law. The term "parish" has no significance in civil law, and if used in ecclesiastical divisions it has just such importance and significance as may be given it under ecclesiastical regulations. In a case involving two national parishes, the Supreme Court of Pennsylvania, March 22, 1922, accepted the testimony in the appellee's behalf, that, under the canon law of the Roman Catholic Church, the members of the respective parishes thus created had no right to determine for themselves to which church they belonged after the division of a parish. Those within the established boundaries belonged to the church established for them. Under the laws of the Church, the proper authorities made the division of the parish, and since ecclesiastically the two parishes were held to be separated, they were also considered so by the civil court.[176]

It does not appear that this recourse to the Holy See would be necessary in such cases as involve merely a change in the administration of the parish and in the parochial functions. When the bound-

[174] Eppstein, *The Catholic Tradition of the Law of Nations,* p. 384.

[175] The extinctive union of all benefices as well as their suppression is reserved to the Holy See by the Code. Canons 1419, 1°; 1422.

[176] Cf. 117 Atl. 219.

aries between two or more parishes have not been clearly defined, the bishop can determine them without substantially changing the status of the parishes.[177] The Holy See need not be consulted when, in addition to the foreign idiom, it becomes necessary to introduce English in the national parishes in sermons, in teaching catechism and in hearing confessions, provided that the spiritual welfare of those who use the other language is not neglected.[178]

Article VI. Parishes for Colored People

Before the Plenary Councils of Baltimore there was little organized activity among Catholics regarding the care of Negroes in the United States. It was left to the individual bishops to make proper provision according to the situations that arose in their dioceses.[179] In the decrees of the II Plenary Council of Baltimore (1866) a whole chapter was devoted to the spiritual welfare of the Negroes.[180] In the preliminary instruction, the Sacred Congregation for the Propagation of the Faith had expressed great concern for the spiritual welfare and the education of the emancipated Negroes, and recommended it to the bishops as a most necessary province of pastoral care.[181]

The Fathers of the Council wholeheartedly acknowledge this recommendation, admitted that there was a danger of losing a large number of souls to the faith, and observed that it was their particular responsibility to watch over all committed to their care, making available for them the benefits of Redemption. But they realized also that a general uniform rule for all the dioceses could not be adopted because of the entirely different conditions in various parts of the country. They thought it better to leave the matter to the zeal and prudence of the respective bishops, so that if, after due consideration,

177 *S.R.R., in causa Annecien. Finium Parochialium,* 5 feb. 1918, *coram R.P.D. Ioanne Prior,* Dec. III—*S.R.R. Decisiones,* X (1918), 18-26.

178 Studies and conferences, "Pastor Halloft and Foreign-born Catholics" —*AER,* LXXII (1925), 85.

179 About 1832 St. Mary's Church was designated for the use of the colored Catholics in St. Louis—Shea, *History,* III, 683.

180 II Conc. Plen. Balt., Tit. X, cap. IV, nn. 483-491—*Acta et Decreta,* pp. 243-247.

181 II Conc. Plen. Balt., instr., 31 ian. 1866—*Acta et Decreta,* p. xxviii, n. 8.

they deemed it necessary to provide a separate church for the colored people, they were urged to do so. If on the other hand Negroes could be invited to attend a common church with the others, without subjecting the church to undue criticism, this method could be employed, as long as the sacraments were not denied to any who wished to receive them.[182]

The Fathers of the Council urged that more particular provisions be diligently made in the provincial councils soon to be held, particularly in those provinces in which there were large numbers of colored people.[183] They decreed that in those places missions should be established exclusively for Negroes in order that they might be taught the word of God. The Fathers confessed that there was an insufficient number of priests to carry on the work properly, but ardently exhorted priests to devote themselves to this work, even entirely if possible, and sought the aid of religious superiors in designating priests who might aid the bishops.[184]

Even before the II Plenary Council of Baltimore there existed separate churches for the colored people,[185] but because of the peculiar conditions that arose immediately after the Civil War, and in view also of political animosities along with racial and religious prejudice, it was especially difficult to make any general provision for the whole country. The III Plenary Council, however, approved the decrees of the II Plenary Council, and noted that a number of separate churches and schools had been built, and that in other places the spiritual needs of the colored people were provided for together with the rest of the members of the congregation at the church they attended.[186] The Fathers of the Council then decreed that wherever possible the bishops should erect churches, schools, orphanages and poor-homes for the use of the Negroes. In other places the Negroes were to be accommodated in the local church, and were to be per-

[182] II Conc. Plen. Balt., n. 485—*Acta et Decreta,* p. 244.

[183] II Conc. Plen. Balt., n. 491—*Acta et Decreta,* p. 247.

[184] II Conc. Plen. Balt., n. 488—*Acta et Decreta,* p. 245.

[185] A universalist church in Baltimore which was purchased by the colored Catholics was dedicated to God February 21, 1864, by the Very Rev. Administrator under the invocation of St. Francis Xavier—Shea, *History,* IV, 393.

[186] III Conc. Plen. Balt., n. 237—*Acta et Decreta,* p. 133.

mitted to receive the Sacraments without any discrimination against them.[187]

The work of the spiritual emancipation of the colored people had begun seriously with the II Plenary Council. In 1871 some of the first missionaries devoted to this work were sent to Baltimore, at the request of Pope Pius IX and Archbishop Spalding, from the newly founded Society of Mill Hill in England. They took over St. Francis Xavier Church, and when the III Plenary Council had again emphasized the need of an organized apostolate, St. Joseph's Seminary was founded in Baltimore to train young men for continued work in this field.[188]

The III Plenary Council also decreed the establishment of a permanent commission to aid the Negro and Indian missions,[189] and when the acts and decrees of the Council were formally promulgated on January 6, 1886, the Commission for Catholic Missions among the Colored People and the Indians became a fact. Thus not only spiritual but also material aid was insured by yearly collections that were to be taken up for this purpose. There were already, besides a number of missions, parishes for colored people in Baltimore, Washington, Charleston, Louisville, New York, Richmond and St. Louis.[190]

As to the number of Catholic Negroes at that time, there seems to be no definite figure, but since the slaves generally accepted the religious affiliation of their masters, it may be significant to note that "of the four million slaves in the United States in 1863 probably not more than five per cent, certainly less than ten per cent, had Catholic masters." [191] The first fairly accurate report on the number of Negro Catholics was published by the above mentioned Commission in 1888, and gave the number as 138,213.[192]

[187] III Conc. Plen. Balt., n. 238—*Acta et Decreta,* p. 133.

[188] Murphy, "The Colored Harvest"—*AER,* LXXIX (1928), 496-508, especially p. 498.

[189] III Conc. Plen. Balt., nn. 242-243—*Acta et Decreta,* p. 135.

[190] Gillard, "A Significant Jubilee for Negro Catholics"—*AER,* XCII (1935), 235-251, especially p. 239.

[191] Butsch, "Negro Catholics in the United States"—*CHR,* III (1917), 33-51, especially pages 36 and 45.

[192] Gillard, "A Significant Jubilee for Negro Catholics"—*AER,* XCII (1935), 235-251, especially p. 237.

For various reasons the growth among the Catholic colored was not at all in proportion to their natural increase, whereas the accommodations, though still inadequate, were multiplied. There were 25 exclusively colored churches in 1890, 105 in 1917, and 228 resident missions in 1941.[193] In 1943 the colored Catholics were estimated to number some 300,440, out of a total population of 12,865,518,[194] with the largest distribution throughout Mississippi, South Carolina, Louisiana, Alabama and Georgia, and the largest single centers in New York, Chicago and Philadelphia.[195]

From what had been said it is apparent that this definite portion of our population has been the object of solicitude not only to the American clergy, but also to the Holy Father.[196] Separate churches were erected for them, and about half the Negro Catholics in the United States worship in churches that can be designated as exclusively for the colored. Unquestionably the mind of the Church is that no distinction be made as to racial differences in the common bond of Faith, and this has been successfully practiced in the past. But it is necessary to keep in mind that the United States is not a Catholic country. Bi-racial problems are the cause of situations that, humanly viewed, are difficult to overcome. The Church has to accept human nature as it is and seek to mold it in the pattern of Christ. If the Church has found it necessary to erect separate churches for these people, one can only interpret this arrangement as being equally advantageous for all concerned.

Since the promulgation of the Code, however, all parishes which are exclusively for the use of a particular language or national group in the same city or territory, or which are merely personal or family parishes, may not be established without a special apostolic indult.

[193] Gillard, *Colored Catholics in the United States* (Baltimore: The Josephite Press, 1941), p. 134.

[194] Tennelly, "Catholic Negro Missions"—*The National Catholic Almanac* (Paterson, N. J.: St. Anthony Guild, 1943), pp. 403-405.

[195] Gillard, *Colored Catholics in the United States*, p. 136.

[196] Moroney, "Catholic Activity in behalf of the Negro"—*AER*, LXII (1920), 45-56; Murphy, "The Colored Harvest"—*AER*, LXXIX (1928), 499; Gillard, "A Significant Jubilee for Negro Catholics"—*AER*, XCII (1935), 235-251; Gillard, "The Catholic Clergy and the American Negro"—*AER*, XCIV (1936), 144-158; Walsh, "Nigra Sum sed Formosa"—*AER*, CV (1941), 493.

Strictly taken, parishes erected for the colored are neither lingual nor national, because quite generally in the United States the Negroes use the language of the country, which is English, and by the fact that they were born here they are its citizens. In a wider sense, however, they can be classified as national parishes by reason of the racial origin of the members. In the first case nationality is considered from the standpoint of political unity, and in the second as a characteristic of people of a common origin. Such parishes could be included, then, in the general classification of those which are designated with the wording, *pro diversitate nationis*. But since the primary reason for establishing national parishes seems to be the diversity of language, it would be more appropriate to refer to colored parishes under the general classification of personal parishes, either strictly personal or cumulatively territorial.[197]

The norm established by the Code is that the diocese is to be divided into distinct territorial parts which are to be called parishes. Only one parish ordinarily is to exist within the same territory according to this principle, and only one pastor for the people within that territory.[198] If another parish for a certain group of people extends over the same territory it cannot be considered as strictly territorial, but personal, with territoriality as the secondary factor. In the case of colored parishes, the distinction is based not on the difference of language and nationality, but rather on the racial characteristics of the people who belong to it. By reason of this difference they are withdrawn from the jurisdiction of the territorial parish and affiliated with their own church. On the other hand, if a certain district is inhabited entirely by colored people, a strictly territorial parish serving only the Colored might exist.

Regarding those exclusively colored parishes which were erected before the Code, since, as has been shown, they are personal parishes

[197] Cappello, *Summa Iuris Canonici*, Vol. II (Romae, 1930), n. 488; Bastnagel, "Is a Parish for Colored People a 'National' Parish?"—*AER*, CVIII (1943), 383. Connolly does not think that they are personal in the limited sense of the Code "because membership in them embraces a whole class of people and is generic, whereas the personal type of parishes seems to embrace a more specific and individual membership."—*The Canonical Erection of Parishes*, p. 107.

[198] Canon 460.

within the contemplation of the law, the law provides that their status is not to be changed without consulting the Holy See. Since the Code, the erection of national, lingual and personal as well as family parishes has been restricted. To erect such parishes a special apostolic indult is required. But since the ordinary has the authority to establish strictly territorial parishes in districts where there is an exclusively colored population, he can, without such an indult, erect a parish in that territory and make any subsequent changes according to the prescriptions of Canon Law. If, however, a parish church is intended for the use of a colored congregation to the exclusion of all others who might live within the same territory, or district, then, according to the prescriptions of law, it must be considered a strictly personal parish requiring a special apostolic indult for its erection.[199]

The same principle would apply to parishes erected for other groups distinct by reason of racial characteristics (Indians, Chinese). Past experience has warranted the existence of such parishes, or at least missions, and there should be no difficulty in obtaining the required indult if the circumstances seem to make it advisable. It may even be possible, where the conditions are quite general, as in some of the southern States, to obtain a general permission to erect such parishes, thus obviating the necessity of recourse to the Holy See in each case.

[199] Bastnagel, "Is a Parish for Colored People a 'National' Parish?"—*AER*, CVIII (1943), 384; Studies and Conferences, "Parishes for Colored People"—*AER*, LX (1919), 85.

CHAPTER V

THE PARISHIONERS

SINCE the parishioners constitute an essential element of a parish, it is necessary to determine who the parishioners of a national parish are, and under what conditions they cease to be its members. Parishioners quite generally are the persons who have a domicile or a quasi-domicile within the limits of a parish, or those who are actually in the parish without having domicile or quasi-domicile anywhere.[1] In the case of national parishes, in which the personal title of nationality or language is a primary consideration, and the territorial principle is secondary, the parish to which a person is supposed to belong can be determined according to the national or lingual group of which he happens to form a part. This is especially true in regions where there are several national parishes which all have their fixed boundaries.[2] But because of the peculiar nature of such parishes and the authoritative ruling that has been made with regard to the people who are to belong to them, it is necessary to consider separately foreign-born Catholics and their children in relation to the parish to which they belong.

ARTICLE I. FOREIGN-BORN CATHOLICS

National parishes were first generally established in the United States by reason of great necessity and utility. The large numbers of immigrants who came to this country made it practically necessary to provide churches and priests to minister to them in their own idiom. The English-speaking pastor was unable to shepherd them in his already numerous flock, to preach the word of God and minister the sacraments to them. These parishes increased and multiplied with the advent of more people. Because of their exclusive knowledge of one language, their affiliation with a particular national parish was easily accepted and recognized. Since language was the principal factor in

[1] Canon 94.

[2] Michiels, *De Personis,* p. 176.

determining the parish to which they were to belong, there were no difficulties with regard to jurisdiction until these people, for whom the parish was originally established, learned English and no longer labored under the language difficulty. Because of the existing conditions, it was necessary for the Sacred Congregation for the Propagation of the Faith, to whose jurisdiction this country was still subject, to issue a definite rule that could serve as a guide for the future.

The question was proposed to the Sacred Congregation by the Apostolic Delegate, Cardinal Martinelli, who thought that, since the matter was of such grave import, it should be submitted to a superior authority. He pointed out that since there were in the United States, within the same territory, several quasi-parishes to accommodate people of different nationalities, certain questions had arisen regarding the claims of jurisdiction over the children born of parents belonging to these churches, as well as over immigrants who, though coming from foreign countries, spoke English. The reply of the Sacred Congregation, dated April 26, 1897, followed the resolutions previously given April 11, 1887, and considered both points separately. (1) "The children, born in America of parents who are not American and who speak a language other than English, upon becoming emancipated, are not obliged to join the quasi-parish to which their parents belong, but have the right to join a quasi-parish in which the language of the country, that is, English is used." (2) "Catholics who were not born in America but who know English, have the right to become members of the church where the English language is used, and cannot be obliged to subject themselves to the jurisdiction of the rector of the church which was established for the people who speak the language of their own country." [3] This reply was sent out in a circular

[3] For the full text of this letter cf. *ASS,* XXX (1897), 256; *AER,* XVII (1897), 87. The Latin text of the two resolutions reads as follows: 1. Filios ex parentibus non-americanis linguam ab Anglica diversam loquentibus, in America natos, non teneri cum emancipati sint ad sese iugendos quasi-paroeciae, ad quam pertinent parentes, sed iure frui sese uniendi quasi-paroeciae in qua regionis lingua, seu Anglica, adhibetur. 2. Catholicos qui in America nati non sunt, qui tamen linguam anglicam noscunt, ius habere membra fieri illius ecclesiae in quae anglica lingua in usu est, nec obligari posse ad sese subiiciendos iurisdictioni rectoris ecclesiae erectae pro populo linguam propriae nationis loquente.

letter from the Apostolic Delegation under the date of May 12, 1897. Although the Sacred Congregation realized the importance of the question in the United States, and the necessity of national parishes for the spiritual care of souls, it recognized the fact that such a state of affairs gave rise to frequent conflicts, and would impede the progress of national and religious unity. Consequently, even though it wanted to preserve the status of national parishes destined for the use of foreigners, it had to favor the position of those who spoke the language of the country and became its citizens.[4]

This instruction was considered to be in force before and after the Code,[5] and received added force from the recent circular letter which was sent February 17, 1938, to all the members of the hierarchy of the United States by the Apostolic Delegation. This letter of His Excellency, the Most Reverend Amleto G. Cicognani, Apostolic Delegate, contained the two resolutions of the Sacred Congregation for the Propagation of the Faith, with the observation that "a misunderstanding seems to have arisen in regard to the proper interpretation of these declarations. In certain sections some foreign-born Catholics and their children, whose cases are covered by these declarations, interpret them in the sense that they are free to affiliate with any parish, even another national parish, in which the English language is spoken. The matter was duly referred to the Holy See, and under the date of January 15, 1938, the Sacred Congregation of the Council declared that: 'When foreign immigrants and their children speak the English language and do not wish to belong to their own national parishes they must affiliate with the American territorial parish in which the English language may be spoken.' "[6]

The wording of this declaration and the principle enunciated are quite clear and understandable, even though the application in individual cases may prove somewhat difficult. For instance, in many places in this country national parishes have become partly, or even entirely, English speaking, in the sense that all of the important parochial functions involving the use of language are conducted in

[4] *Analecta Ecclesiastica,* V (1897), 292, in nota; *Le Canoniste Contemporain,* XX (1897), 615.

[5] *AER,* LXXX (1929), 89.

[6] Bouscaren, II, 78, under canon 216.

English or alternately with the foreign idiom. Would a person who does not wish to belong to his own national parish any longer because of the great inconvenience (e.g. distance), have to be refused admission into another nearby parish where English is used, at least proportionately to the need, just because there happens to be no territorial parish within reasonable distance? It does not seem to be the mind of the Church to impose hardships upon its subjects and penalize them when they wish to worship in the language of the country in a nearby national church, which for all practical purposes might serve the territory, but as yet cannot be made exclusively territorial. It rather seems that such a fusion of nationalities would even more easily promote the eventual establishment of parishes according to territorial lines.

The above mentioned declaration of the Sacred Congregation of the Council favors the language of the country since it is the language of its government, of public education, of commerce, of industry and finance. Moreover, since that language is the language in which the laws of this country are promulgated, the knowledge of it promotes peace and order in the social lives of the country's citizens. The Church, though providing for the individual needs of language groups, does not seek to perpetuate an abnormal condition beyond the bounds of necessity or of immediate expediency, and therefore declares that those who no longer wish to belong to their own national parishes must affiliate themselves with the American territorial parish in which they have their domicile.[7] From what has been said it is clear that even though foreign-born Catholics are not bound to remain in the national parish once they have learned English, they are in no way obligated to leave it, even after the immediate necessity of the use of their native language has passed. Many parishioners of national parishes are equally conversant with both languages, and may even be more fluent in English than in their native tongue. Nevertheless they still retain the right to belong to the national parish, because the declaration of the Sacred Congregation states that only when they no longer wish to belong to the national parish does it become

[7] Studies and Conferences, "Parish Rights of Foreign Immigrants"—*AER*, XXXVIII (1908), 65-69, especially p. 68; Studies and Conferences, "Why the Discrimination?"—*AER*, XXXVIII (1908), 208-211.

necessary for them to join the territorial parish.[8] They should not therefore be solicited or compelled to join the territorial parish, and it would seem that even if they moved to another city in which there is a national parish of the same language group, they can affiliate themselves with it.

If a parishioner of a national parish decides to join another parish he must not affiliate himself with any other national parish in which the English language is spoken. If he joins the territorial parish in which he has his domicile it seems that he may return again to his own national parish since the Sacred Congregation mentions only affiliation "with any other parish in which the English language may be spoken," and says nothing against returning to the former parish. But since the common law of the Church as stated in canon 216 considers national parishes as more or less exceptional, persons who speak a foreign idiom are, as it were, dispensed from belonging to territorial parishes. If later, when they have learned English, they join a territorial parish because they have found it no longer necessary, as far as language is concerned, to belong to a national parish, the motivating reason for this exception is presumed to have disappeared, and consequently can no longer be used.[9]

Since the greatest liberty is given by the Sacred Congregation to those parishioners of a national parish who speak English to make this change themselves, it would seem that the authority of both the territorial and the national pastor is restricted. No pastor may determine in this respect who shall or shall not be a member of his parish.[10] If a parishioner of a national parish chooses to affiliate himself with a territorial parish in which he has domicile, the pastor of the national parish cannot oblige him to remain, nor can the pastor of the English-

[8] Studies and Conferences, "Pastor Halloft and Foreign-Born Catholics" —*AER,* LXXII (1925), 85.

[9] Canon 86. Cf. Studies and Conferences, "National and Canonical Parishes in the United States"—*AER,* LXXVI (1927), 90, where it is considered as a privilege.

[10] Studies and Conferences, "National and Canonical Parishes in the United States"—*AER,* LXXVI (1927), 90; Studies and Conferences, "Pastoral Care of Foreign Catholics in America"—*AER,* LXX (1924), 176-181; Studies and Conferences, "Nationalism and Catholicity of the Clergy in the United States"—*ibid.,* 295.

speaking territorial parish refuse admittance.[11] Casual attendance at a territorial church does not necessarily indicate a person's intention of joining the parish. Such an intention would have to be expressed to the pastor of the territorial parish and shown by inscription in the parish records, and by the assumption of the regular obligations of parishioners in the reception of the sacraments, and contributions to the support of the church.

Article II. The Children of Foreign-born Catholics

Both the declaration of the Sacred Congregation for the Propagation of the Faith and the declaration of the Sacred Congregation of the Council, made explicit mention of the children of foreign-born Catholics who have learned English.[12] The freedom of choice that has been accorded the parents is *a fortiori* given to their sons and daughters, even though they have been born, baptized and reared in a national parish. If they speak the language of the country, they may if they wish, as soon as they become emancipated from parental authority, affiliate themselves with the territorial parish in which they have their domicile. Children who are under age, however, must follow their parents in parochial affiliation until they have been emancipated. Then they are free to make their own choice.[13]

According to the Code a person reaches the age of majority after having completed the twenty-first year. Before that he is considered a minor, and if he has not reached the age of reason, an infant.[14] A major person enjoys the full exercise of his rights, whereas a minor is subject to the authority of his parents or guardians unless he is exempt by law.[15] Since the exercise of only the acquired rights of the minor is the object of this subjection to parental authority,[16] one

[11] Studies and Conferences, "American and National Parishes"—*AER*, LXXII (1925), 521-526.

[12] Bouscaren, II, 78.

[13] Studies and Conferences, "Parish Rights of Foreign Immigrants"—*AER*, XXXVIII (1908), 68.

[14] Canon 88, § 1, § 3.

[15] Canon 89.

[16] Michiels, *De Personis*, p. 45.

may say that the law is a purely canonical one,[17] and is not to be considered here from the standpoint of divine law, because it refers rather to the canonical incapacity of a minor to act, and not the subjection that is due to parents from the positive or natural law of God.

The law provides for minors exemptions from parental control either explicitly or implicitly. Minors are exempt explicitly when they are mentioned expressly in the canons as authorized to act independently, for instance, in choosing the church for their funeral, the place of burial, and in placing other acts.[18] They are implicitly exempt when the law not only does not require, but even excludes the necessity of the intervention of this authority.[19]

This can happen: (a) when the minor is obliged to act either by divine or ecclesiastical law, as for example, in receiving the sacraments and catechetical instructions, and attending divine services. In these things the authority of the parents is superseded by divine and ecclesiastical authority which grants the minor the free exercise of his spiritual rights. The parents have the responsibility of directing the manner in which these rights are to be exercised, in as much as it is consonant with the good of the whole family or of the children. If they restrict the actual exercise of these fundamental rights, they transgress their authority; (b) when a person is declared capable by ecclesiastical authority validly and licitly to perform some act at an age less than that of majority. Such exemption would be employed, for example, in entering a state of life—clerical, religious or matrimonial.[20]

In view of what has been said, it would be possible to assume that since the original declaration of the Sacred Congregation for the Propagation of the Faith does not explicitly mention minors, and the later declaration of the Sacred Congregation of the Council does not mention emancipation at all, the children of foreign-born Catholics can be at most only implicitly exempt. Minors who have reached the

[17] For the civil effect cf. Vermeersch-Creusen, *Epitome,* I, n. 209; Coronata, *Institutiones,* I, n. 120; Maroto, *Institutiones,* I, n. 441.

[18] Canons 1223, § 2; 1648, § 3; 93, § 2.

[19] Vermeersch-Creusen, *Epitome,* I, n. 209.

[20] Cf. canons 108; 543; 968; 1352; 1035; 1038-1039.

age of puberty, however, as in the case of minors who seek to contract marriage,[21] should see that their parents are not reasonably opposed to such an action, because the spiritual good of the descendants of foreign-born Catholics can be amply provided for in many national parishes today where both English and the foreign idiom are used.

It is evident that when minors marry they become emancipated from parental authority. If the persons who marry are members of a national parish they may retain their affiliation with the parish. In cases where one of the persons is from a national parish and the other from a territorial parish, another solution must be sought. Neither the Code nor the private declarations mention explicitly what is to be done, but in line with the general principle of law one can form a conclusion. The law states that unless some other provision is made,[22] a wife partakes of the status of the husband with regard to canonical effects.[23] Thus, if she is not lawfully separated from her husband, she is considered as one with his person, necessarily retaining his domicile,[24] and in general being subject to the same ecclesiastical superior. The pastor of the husband would also logically, therefore, be the pastor of the wife. Canon 98, § 4, permits a woman to change to the rite of her husband at the time of marriage or any time during it, and to return to her own rite when the marriage is dissolved. Though the privilege of changing one's rite is something entirely different, one can by analogy say that also in the case of marriage between two parishioners of different national parishes, or between a parishioner of a national parish and one of a territorial parish, the bride may chose the parish of her husband with the right of returning to her former parish when the marriage is dissolved, if she chooses to do so. The general conclusion is, that the wife partakes of the status of her husband and becomes a member of the parish in which he has his domicile.

[21] Canon 1034.

[22] This is done in canons 98, § 4; 1223, § 2; 1456.

[23] Canon 112; 1229, § 2.

[24] Canon 93, § 1.

CHAPTER VI

THE PASTOR

Article I. The Appointment

The pastor according to Canon Law is defined as a priest or a moral person upon whom a parish has been conferred in title, with the care of souls to be exercised under the authority of the local ordinary.[1] A parish is regularly understood to be a distinct territorial division of a diocese with its own church, pastor and congregation.[2] The title is determined by the territory over which the pastor has jurisdiction.[3]

But the law also recognizes the existence of parishes constituted according to the principle of personality, whereby people who speak a certain foreign language, or who themselves are foreigners or descendants of foreign immigrants, may belong to the church established exclusively for them, and are not required to join the territorial parish in which they happen to reside. In this case the title derives directly from the persons themselves, or is intimately connected with them.[4] A priest to whom such a parish is conferred by legitimate authority, and who has the spiritual care of the people belonging to his church is known as the pastor of a national parish, as distinguished from the local pastor.[5]

To be a pastor in the true sense he must hold the parish in title, that is, it must be canonically his in that he administers the parish not as a mere delegate of the bishop, but in his own name. Thus he has the ordinary power attached to the office and defined by canon law, and cannot, without legitimate reason, be restricted in exercising it. He is not completely independent, however, because the bishop possesses and can exercise ordinary jurisdiction in any part of the

[1] Canon 451, § 1.
[2] Canon 216, § 1.
[3] Cappello, *Summa,* II, n. 488.
[4] Cappello, *loc. cit.;* Wernz-Vidal, *Ius Canonicum,* II, n. 720.
[5] Wernz-Vidal, *loc. cit.*

diocese.[6] National parishes are recognized in the Code, and since a pastor is one to whom a parish is conferred in title, the pastor of a national parish is a pastor in the true sense, with all the corresponding rights and duties, unless they are expressly restricted.

A parish must be conferred upon a person, either physical or moral. The physical person must be a priest,[7] but since moral persons are not excluded, it may happen that a national parish is given not to a particular individual but to a religious community, in which case the moral person has the title of incumbency, but then acts through a vicar who takes care of the actual spiritual welfare of the parishioners.[8] The bishop ordinarily is the one who confers the benefices that exist in the diocese, unless they happen to be reserved.[9] This he can do even before his consecration as long as he has taken canonical possesion of his diocese,[10] for the act of conferring a benefice is not an act of orders, but one of jurisdiction.[11] But the choice of a pastor is regulated by certain rules that have been incorporated into the Code from the Council of Trent and correlative constitutions. Under grave obligation the ordinary must appoint the priest most suitable for a particular parish without partiality.[12] According to the prescriptions of the Code, if, without sufficient reason, a benefice is not conferred by the ordinary within six months after he has received news of the vacancy, the Holy See reserves to itself the right to confer such a benefice.[13] Ordinarily, then, the bishop should strive to appoint a suitable pastor within the allotted time, unless in his prudent judgment, in view of certain circumstances, he deem it necessary to postpone the appointment.[14]

From the time of the Council of Trent [15] the bishops has been guided in their appointments by the *concursus*, a competitive quali-

[6] Canon 334, § 1.
[7] Canon 154; 453; 1442.
[8] Cf. canons 452, § 2; 471.
[9] Canon 335.
[10] Canon 334, §§ 2, 3.
[11] D'Angelo, *Parroco e Parrocchia*, p. 47, note 2.
[12] Canon 459, § 1.
[13] Cf. canons 1432, § 3; 155.
[14] Canon 458.
[15] Sess. XXIV, *de ref.*, c. 18.

fication examination which was to be in writing. It was necessary for the validity of the candidate's appointment, and the bishop was obliged to appoint the one who had qualified best among those who were approved by the examiners, but the candidate's other qualifications had to be taken into consideration also.[16]

In the United States up to the III Plenary Council of Baltimore (1884) all of our rectors were removable. Nevertheless the *concursus* was adopted by the II Plenary Council (1866) for all such rectors.[17] In the III Plenary Council it was decreed that one rector out of every ten should in the future be made irremovable,[18] and that the rules of the *concursus* be applied in their appointments, with certain exceptions that were provided in the decree.[19] These provisions of the Baltimore Councils were in force before the Code, and since the Code explicitly mentions that until the Holy See makes other provisions the past regulations concerning the *concursus* be retained wherever they were in use,[20] and since they did not conflict with the Code, but were rather *praeter ius*, they were to be considered in force also after the promulgation of the Code, though not under the pain of nullity.[21]

Because of the numerous difficulties accompanying a *concursus*, the Archbishops and the Bishops of the United States, through His Eminence, the Cardinal Archbishop of Boston, petitioned the Holy See to abrogate the provisions made in the III Plenary Council of Baltimore (1884), and to permit that the appointments to all parishes be made according to canon 459, § 3, of the Code of Canon Law. In a private decree of the Sacred Congregation of the Council issued through His Excellency, the Apostolic Delegate, and dated June 24, 1931, this petition was granted and the provisions of the Plenary Council were abrogated, and all appointments to parishes in the United States, whether removable or irremovable, are for the future

[16] Smith, *Elements*, I, n. 647.

[17] II Conc. Plen. Balt., n. 126—*Acta et Decreta*, p. 80.

[18] III Conc. Plen. Balt., n. 40—*Acta et Decreta*, p. 25.

[19] *Acta et Decreta*, nn. 35-37, 41, 43, 52, 57.

[20] Canon 459, § 4.

[21] Coady, *The Appointment of Pastors*, p. 121; Studies and Conferences, "Irremovability and Concursus"—*AER*, LXI (1920), 294.

to be made according to canon 459, § 3, of the Code, all things to the contrary notwithstanding.[22] In this country, then, the holding of the *concursus* is no longer necessary for the appointment of removable or irremovable pastors.[23]

In the appointment of pastors for national parishes, the bishop should keep in mind, besides the other requirements enacted in the law, their relation to the particular parish that happens to be vacant. He should consider the qualifications of the priest to be appointed and the specific requirements of the parish that is vacant. In other words, he is not obliged to choose a priest who already has an ecclesiastical office. He may even prefer others to those who are very suitable for the particular vacant parish, but who, in his opinion, will be more useful and necessary in another capacity or in another parish not yet vacant.[24]

On the other hand, from the point of view of the vacant parish itself, the qualifications of the candidate are to be judged not merely on the basis of his knowledge and experience, but also on the basis of the peculiar condition and needs of the parish. Thus one who is less learned or younger in service may be suited for a particular parish because of its social conditions or in view of his knowledge of the language of the people.[25] To fulfill the pastoral duties according to the divine command,[26] the pastor should first be able to understand the language of his parishioners. This knowledge was considered so important that some thought it was necessary for the validity of his appointment.[27]

If the people of a language group belonged to the local parish, the pastor of that parish was obliged to provide a priest of their language at least a few times a year in order that such parishioners

[22] Cf. Bouscaren, I, 249; also in *AER*, LXXXV (1931), 383.

[23] There were also permanent rectors of national parishes before the Code and irremovable pastors appointed for national parishes after the Code. Cf. Studies and Conferences, "National Churches and the Boston Synod"—*AER*, LXI (1919), 182-184.

[24] Wernz-Vidal, *Ius Canonicum*, II, n. 729.

[25] Studies and Conferences, "The Recent Rescript on Appointment of Irremovable Pastors"—*AER*, LXXXV (1941), 388-391.

[26] Conc. Trident., sess. XXIII, *de ref.*, c. 1.

[27] Cf. Riganti (1661-1735), *In Regulas Cancelleriae*, Reg. XX, n. 1-2.

could avail themselves of a proper opportunity to go to confession to him.[28] It is important, then, with reference to the prospective candidates for the vacant national parish, that the bishop consider the relative needs of that particular parish and select the more suitable and worthy candidate. This choice is left entirely to him. From among all those who appear suitable and worthy, the bishop is free to choose one who to him appears to be more worthy or more suitable than the rest. This is true notwithstanding the opinion of the examiners in favor of another candidate, for the bishop alone is the responsible judge of the needs of the particular parish in question.[29] Though the condition of the parish may help determine the choice of the pastor, the parishioners themselves have no right, according to the Code, either to elect or to present their own candidates.[30]

It does not appear necessary in every case to appoint a pastor who speaks the language of all of his parishioners, or even of a large number of them. According to the provisions of Canon Law, priests may be appointed as assistants to the pastor not only because of the excessive number of parishioners, but also for other reasons to be weighed by the bishop.[31] An assistant can be appointed for the parish in general, or for a particular part of the parish.[32] Thus if a particular portion of the parish is composed of a number of people speaking a foreign language, an assistant could be appointed to care for that particular group of people at least until such time that the pastor learned the language.[33]

Besides appointing pastors to national parishes, the bishop may find it necessary to remove them. As far as the rights and duties are concerned, there is no practical difference between removable and irremovable pastors. But there is a notable difference when their

[28] Cf. *Statuta Provincialia et Dioecesana* (Philadelphiensia), p. 48, n. 17; also the circular letter of Pius X to the American Ordinaries concerning Italian immigrants—*AER*, LII (1915), 585.

[29] Canon 459, § 1; cf. D'Angelo, *op. cit.*, p. 151.

[30] Augustine, *Status of Catholic Parishes*, p. 212.

[31] Canon 476, § 1.

[32] Canon 476, § 2; Augustine, *Commentary*, II, 573.

[33] Bastnagel, *The Appointment of Parochial Adjutants and Assistants*, The Catholic University of America Canon Law Studies, n. 58 (Washington, D. C.: The Catholic University of America, 1930), p. 127.

removal and transfer is concerned. The Code requires a certain stability in connection with the parochial office, but this stability does not prevent the removal of the pastor from office for a sufficient canonical reason.[34] The bishop, therefore, can remove both the removable and irremovable pastors of national parishes according to the provisions of law.[35]

An irremovable pastor cannot be deprived of his parish except for the reasons expressly stated in the law as requiring such a penalty, and in strict observance of the procedure prescribed.[36] Thus the hatred of the people directed against the pastor, even though he is in no way at fault, exists as a canonical cause for the removal, for such hatred can, and in all probability will, seriously impede his usefulness to the spiritual progress of the parish.[37]

The removable pastor can be deprived of his office by the ordinary for the same just reasons, but in this case also the rules of the Code should be followed. The difference between the procedure in relation to pastors enjoying the diverse status is that the irremovable pastor is given recourse to the bishop against the decree of removal in canon 2153.[38] The transfer, but not the administrative removal for a canonical cause, of an unwilling irremovable rector requires a papal indult,[39] but a removable pastor may be transferred even against his will according to the provisions of canons 2162-2167. As for penal removal of pastors, this may be effected by an act of deprivation, deposition and degradation.[40]

To safeguard the discipline of the Church, there is a penal sanction attached to any wilful attempt on the part of the priest to arouse the congregation in sermons or writings, or by soliciting support against the lawfully decreed removal.[41] In civil law also, the general attitude is that the bishop is the priest's superior, and that it is his province

[34] Canon 454, § 1.

[35] Canons 192; 2148.

[36] Canons 2142-2156.

[37] Canon 2147, § 2, n. 2.

[38] Canons 2157-2161.

[39] Cappelo, *Summa*, II, n. 545.

[40] Cf. Cappello, *Summa*, II, 552; canons 2303, 2305.

[41] Canon 2337.

to designate the place for the priest to exercise his priestly functions, and to prescribe the necessary rules for his guidance and control.[42] The State, therefore, will not interfere in the lawful exercise of episcopal rights, because the civil courts claim no authority to inquire into the rightfulness of ecclesiastical decisions affecting only ecclesiastical affairs.[43]

Article II. Rights and Duties

The functions of a pastor may be described as partly spiritual and partly temporal, but the temporal are based more or less on the spiritual office according to the principal, ***beneficium propter officium.*** The spiritual rights of the pastor extend to the administration of the sacraments and the sacramentals. Thus he has a right to confer solemn baptism, to carry the Blessed Sacrament publicly to the sick within the parish, to administer Holy Viaticum and Extreme Unction, to publish the promotion to sacred orders and the banns of marriage, to assist at marriage and give the nuptual blessing, to bury his parishioners, to bless houses on Holy Saturday or any other day sanctioned by custom, to bless the baptismal font on Holy Saturday, and to hold public processions and solemn blessings outside of the church.[44] His temporal rights are concerned with the offerings of the faithful and the stole fees. Since the pastor is entitled to a just support, he has a right to the fees and dues that have been approved by custom or lawful taxation according to diocesan statute or episcopal approbation. If, however, he exacts more than the law or custom allows he is obliged to make restitution.[45]

On the other hand, the pastor has certain obligations and duties which he must fulfill, and these include duties arising from promoting

[42] *"Religious Societies"*—29 *American Jurisprudence* (48 vols. Rochester, N. Y.: The Lawyers Co-operative Co., 1936—); cf. Ross v. Vertin, 46 Mich. 457, 9 N. W. 491; Baxter v. McDonnell, 155 N. Y. 83, 49 N. E. 667; Twigg v. Sheehan, 101 Pa. 363; Formanski v. Iwanowski, 108 Atl. 27.

[43] O'Donovan v. Chatard, 97 Ind. 421; Stack v. O'Hara, 98 Pa. 213; Watson v. Jones (1871), 80 U. S. (13 Wall.) 679, 714, 20 L. Ed. 666. Cf. Zollman, *American Civil Church Law*, p. 336.

[44] Canon 462.

[45] Canons 463, § 2; 1507; 2408.

the spiritual welfare of the faithful committed to his care, as well as from the temporal administration of the parish. These obligations are the profession of faith, residence in the parish, the official mass for the people, the preaching of the word of God, the celebration of the divine offices, the administration of the sacraments, pastoral vigilance and zeal particularly with regard to the education of the young,[46] the care of the sick and the poor, and the care of parish books and archives.[47] Competent and reliable authors have written at length concerning the various rights and duties of pastors, so it is not necessary to speak of them in detail here. These rights and duties pertain also to pastors of national parishes.[48] But since these rights and duties are to be exercised only according to the jurisdiction of the pastor over his parishioners it is important to recall just how this jurisdiction is determined.

When a parish has definite boundaries, the pastor's jurisdiction extends over the whole territory and includes all those who reside within that territory, unless they happen to be exempt. He can, therefore, exercise his jurisdiction in favor of his parishioners even if he is outside of his territory, and can absolve and dispense them (e. g. from fasting) in any place where they happen to be. This emphasizes by an indirect argument the importance of determining parish boundaries.[49]

If a parish is more personal than territorial and established for the people of a certain language group, it is necessary to make a distinction based on the status of the parish. Such a parish is strictly personal in the sense that it includes persons of that language group in a certain diocesan district without respect to territorial boundaries. But most likely the personal parish is also territorial inasmuch as it includes the faithful of a certain language group within a given territory. In this case, the pastor may, within the limits of his territory,

[46] Studies and Conferences, "Children of Foreign-speaking Parents"—*AER*, LXII (1920), 690.

[47] Canons 464-470.

[48] Wernz-Vidal, *Ius Canonicum*, II, 782-795; Coronata, *Institutiones*, I, 579-589; Vermeersch-Creusen, *Epitome*, I, 395-407; Augustine, *Commentary*, II, 536-559; Ayrinhac, *Constitution of the Church*, 327-351; Cappello, *Summa*, II, 32-81; Fanfani, *De Iure Parochorum*, 184-343; Ferreres, *Institutiones*, I, 325-333; Cocchi, *Commentarium*, III, 398-425.

[49] Cappello, *Summa*, II, n. 505.

even though it be cumulative with other parishes, exercise his jurisdiction over all his parishioners of a particular language group who have not affiliated themselves with the territorial parish of the place.[50]

In connection with this matter of jurisdiction and status of national parishes in the United States several problems have arisen, and these will be considered separately.

1. *The Obligation of the Official Mass for the People*

There has existed considerable controversy in the United States concerning the obligation of applying the official mass for the people. According to the prescriptions of canon 466, it is quite evident that all pastors are bound by the obligation, but since the status of parishes in this country was not clearly understood, it was contended that the obligation did not extend to the pastors of these parishes, especially when they were under the jurisdiction of the Sacred Congregation for the Propagation of the Faith. The question was ardently debated in American ecclesiastical publications shortly after the promulgation of the Code,[51] and has been brought up again most recently.[52] Since the responses of the Holy See on the status of parishes in the United States, there can be no longer any doubt about the obligation of pastors in charge of those parishes to apply the official mass for the people.[53] The prevailing opinion of canonists, that the obligation existed, was thus confirmed.[54]

The question was settled as far as territorial parishes are concerned, but since there was no mention made in the responses about national parishes there were doubts expressed concerning the obliga-

[50] Cappello, *Summa,* II, nn. 488, 505.

[51] *Homiletic and Pastoral Review,* XIX (1919), 722; XX (1920), 124, 155; *AER,* LXVIII (1918), 563; LIX (1918), 304; LX (1919), 182; LXIII (1920), 343.

[52] *Homiletic and Pastoral Review,* XLIV (1943), 138.

[53] S. C. Consist., decl., 1 aug. 1919—*AAS,* XI (1919), 346; Letter of the Apostolic Delegate, U. S., 10 nov. 1922—Bouscaren, I, 149; S. C. Conc., resol., 5 mart. 1932—*AAS,* XXV (1932), 436.

[54] Sabetti-Barrett, *Compendium Theologiae Moralis* (27 ed., New York, 1919), p. 653; Studies and Conferences, "The Mass pro Populo—A Bishop's View"—*AER,* LX (1919), 182-183; Woywod, *A Practical Commentary on the Code of Canon Law* (2 vols., New York: Wagner, 1939), I, n. 344.

tion of such pastors.[55] Ayrinhac (1867-1930) concluded from the responses that, since national parishes have no strict boundaries, their pastors do not have all of the obligations of canonical pastors.[56] This statement cannot be accepted as entirely correct because it is not correct if applied to national parishes in general, as Donnellan points out.[57] National parishes, though they may extend over two or more territorial parishes, generally have besides a definite people, an assigned territory.[58] Therefore, pastors of such parishes are certainly bound by the obligation of applying the official mass for the people even on the strength of the responses.

In cases in which national parishes do not have clearly defined boundaries, but have a definite congregation, one has to deduce the reasons from the Code itself. Since national parishes were in reality established before the Code was promulgated, and the local ordinary is forbidden to change them without first consulting the Holy See, they must also now be considered as canonically established.[59] A pastor is a priest to whom a parish is entrusted in title with the care of souls which is to be exercised under the authority of the ordinary of the diocese.[60] In fact, every parish should be entrusted to such a parish priest,[61] and since personal parishes are assumed by the Code to exist, those upon whom they are conferred must be considered as pastors. One must conclude, then, that pastors of national parishes, whether strictly personal or territorial, have the obligation of applying the official mass for the people.[62] The Code does not ex-

[55] Studies and Conferences, "National Parishes in America"—*AER*, LXXVII (1927), 523; Studies and Conferences, "The Obligation of Pastors of National Parishes to Apply Mass 'pro Populo'"—*AER*, LXXXIV (1931), 78.

[56] *Constitution of the Church*, p. 25.

[57] *The Obligation of the Missa pro Populo*, The Catholic University of America Canon Law Studies, n. 155 (Washington, D. C.: The Catholic University of America Press, 1942), p. 73.

[58] Studies and Conferences, "National Pastors and Assistance at Marriage"—*AER*, LXXX (1929), 88-94.

[59] Woywod, *Commentary*, I, n. 169. Cf. supra, pp. 90-100.

[60] Canon 451, § 1.

[61] Augustine, *Commentary*, II, 510.

[62] Studies and Conferences, "They are Canonical Pastors"—*AER*, LIX (1918), 304.

plain the meaning of the words *"in titulum,"* and since no pastor can be considered as the owner or proprietor of a parish, the meaning must apparently be restricted to the concept of possession by a legitimate claim, which in the case of national parishes derives from the quality of the persons who are the parishioners.[63]

This obligation of applying the official mass for the people is a personal one, and obliges *sub gravi* and *ex iustitia* by reason of the pastoral office which involves the care of souls. It was even considered as based upon the divine law in the Council of Trent.[64] All who are the proper pastors of a definitely assigned congregation, whether they are removable or irremovable, or appointed for only a short time, must fulfill this obligation. This applies also to those who take the place of pastors in the care of souls, as permanent vicars and temporary administrators *(vicarii oeconomi)*. Quasi-pastors are bound only insofar as it expressed by the law.[65] This obligation exists even in places where there is little or no income, even though it thus places an unusual burden on the pastor,[66] but when it becomes too burdensome recourse may be had to the Holy See for relief by way of reduction.[67]

This is a grave obligation of justice, and therefore, if the mass is not applied on the day required, either intentionally or inadvertently, it should be supplied as soon as possible. The ordinary, for a just cause, may allow the pastor to celebrate the official mass on some other day.[68] Pastors who may not have performed this obligation in good faith thinking that they were not canonical pastors, would still be obliged to supply the masses, for good faith, though it precludes sin, does not satisfy the obligation of justice. It may well be that the

[63] Augustine, *Commentary*, II, 510.

[64] "Cum praecepto divino mandatum sit omnibus quibus animarum cura commissa est, oves suos agnoscere, pro eis sacrificium offerre . . ."—sess. XXIII, *de ref.*, c. 1; some refer to it as hypothetically based on the divine law by the fact that the Church commits the care of certain people to the pastor. Thus Cappello, *Summa*, II, n. 528; Sipos, *Enchiridion Iuris Canonici* (Pečs, 1936), p. 260; cf Bouscaren, I, 254.

[65] Canon 306.

[66] Sipos, *Enchiridion*, p. 319.

[67] S. C. Consist., decl., 1 aug. 1919—*AAS*, XI (1919), 346, n. 5.

[68] Canon 466, § 3.

supplying of the omitted masses causes an extraordinary burden for the pastor. It may also be that the parishioners will feel inconvenienced if they cannot have mass said in the parish according to their intentions on certain days through the fact that the official mass for the people is offered. But since the ordinary does not have the authority to commute or condone the obligation of celebrating the masses,[69] recourse must be had to the Holy See, e.g. to the Sacred Penitentiary.[70]

2. *Right of Conferring Baptism*

One of the functions reserved to the pastor is the solemn conferring of baptism upon all who are his parishioners.[71] Pastors of national parishes enjoy the same right with regard to the people who belong to their parish. The law is very forceful and explicit in its insistence upon baptismal fonts in all parochial churches.[72] The pastor of the territorial parish is restricted in his rights over certain people who live within his territory if there exists a national church for them within reasonable distance, and if they have not yet affiliated themselves with the local English-speaking parish. The jurisdiction of the pastor of the national parish, on the other hand, is not coextensive with that of the other parishes, but is limited to persons of the language group for whom the church is erected, and who do not belong to the territorial parish. It seems reasonable to suppose, then, that if a family of a language group takes up its residence within the limits of a territorial parish and wishes to belong to the national parish erected for persons

[69] Cardinal Gibbons had obtained a rescript from the S. Consistorial Congregation, December 5, 1919, granting the faculty to all the bishops in the United States to dispense from the obligation of the *missa pro populo* for five years. This was later renewed in January 20, 1924, and November 13, 1929, by the same Sacred Congregation for a period of five years, giving the Apostolic Delegate the power to authorize all bishops of the United States to reduce, at their prudent discretion, the obligation of the official mass for the people, in poor parishes to the number required by canon 306—Bouscaren, I, 256. The exercise of these faculties did perhaps cause some confusion as to the nature of the obligation of pastors in particular cases.

[70] Wernz-Vidal, *Ius Canonicum,* II, n. 736.

[71] Canon 462, 2°.

[72] Canon 774, § 1; C.P.I., 12 nov. 1922, ad IV—*AAS,* XIV (1922), 662.

speaking its language within those same limits, the pastor of the national parish will have the right to baptize the children. If the family affiliated itself with the territorial parish, then the pastor of the territorial parish would have the right. The declaration of the Sacred Congregation of the Council already mentioned,[73] points out quite clearly that they are not to affiliate themselves with any other national parish, but only with a parish of their own nationality.[74]

Another question arises with regard to the baptism of converts. It may be noted that the baptism of adults, including converts, is to be referred to the ordinary when it can conveniently be done, in order that the baptism may be more solemnly conferred either by the ordinary himself or by his delegate.[75] This is not commonly done in the United States inasmuch as such a baptism is frequently mentioned in the synodal statutes as not being reserved to the bishop, and permission for the conferring of it is given to the priests throughout the diocese. Augustine maintains that a pastor of a national parish can in justice baptize a convert of another nationality,[76] unless he be restricted by diocesan statutes or lawful custom to the contrary. The evident explanation for this is that no pastor can claim anyone as his subject before baptism, according to canon 87 and 12. But it seems that, indirectly, the Church can oblige those who are not baptized, because it ordinarily obliges strangers who belong to another parish to be baptized by their own pastor,[77] and it commends non-Catholics in the parish to the care of respective pastors.[78] Therefore, since the pastor of a national parish is limited in his jurisdiction not only as to territory but also with regard to certain members in that territory, he is permitted according to the common

[73] Cf. supra p. 153.

[74] Augustine, on the contrary, seems to conclude that a pastor of another national parish may claim as much right over them as a pastor of the territorial parish by reason of territory or parochial district, but this is not justified according to the proper interpretation of the declarations at hand. Cf. *Commentary*, IV, 41; *The Pastor According to the New Code of Canon Law* (St. Louis: Herder, 1924), p. 57.

[75] Canon 744.

[76] *Commentary*, IV, 41.

[77] Canon 738, § 2; Ayrinhac, *Legislation on the Sacraments*, p. 18.

[78] Canon 1350.

law to baptize only those converts who belong to the language group for which the parish was erected.[79] But because of the immemorial custom that has been practiced and recognized in this country since missionary days, it seems that converts can be baptized by those from whom they have received their instructions even though they may belong to another parish.[80] By baptism, then, the convert does not necessarily become a member of the national parish, but, according to the disposition of the Holy See, only if he is an immigrant or descendant of immigrants, in which case he may join the parish for his particular language group, and cannot be compelled to join the territorial parish.[81]

3. *The Pastor and Marriage*

As in other matters of jurisdiction, the proper pastor for marriage is determined according to the principles already outlined. In general these are the principles which are based on the elements of territory and of personal subjection, according to which pastors have the right to administer the sacraments to those who are their parishioners. The practice of the Church has been uniform with regard to personal and territorial parishes, and on the basis of this practice, and the responses given by the Sacred Congregations in this connection, one can outline the present law.

In the Archdiocese of New York as early as 1842, it was required that marriages be celebrated in the parochial district to which at least one of the parties belonged, whereas the marriages of persons of a foreign language group were to take place before the priest who had charge of such persons.[82] In the course of time, as national parishes became more numerous, particularly in the larger cities, it became necessary to give them distinct territorial limits,

[79] Waldron, *The Minister of Baptism,* The Catholic University of America Canon Law Studies, n. 170 (Washington, D. C.: The Catholic University of America Press, 1942), p. 101; Studies and Conferences, "National Parishes: Affiliation and Separation"—*AER,* LXXXVII (1932), 531.

[80] Cf. S. C. Conc., 31 jan. 1927—Bouscaren, II, 184, can. 778.

[81] Cf. Studies and Conferences, "Unfair Dissociation from National Parish" —*AER,* LXXXVIII (1933), 315.

[82] Synod of New York, August 28, 1842—Shea, *History,* III, 538.

so that such parishes became not only personal but also territorial. This practice became quite general in cities, towns, and other divisions of the diocese, so that it can now be said that in most cases such parishes are also territorial.[83]

When the decree *"Ne Temere"* was promulgated in the United States, the question of the pastor's competence with regard to valid assistance at marriages in a cumulative territory was at once brought up. The Holy See evidently had this situation in mind when to a proposed doubt it replied that pastors who held their territory cumulatively with others could validly assist at marriages within that territory.[84] In view of the fact that most of the national parishes have such a cumulative territory,[85] the pastors can validly assist within their respective territory at all marriages of Catholics, even those who are not their parishioners.[86] Such would be the case if one or more national parishes extended over the same territory constituting the local parish. Each of the pastors could validly assist at the marriages of all in their territory as well as of any Catholics if the marriage occurs in the parochial territory.[87]

A different situation would arise if a pastor had a few persons or families living outside of his own territory, and within the territory of another parish. He could then validly assist outside of his territory only at the marriage of those people.[88] It is evident from

[83] There have been various objections to this view on the grounds that all national parishes are strictly personal, and cannot be otherwise, since they have no definite territory, and because the law requires that there be only one pastor of a given territory. Cf. *Periodica,* XVI (1927), 261.*

[84] Response of the Sacred Congregation of the Council, February 1, 1908, to doubt VIII: "Ubinam et quomodo parochi qui territorium exclusive proprium non habentes cumulative territorium cum alio vel aliis parochis retinent matrimoniis adsistere valeant." Resp.: "Affirmative in territorio cumulative habito."—*ASS,* XLI (1908), 109.

[85] Cf. *Le Canoniste Contemporain,* XXXI (1908), 132.

[86] Canon 1095, § 1, 2°. Cf. Wernz-Vidal, *Ius Canonicum,* V, n. 535; De Smet, *De Sponsalibus et Matrimonio* (4 ed., Brugis: Beyaert, 1927), n. 108; Ferreres, *Institutiones,* I, 802.

[87] Vermeersch-Creusen, *Epitome,* II, n. 393; Sipos, *Enchiridion,* p. 611; McNicholas, "Difficulties of the New Marriage Legislation"—*AER,* XXXIX (1908), 24-38, especially p. 29.

[88] The Sacred Congregation of the Council, February 1, 1908, in the response

canon 1094 that these persons can also validly be married by the pastor in whose territory they reside.[89]

In the case of cumulative territory it could appear that, because of the extensive competency which pastors of national parishes have with regard to marriage within the limits of their territory, there exists a great danger of conflict of rights. It is to be borne in mind that the intention of the Church was to safeguard the sanctity of the marriage at its very celebration by making it valid if contracted in parishes held cumulatively. The purpose of the decree *"Ne Temere"* and of the Code [90] was to provide precise and clear rules whereby the validity of the marriage can be judged. It is not to be considered as a favor bestowed upon the pastor, but a prudent provision on the part of the Church. Therefore, if neither party is subject to the pastor by whom they are to be married, to assist lawfully or licitly, he must follow the conditions enacted by the Code, that is, he must obtain the permission of the pastor of at least one of the parties, or there must be some grave necessity or reasonable excuse for not obtaining that permission.[91] Since the jurisdiction of the pastor of a national parish is restricted to the faithful of a respective language group, it cannot be said that domicile or quasi-domicile, or a month's residence within the cumulative territory grants him the right to marry anyone also licitly.[92] He cannot do this any more than the pastor of a territorial parish has the right under the same circumstances with regard to families or persons belonging to the national parish.

If the national parishes happen to be strictly personal, the principle of personal subjection is applied, and the pastor can validly and lawfully assist at the marriage of his own subject wherever it

to doubt IX: "Ubinam et quomodo parochus qui in territorio aliis parochis assignato nonnullas personas vel familias sibi subditas habet, matrimoniis adsistere valeat." Resp.: "Affirmative, quoad suos subditos tantum, ubique in dicto territorio, facto verbo cum Ssmo."—*ASS,* XLI (1908), 109.

89 In a reply to the East Indies, the Sacred Congregation of the Sacraments, June 2, 1910, said that *because of the peculiar circumstances* the people had to be married by the personal pastor for validity.—*AAS,* II (1910), 448.

90 Canons 1094 and 1095.

91 Canon 1097, § 1, n. 3.

92 Canon 1097, § 1, n. 2.

is celebrated.[93] They cannot validly assist at the marriages of those who are not their parishioners.[94] The question whether in the case of strictly personal parishes the right is exclusively the pastor's, or is cumulative with that of ordinary local pastors, will have to be determined by the rescripts of the Holy See in individual cases. The presumption seems to be in favor of cumulative competence for the valid assistance, because exclusive competence is a notable derogation of the common law.[95] In the cause of harmony, since the bishop cannot withdraw certain persons and families from the jurisdiction of one pastor and assign them to another parish, pastors may agree among themselves to cede to each other their parochial functions with regard to certain families or persons. But since these people have the right to demand the ministrations of their own pastors, their consent would have to be presupposed.[96]

[93] The Sacred Congregation of the Council, February 1, 1908, to doubt VII: "Ubinam et quomodo cappellani castrenses, vel parochi nullum absolute territorium nec cumulative cum alio parocho habentes, at iurisdictionem directe exercentes in personas aut familias, adeo ut has personas sequantur quocumque se conferant, valide matrimoniis suorum subditorum adsistere valeant." Resp.: "Quoad cappellanos castrenses aliosque parochos, de quibus in dubio, nihil esse immutatum."—S. C. C., *Romana et aliarum*, 1 febr. 1908, I-XII—*AAS*, XLI (1908), 108; *Fontes*, n. 4344. The editors added to this reply the following note: "Hinc illius generis parochi retinent, prout sub iure Tridentino, potestatem personalem quoad sponsalia et matrimonia suorum tantum subditorum, quos ubilibet coniungere valeant."

[94] Cf. *ME*, XXXVIII (1926), 190.

[95] Wernz-Vidal, *Ius Canonicum*, V, n. 535; Cappello, *De Sacramentis* (Vol. III, *De Matrimonio*, 3. ed., Taurinorum Augustae: Marietti, 1933), III, n. 667; De Smet, *De Sponsalibus et Matrimonio*, n. 108; Canon 1095, § 1, 2°.

[96] Cappello, "Nonnullae Questiones"—*Periodica*, XVIII (1929), 149.*

CHAPTER VII

ORIENTALS IN THE UNITED STATES

Article I. Rome and the Oriental Rites

The attitude of the Catholic Church regarding the Orientals can be gathered fully from her toleration and encouragement of the distinct rites [1] and customs of the various branches of Oriental Catholics.[2] Under such favorable conditions, these different rites have maintained their identity distinct from the Latins and other branches of the Oriental Church.[3]

The Popes have staunchly protected the Orientals and favored them, perhaps not without a well-founded hope of seeing eventually, with the grace of God, a union among all dissidents. The Eastern Church was ancient in its established tradition of language and rite, as well as in its history and culture. The Church realized this, and consequently respected the accidental liturgical differences as long as there remained an essential unity of faith between the rites. This idea of unity has pervaded the legislation concerning the Oriental Church, and that is why in the IV Lateran Council (1215) the Church legislated to provide for the people of different rites living

[1] Cf. Herman, "De Conceptu 'Ritus' "—*The Jurist,* II (1942), 333-345.

[2] *Statistica con Cenni Storici della Gerarchia e dei Fedeli di Rito Orientale* (Roma: Tipografia Poliglotta Vaticana, 1932), pp. 33-257. In these pages of the work published by the Sacred Congregation for the Oriental Church there are excellent historical sketches of the individual rites.

[3] Cf. Cicognani, *Canon Law,* pp. 445-460, for a very good outline on the status of Oriental Catholics; Duskie, *The Canonical Status of Orientals in the United States,* p. 19; Petrani, *De Relatione Iuridica inter Diversos Ritus in Ecclesia Catholica* (Taurini: Marietti, 1930), pp. 14-25; Dausend, *Das interrituelle Recht in Codex Iuris Canonici* (Paderborn, 1939), pp. 66-77; Attwater, *The Catholic Eastern Churches* (Milwaukee: Bruce, 1935), pp. 13-40; Senyshyn, *One Fold and One Shepherd* (Stamford, 1944), pp. 9-10; *Studi Storici sulle Fonti del Diritto Canonico Orientale* (Roma, 1932), Vol. VIII.

under the jurisdiction of the Latin Ordinaries.[4] Rite and language had long been considered secondary in the broad plan of salvation,[5] and since the Church herself regarded as lawful the establishing of a legitimate custom, it is not surprising that she permitted, and even insisted upon, the observance of these customs also among the Orientals.[6] When there was danger to faith or morals, however, she did not hesitate to legislate accordingly.[7]

The same solicitous care was expressed by the Church in the II Council of Lyons (1274) under Gregory X (1271-1276),[8] and at the Council of Florence (1439-1445) under Eugene IV (1431-1447),[9] in which a sincere attempt was made to effect a permanent union with the Byzantine Church.[10] The Popes kept in mind above all that the Church was neither Latin nor Greek, but that it was Cath-

[4] Canon 9—Mansi XXII, 998; this canon was accepted into the Decretals of Gregory IX—c. 14, X, *de officio iudicis ordinarii*, I, 31.

[5] Cf. c. 3, D. XII. The first part of this chapter is taken from the epistle of Leo IX (1049-1054) to Michael and Leo, Bishops—JL, n. 4302; Mansi XIX, 635; the second part is from an epistle of Nicholas I (858-867) to Photius—JE, n. 269; Mansi XV, 174; XVI, 68.

[6] Cf. c. 32, X, *de decimis, primitiis et oblationibus*, III, 30—Compilatio IV, c. 5, III, 9; c. 80, D. IV, *de cons.*; c. 6-7, D. XI; c. 3, X, *de cognatione spirituali*, IV, 11; In the Code of Canon Law there are numerous places in which this concern for the Orientals is expressed. Cf. Canons 1; 98; 733, § 2; 782; 804; 864; 866; 955, etc.

[7] ". . . illis deferre non volumus, nec debemus, quae periculum generant animarum et ecclesiasticae derogant honestati."—IV Lateran Council, canon 4—Mansi XXII, 990; c. 6, X, *de baptismo*, III, 42—Compilatio IV, c. un., III, 16; cf. letter of Celestine III (1191-1198) to the Archbishop of Otranto—JL, n. 17629—c. 9, X, *de temporibus ordinationum et qualitate ordinandorum*, I, 11—Compilatio IV, c. 1, I, 7.

[8] Pars II, cap. 9—Mansi XXIV, 129.

[9] Mansi, XXXI A, 1031.

[10] Not only in the East were the rites honored and recognized, but also in the West. In Toledo, Spain, at the end of the fifteenth century, six Mozarabic parishes had survived the domination of the Moors, and after 1495, under Francis Cardinal Ximenes de Cisneros, they enjoyed many privileges. Cf. *MPL*, LXXXV, 11; Florez, *Espana Sagrada*, III (Madrid, 1748), 190 sq.; Ferreres, *Institutiones*, I, n. 732.

olic, and they expressed these sentiments in various documents concerning the Eastern rites.[11]

Oriental Catholics were, however, to preserve their rites and customs wherever they happened to be, even under the jurisdiction of Latin ordinaries. This is certain from many pronouncements of the Popes during the past centuries and in more recent times.[12] The dispositions of Benedict XIV (1740-1758) were of particular importance in consolidating the basic norms of the Church's legislation concerning the Oriental rites. In the constitution *"Etsi pastoralis"* he established the rules regarding the jurisdiction of the Latins and Greeks in southern Italy, summing up the previous legislation on this point.[13] Later he extended a similar application to other Eastern Catholics in the encyclical letter *"Demandatam"* to the Patriarch of Antioch, and defended the cause of the Oriental Slavs among the Latins,[14] as well as that of the Orientals of Asia

[11] Benedictus XIV, const. *"Etsi Pastoralis,"* 26 maii 1742—*Fontes,* n. 328; Pius IX, const. *"Romani Pontifices,"* 6 ian. 1862—*Fontes,* n. 531; litt. encycl. *"Amantissimus,"* 8 apr. 1862—*Coll.* I, n. 1226; Leo XIII, const. *"Orientalium dignitas,"* 30 nov. 1894—*Fontes,* n. 627; Benedictus XV, *"Dei providentis,"* 1 maii 1917—*AAS,* IX (1917), 529; const. *"Sedis huius,"* 14 maii 1919—*AAS,* XII (1920), 318; Pius XI, litt. encycl. *"Ecclesia Dei,"* 12 nov. 1923—*AAS,* XV (1923), 573.

[12] Innocentius IV, ep. *"Sub Catholicae,"* 6 mart. 1254—*Fontes,* n. 34; Pius IV, const. *"Romanus Pontifex,"* 16 febr. 1565—*Bull. Rom.* VII, 271; Paulus V, decl., 10 dec. 1615—*Bull. Rom.* XII, 341; Benedictus XIV, const. *"Etsi Pastoralis,"* 26 maii 1742—*Fontes,* 328; const. *"Allatae sunt,"* 26 iul. 1755—*Fontes,* n. 434; const. *"Romana Ecclesia,"* 18 mart. 1743; ep. encycl. *"Demandatam,"* 24 dec. 1743—*Fontes,* n. 338; Leo XIII, litt. ap. *"Orientalium Dignitas,"* 30 nov. 1894—*Fontes,* 627. Those applying particularly to the Ruthenians are: Clemens VIII, bull. *"Magnus Dominus,"* 23 dec. 1595—*Bull. Rom.* X, 239; Pius X, litt. ap. *"Ea semper,"* 14 iun. 1907—*ASS,* XLI (1908), 3; const. *"Tradita ab antiquis,"* 14 sept. 1912—*Fontes,* n. 698—*AAS,* IV (1912), 616; S. Cong. de Prop. Fide pro Neg. R. Or., decr. *"Cum Episcopo,"* 17 aug. 1914—*AAS,* VI (1914), 458; decr. *"Fidelibus Ruthenis,"* 18 aug. 1913—*AAS,* V (1913), 393; S. C. Or., decr. *"Cum data fuerit,"* 1 mart. 1929—*AAS,* XXI (1929), 152; decr. *"Qua sollerti,"* 23 dec. 1929—*AAS,* XXII (1930), 99; *AAS,* XXIX (1937), 342-343.

[13] Cf. Ploechl, *"Two Hundred Years—'Etsi Pastoralis'"—The Jurist,* II (1942), 211-213.

[14] Const. *"Militantis ecclesiae,"* 9 nov. 1754—*Bull. Rom. Cont.,* IV, 205.

Minor in a letter to the missionaries of the Orient.[15] One can be assured from this attitude of the Church, both in fact and in law, that the position of Oriental Catholics in places where the Latin rite predominates is safeguarded and protected.

Article II. The Division of Rites

In speaking of parishes and Orientals of another rite [16] one must well understand the meaning of the term. It is used throughout the Code of Canon Law without being defined, and is used now in one sense and now in another. In its restricted sense the term can be used to designate the proper manner in which liturgical functions and ceremonies are to be performed.[17] This is merely a liturgical definition and must be elaborated to correspond to its full juridical significance. The definition must include not only the manner of performing these functions but also all the sacred functions proper to some church, as well as its hierarchical constitution and discipline binding the faithful under one rule.[18] This is what Herman has in mind when he defines rite: "Coetus fidelium qui propriis regitur legibus et usibus antiqua traditione innixis, non solum quod ad res liturgicas sed etiam ad canonicam disciplinam attinet, et qui tamquam autonomus et a ceteris distinctus a Sancta Sede agnoscitur." [19] In this definition the faithful, both priests and laity, are determined with respect both to liturgical functions according to their proper form and language, and to the discipline established for

[15] Const. *"Allatae sunt,"* 25 mart. 1755—*Fontes*, n. 434.

[16] Unless otherwise specified, the reference is to the Catholic Rites.

[17] Michiels, *De Personis*, p. 260; Wernz-Vidal, *Ius Canonicum*, II, n. 21; Vermeersch-Creusen, *Epitome*, I, n. 220; Duskie, *The Canonical Status of Oriental Catholics in the United States*, p. 13.

[18] Cf. Petrani, *De Relatione Iuridica inter Diversos Ritus in Ecclesia Catholica*, p. 1; Dausend, *Das interrituelle Recht in Codex Juris Canonici*, p. 53.

[19] Herman, "De Conceptu 'Ritus'"—*The Jurist*, II (1942), 333-345, especially p. 339. Thus he altered the former definition given in the *Orientalia Christiana*, XXXII (1933), 105: "Ritus est ordo iuris ecclesiastici quo non solum res liturgicae sed universa quoque disciplina unius partis Ecclesiae universalis ordinatur."

a certain part of the Church, approved by legitimate authority and custom, and recognized by the Holy See.[20]

Generally, the manner in which the Holy Sacrifice is celebrated determines the rite,[21] and the broadest division on this basis is into the disciplines of the Oriental and the Latin Churches.[22] The Latin Church includes under one uniform discipline the Roman, Ambrosian (in Milan), Lyonese (in Lyons), and the Mozarabic (in Toledo and Seville) rites.[23] The Oriental Catholics are divided into various rites under the five disciplines which are the original rites used by the Oriental Church. These are the Armenian, Alexandrian (Coptic and Ethiopian), Antiochene (Pure Syrian, Maronite, Malankarese), Chaldean (Malabarese), Byzantine (Greek, Ruthenian, Rumanian, Russian, Melchite, Georgian, etc.).[24] In the Latin Church therefore a difference of rite does not imply a change of discipline, whereas in the Oriental Church each discipline is under the jurisdiction of patriarchs and bishops, and a change of rite involves a change of discipline also.

Article III. Provisions for Various Rites

1. The Greek-Ruthenians

The presence of a large number of Catholics of the Oriental rite in this country is of comparatively recent development. The Greek-Ruthenians first began to come in large numbers about the year 1879, originally settling in Pennsylvania. A priest was requested by the colony in Shenandoah, and under the care of the Rev. Ivan

[20] Cf. Michiels, *De Personis*, p. 260.

[21] Cicognani, *Canon Law*, p. 447.

[22] Petrani, *op. cit.*, p. 1.

[23] Cicognani, *Canon Law*, p. 444; Vermeersch-Creusen, *Epitome*, I, n. 220.

[24] *Statistica*, p. 29; Cicognani, *Canon Law*, p. 446; Duskie, *op. cit.*, p. 19; Dausend, *Das interrituelle Recht*, p. 66; Coronata, *Institutiones*, I, n. 134; Gulovich, "Matrimonial Laws of the Catholic Eastern Churches"—*The Jurist*, IV (1944), 202; Korolewskij—*Fonti VIII*, pp 15 sq. Michiels (*De Personis*, p. 264) and Vermeersch-Creusen (*Epitome*, I, n. 220) divide the Orientals into four disciplines combining the Antiochene and the Chaldean, while Petrani (*op. cit.*, p. 2) enumerates six, separating the Antiochene into the Syrian and Maronite.

Valansky, who arrived in 1885, the first church of the Byzantine rite in America was dedicated to St. Michael.[25] As the number of Greek-Ruthenians grew, it became necessary to establish certain regulations to avoid abuses and to protect the freedom of rite.[26]

By 1910 there were estimated to be as many as 371, 500 Ruthenians in the United States.[27] On March 26, 1907, Pius X appointed the titular Bishop, Stephan Ortynsky, as the Vicar of the Greek-Ruthenians, under the jurisdiction of the Latin Ordinaries, thus giving members of this rite a status distinct from that of the other Orientals in this country.[28] This dependence upon the Latin ordinaries lasted until 1913, when a separate diocese was established for the Greek-Ruthenians in the United States. The Ruthenian Bishop received full jurisdictional powers over the faithful and the clergy of the Greek-Ruthenian rite, and became directly dependent upon the Holy See.[29] This provision necessitated another change in the previous legislation made for the Ruthenians, and a new decree was issued by the Holy See.[30]

After a brief career fraught with many difficulties due to national and political differences among the people belonging to this rite, but not without some successes,[31] Bishop Ortynsky died March 28, 1916.[32]

Two priests were appointed administrators by the Apostolic Delegate, April 11, the same year, the Rev. Gabriel Martyak for the Podcarpathians, and the Rev. Peter Poniatyshyn for the Galicians. After the World War the Holy See prudently appointed two bishops for the Greek-Ruthenians, Bishop Constantine Bohachevsky

[25] *Statistica*, p. 213.

[26] Cf. S. C. de Prop. Fide, decr., 1 maii 1897—*Coll.*, n. 1966; litt. encycl., 1 oct. 1890—*Coll.*, n. 1966, in nota 2.

[27] *Statistica*, p. 214. This is according to the United States census report.

[28] Litt. ap. *"Ea semper,"* 14 iun. 1907—*ASS*, XLI (1908), 3.

[29] Cf. "Extension of Jurisdiction of the Ruthenian Bishop for the United States"—*AER*, XLIX (1913), 473.

[30] S. C. de Prop. Fide, decr. *"Cum Episcopo,"* 17 aug. 1914—*AAS*, VI (1914), 458.

[31] Cf. Attwater, *The Catholic Eastern Churches*, p. 86; Halich, *Ukrainians in the United States* (Chicago: The University of Chicago Press, 1937), p. 102.

[32] *Statistica*, p. 215.

for the Ukrainian Catholic Diocese, which included the Galicians, and Bishop Basil Takach for the Podcarpathians.[33] There are about 278,171 Catholics belonging to the latter diocese (Homestead, Pa.),[34] and about 305,726 to the Ukrainian Greek Catholic Diocese (Philadelphia).[35]

The Greek-Ruthenians were first governed by the Apostolic letter *"Ea semper"* of June 14, 1907. With the appointment of their own bishop, the former provisions proved unsatisfactory, and a new decree *"Cum Episcopo"* was issued August 17, 1914, to be effective for a period of ten years. It was renewed for an indefinite time on June 21, 1924, by the Sacred Congregation for the Oriental Church,[36] and was finally supplanted by another decree of the Sacred Oriental Congregation, March 1, 1929, the *"Cum data fuerit,"* which is still in force in the United States.[37]

According to the *"Cum data fuerit"* the appointment of the Greek-Ruthenian bishops for the United States is reserved to the Apostolic See, and they are under its immediate jurisdiction and power. They can thus exercise full ordinary jurisdiction over all the faithful of their rite according to the place of origin. This jurisdiction is much like that of the Latin ordinaries, except that it is both personal and territorial. They have the right to rule and govern their own flocks, and to establish laws and statutes in matters not contrary to the common law. They are to maintain particular vigilance over doctrine

[33] *AAS,* XVI (1924), 243.

[34] There are 154 priests and 153 resident churches, principally in Pennsylvania, Ohio, and New Jersey.—*The Official Catholic Directory* (New York: Kenedy, 1946), pp. 793-796.

[35] The total number of priests is 133, and there are 96 resident churches, especially in Pennsylvania, New York, and New Jersey.—*The Official Catholic Directory,* pp. 797-801. It may be noted in passing that the titles of the dioceses as found today are not in exact accord with the decree *"Cum data fuerit."*

[36] Cf. Duskie, *op. cit.,* p. 43.

[37] *AAS,* XXI (1929), 152-159. With slight modifications in articles 15 and 39 it was confirmed for another ten years by the same Congregation on November 23, 1940—*AAS,* XXXIII (1941), 27. The Ruthenians in Canada, originally guided by the decree *"Fidelibus Ruthenis"* (1913), are now guided by the decree *"Graeci-Rutheni ritus"* of May 24, 1930, issued by the Sacred Oriental Congregation—*AAS,* XXII (1930), 346.

and morals, as well as the rite and discipline peculiar to their Church, in order that there may in the latter, among all the faithful committed to their care, exist complete uniformity. To do this effectively they are required to make a faithful and regular visitation of the parishes entrusted to their care. To insure the temporal welfare of the diocese, they are required to seek the counsel and advice of experts, and to make suitable rules regarding the administration of ecclesiastical property, reporting to the Sacred Oriental Congregation on the state of the diocese every five years. Any controversies that may arise between the Latin and Ruthenian ordinaries are to be referred to the said Congregation.

If a vacant or newly erected parish is to be filled, and native priests are not available, the bishop may obtain such a priest from a European diocese, but only through the agency of the Sacred Oriental Congregation, and the priest thus invited must be a celibate. As rectors of parishes and missions in the United States, the priests are removable at the will of the ordinaries of their rite, but may not be removed without a grave and just reason. Although the Greek-Ruthenian ordinaries exercise jurisdiction only over their own clergy and people, if in any particular place there happens to be a group of faithful of their rite without a mission or priest of their own, the bishops shall communicate their jurisdiction over these people to a priest of the Latin rite in the place, the Latin ordinary having been previously informed.[88]

Mass and Holy Communion. The faithful, though urged to attend their own churches and to follow their own rite, are not obliged to do this in districts where there are no priests or churches of their rite, or when they cannot reach their churches without great inconvenience. In these circumstances, they must fulfill the precepts of the Church by hearing Mass in another Catholic church, and in the latter they may also receive the sacraments.[89] They do not thereby change their rite, even if this is continued for a long time, and no priest of the Latin rite is permitted to induce any member of another rite to transfer to the Latin rite against the

[88] *"Cum data fuerit,"* art. 19—*AAS,* XXI (1929), 156.

[89] *"Cum data fuerit,"* art. 29—*ibid.,* p. 157.

canonical provisions.[40] The faithful are permitted to observe the feasts and fasts according to the place in which they happen to reside, and if holydays of obligation fall on the same day in both rites, they can fulfill the precept by hearing Mass in any Catholic church.[41]

All the faithful may receive Holy Communion consecrated according to any Catholic rite, and in case of necessity it may be administered by a priest of any rite, but according to his own ritual. The precept of Paschal Communion may be fulfilled validly and licitly in any rite, but if it is fulfilled in another parish, the proper pastor should be informed.[42]

Confession. If the faithful of the Latin rite wish to go to confession to a priest of the Greek-Ruthenian rite approved by his ordinary, they may validly and licitly receive sacramental absolution, even if a priest of their own rite is available. The faithful of the Greek-Ruthenian rite are also permitted to confess their sins to an approved Latin priest.[43] However, a priest of the Greek-Byzantine rite approved for confessions by his ordinary, cannot validly and licitly absolve in a church or oratory which is subject to the exclusive jurisdiction of the Latin ordinary unless the latter has expressly granted him faculties.[44] Nor can a Latin priest under the same conditions hear confessions and give absolution in a church or oratory under the exclusive jurisdiction of the Greek-Ruthenian ordinary unless he has express faculties from him.[45] But a Greek-Ruthenian priest who is approved by his proper ordinary for hearing confessions may validly absolve a Latin penitent anywhere in the United States as long as the confession is heard outside of the church.

Latin priests, furthermore, cannot, without proper permission from the Greek-Ruthenian ordinary, absolve the faithful of the Greek-Ruthenian rite from censures and sins reserved to their own

[40] *"Cum data fuerit,"* art. 30—*ibid.*, p. 157.

[41] S. C. Or., decl., 11 iun. 1930—*AAS*, XXII (1930), 354.

[42] *"Cum data fuerit,"* art. 32-34—*ibid.*, p. 158.

[43] *"Cum data fuerit,"* art. 31—*ibid.*, p. 157.

[44] S. C. Or., 26 aug. 1932—*Sylloge*, n. 173, as cited by Bouscaren, *Canon Law Digest*, II, 218, under canon 874.

[45] S. C. de Prop. Fide, 2 dec. 1932—*loc. cit.*

ordinary. The same is true regarding Greek-Ruthenian priests with reference to the reservations which the Latin ordinary has made.[46] But if a person of a rite in which the sin is not reserved confesses to a priest of a rite in which it is reserved, it seems that he can be absolved. To obviate any difficulties the respective ordinaries should notify each other as to what reservations they have made for their subjects.

Marriage. In a marriage between a Latin and a Greek-Ruthenian, the woman may accept the rite of her husband either at the time of the marriage or any time during it, with the privilege of returning to her former rite after the dissolution of the marriage.[47] As to the form, the *"Ne temere"* must be followed and the marriage is to take place before the pastor of the bride, unless the ordinary of the place of the bride for a sufficient reason permits the celebration in the rite of the groom.[48] If a dispensation is needed in marriages of mixed rite, it should be asked from and granted by the bishop of the prospective bride,[49] even if she changes her rite at the time of the celebration of the marriage.

2. *Other Oriental Catholics*

Besides the Greek-Ruthenian, there are also other Oriental Catholics in the United States. Many Italo-Greeks settled in Pennsylvania. There were churches founded for Italo-Greeks in New York in 1904, and in the same year a church for the Rumanians was opened in Cincinnati.[50] Syrians and Melchites who came to this country established churches, and a large number of Maronites worship in their own churches and have their own priests.[51]

One may better understand the need for such parishes which are established according to a difference of rite if one have a general idea of the distribution of these people in the various parts of the country. The *Maronites,* the largest individual group outside of the

[46] *"Cum data fuerit,"* art. 31—*ibid.*, p. 157.
[47] *"Cum data fuerit,"* art. 38—*ibid.*, p. 159.
[48] S. C. Or., 23 nov. 1940—*AAS*, XXXIII (1941), 27.
[49] *"Cum data fuerit,"* art. 40—*AAS*, XXI (1929), 159.
[50] Attwater, *The Catholic Eastern Churches*, pp. 74, 105.
[51] Cf. Attwater, *op. cit.*, pp. 115, 168, 188.

Ruthenians, number about 38,800, and are found especially in the provinces of New York (Buffalo, Syracuse, Brooklyn), Detroit, Boston (Fall River, Springfield), Philadelphia (Pittsburgh, Scranton), Cincinnati (Cleveland), Baltimore (Wheeling, Richmond), and St. Louis. The *Melchites* (about 13,600) are in the province of New York (Brooklyn), Newark, Detroit, Cincinnati (Cleveland, Toledo), Boston (Providence, Springfield); the *Italo-Greeks* (about 10,000) in the province of New York (Brooklyn); the *Rumanians* (about 8,000) are in the provinces of Cincinnati (Cleveland, Fort Wayne), Detroit, Newark (Trenton), and Chicago (Rockford); the *Syrians* (about 6,900) in the provinces of Boston (Hartford), Cincinnati (Columbus), New York (Brooklyn), Newark (Trenton) and Detroit; the *Armenians* (about 3,000) in the provinces of New York (Brooklyn), Newark, Boston (Springfield); the *Chaldeans* (about 800) in the provinces of San Francisco, Chicago and Boston (Hartford).[52]

Although the constitutions and the decrees of the Holy See directed to one of the Oriental rites do not bind the others, unless such an intention is expressed, it will be worth while, nevertheless, to make some general observations concerning the rites in the United States. The Holy See has placed all Orientals in this country, except the Ruthenians, under the jurisdiction of the respective Latin Ordinaries in whose diocese they have their domicile or quasi-domicile.[53] Though they may conform to the Latin rite in their religious practices, they are not permitted to change their rite, even if they acquire a permanent domicile.[54] Since the Code exempts Orientals from the discipline of the Latin Church except in matters which of their very nature pertain also to them, or when they are ex-

[52] This distribution is made according to population and not parishes, and is based on reports from various chanceries. It is practically impossible to make an accurate estimate because of the constant migration of people to different parts of the country, but the general outline given may serve to help understand the necessity of knowing something of the laws governing these Orientals. Cf. *Statistica*, pp. 505-515.

[53] S. C. de Prop. Fide pro Neg. R. O., 17 aug. 1914—*AAS*, VI (1914), 458; cf. Duskie, *op. cit.*, p. 35.

[54] Leo XIII, const. *"Orientalium dignitas,"* 20 nov. 1894, § 9—*Fontes*, n. 627.

pressly mentioned,[55] they are still bound, whenever it is possible, by the liturgical and canonical legislation of their respective disciplines, unless they have legitimately transferred to the Latin rite. It is important to note that there is no general permission granted to transfer at will from one rite to another,[56] and if such a transfer is attempted, it is to be considered as not only illicit, but also null and void, according to the opinion of some canonists.[57] In the past the Holy See has occasionally granted such general permissions either explicitly or implicitly.[58] Other Orientals then, besides the Greek-Ruthenians, are held to the prescriptions of the law of their own discipline, even those who are under the jurisdiction of the Latin ordinaries in the United States, unless they are exempt by the Code or by the provisions of the Holy See.

The Latin ordinary cannot exercise his authority in prejudice to the Oriental rites or discipline. In exercising his power he can grant faculties to the Oriental priests subject to him.[59] He may also establish separate churches and missions for the people of a dif-

[55] Canon 1.

[56] Canon 98, § 3.

[57] Blat, *Commentarium,* II, n. 25; Wernz-Vidal, *Ius Canonicum,* II, n. 24; Michiels, *De Personis,* p. 294; Herman, "De Conceptu Ritus' "—*The Jurist,* II (1942), 343-344. Coronata (*Institutiones,* I, n. 134, C, c) thinks the transfer would be valid as to its juridical effects, but could be rescinded "ad instantiam partis *interesse* habentis."

[58] Cf. Michiels, *De Personis,* p. 295. Beginning January 1, 1929, Legates of the Roman Pontiff, Nuntios, Internuntios, and Apostolic Delegates, or also those temporarily taking their places, had faculties to grant changes from one rite to another if the petition was sent through the ordinary under whose jurisdiction the petitioner happened to be. In places where there were no Apostolic Legates or if the transfer concerned a priest, the petition had to be sent to the Sacred Oriental Congregation. These faculties were revoked by the Holy See in the decree of November 23, 1940, and all matters pertaining to the transfer from one rite to another in the case of clerics and laity are reserved to the Sacred Oriental Congregation, all things to the contrary notwithstanding. Cf. *AAS,* XX (1928), 416; *AAS,* XXXIII (1941), 28.

[59] S. C. de Prop. Fide, 12 apr. 1894—*Coll.,* n. 1866; 1 oct. 1892—*Coll.,* n. 1966, in nota 2.

ferent rite,[60] and appoint priests to take charge of them as pastors, removing them if there is a reasonable cause. According to the decree of 1929, and the instruction of 1932,[61] Oriental priests having the care of souls outside of their Patriarchates and under the jurisdiction of an ordinary of another rite, must send a yearly report to the Sacred Congregation of the Oriental Church on the religious state of the people, and the spiritual ministrations which they give them. This report should be signed by the priests themselves and approved by the ordinary of the place who himself may add suitable annotations before sending it to Rome. Latin ordinaries have general jurisdiction granted by the Sacred Oriental Congregation, but in cases which require the intervention of the Holy See they must have recourse to the Sacred Oriental Congregation.[62]

Since the Holy See has severely prohibited any usurpation of privileges belonging to different rites, a summary outline of the laws governing the administration of the sacraments in places where there are parishes of Latin and Oriental rites may serve a useful purpose here. The fundamental rule to be observed is that in the ceremonies of administering and receiving the sacraments each must follow his own rite.[63]

Baptism. If both parents are of the same rite the children are to be baptized in the same rite,[64] for an Oriental pastor has full competence in fact and in law over all of his parishioners.[65] If circumstances make it necessary for another priest to perform the baptism, then he may do so lawfully, but the baptism does not effect a change of rite.[66] If the parents are of mixed rites, then the bap-

[60] The restrictions of canon 216, § 4, do not seem to apply to the Orientals. Cf. Coronata, *Institutiones*, I, n. 309, p. 367 in nota 4; Maroto, *Institutiones*, II, n. 771.

[61] S. C. Or., decr. 23 dec. 1929—*AAS*, XXII (1930), 99, n. 14; instr., 26 sept. 1932—*AAS*, XXIV (1932), 244, n. 6; decr., 16 nov. 1938—*AAS*, XXXI (1939), 169.

[62] Cf. Duskie, *op. cit.*, p. 69.

[63] Canon 733; cf. Benedictus XIV, *"In superiori,"* 29 dec. 1755, § 3—*Fontes*, n. 437.

[64] Canon 756, § 1.

[65] Dausend, *Das interrituelle Recht*, p. 93.

[66] Canon 98, § 1.

tism is to be administered in the rite of the father unless there is a special provision in particular law,[67] and if they are illegitimate they are generally baptized in the rite of the mother.[68] If only one of the married parties is Catholic then the child is to be baptized in the rite of the Catholic parent.[69] The same rules may be applied to the baptism of children under the care of guardians, but unbaptized adults are free to choose their own rite.[70]

Confirmation. The priests of a majority of the Oriental rites are permitted by immemorial custom to administer the sacrament of confirmation at the time of baptism,[71] but only to those of the same rite or of another Oriental rite which enjoys the same privilege.[72] If they administer this sacrament to a child of the Latin rite, however, it need not be repeated unless they themselves or their parents later insist that it be done, or the persons themselves are to be given the tonsure or admitted to sacred orders, in which case it may be repeated privately and conditionally.[73]

The faculty of administering confirmation has been withdrawn from certain Orientals, and can no longer be exercised by them.[74]

[67] Canon 756, § 2. There is a special provision for the Italo-Greeks under Latin jurisdiction; their children can also be baptized in the rite of the mother if she belongs to the Latin rite. Cf. Clemens VIII, instr. *"Sanctissimus,"* 31 aug. 1595, § 5—*Fontes,* n. 179; Benedictus XIV, const. *"Etsi pastoralis,"* 26 maii 1742, 2—*Fontes,* n. 328; S. C. de Prop. Fide, decr., 6 oct. 1863—*Fontes,* n. 4859.

[68] Petrani, *op. cit.,* p. 63; cf. *"Cum data fuerit,"* art. 41, 43—*AAS,* XXI (1929), 159.

[69] Canon 756, § 3.

[70] Leo XIII, litt. ap. *"Orientalium dignitas,"* 30 nov. 1894, n. XI—*Fontes,* n. 627. Cf. Petrani, *op. cit.,* p. 64.

[71] Benedictus XIV, *De Synodo Dioecesana,* lib. VII, cap. IX, n. 1.

[72] S. C. S. Off., 22 apr. 1896—*Coll.,* n. 1926—*Fontes,* n. 1178.

[73] S. C. S. Off., litt. 16 mart. 1872—*Fontes,* n. 1021—*Coll.,* n. 1381; S. C. S. Off., 2 apr. 1879—*Fontes,* n. 1060—*Coll.,* n. 1515; S. C. S. Off., *Ierosolym.,* 14 ian. 1885—*Fontes,* n. 1090—*Coll.,* n. 1630. Cf. Cases and Studies, "Confirmation by a Priest"—*The Jurist,* II (1942), 374-375.

[74] Cf., for the Italo-Greeks, Clemens VIII, const. *"Sanctissimus,"* 31 aug. 1595—*Fontes,* n. 179—*Coll.,* n. 176, in nota. It is doubtful that those coming from the former kingdom of Cyprus have it, since it was withdrawn there by Innocent IV. Cf. ep. *"Sub Catholicae,"* 6 mart. 1254, § 3 ad 4—*Fontes,* n. 34; S. C. S. Off., 5 iul. 1853—*Fontes,* n. 924—*Coll.,* n. 1095.

The Maronites no longer have this faculty as can be ascertained from the decree of the Synod of Mt. Lebanon (1736),[75] and from the response of the Holy Office given on July 5, 1853.[76] The *"Ea semper"* restricted this faculty for the Ruthenian clerics in the United States,[77] but since the apostolic letter did not conform to the practice of the church as established in the Synod of Zamosč (1720) it was not considered in force.[78]

Confession. All Oriental priests in this country, except the Greek-Ruthenians, are under the jurisdiction of Latin ordinaries, and receive faculties to hear confessions from them. Since the greatest liberty is given the faithful in this matter, it is sufficient to recall that canon 905 permits them to confess to any legitimately approved confessor, even of another rite, and the priest can accordingly both validly and licitly absolve them.[79]

The Holy Sacrifice and Communion. The faithful may fulfill the precept of hearing mass on Sunday and holy days of obligation in a Catholic church of any rite.[80] They may also receive Holy Communion in any rite even if only for the sole reason of devotion,[81] but they should be urged to receive Paschal Communion and Holy Viaticum in their own rite if possible.

Priests of the Byzantine rite, and in general all Oriental priests may be permitted to celebrate mass on altars in Latin churches, but only in their own rite.[82] Because of abuses in the past, Oriental

[75] Pars II, cap. II, can. 15; cap. III, can. 2—*Coll. Lac.* II, 121-123.

[76] *Fontes*, n. 924—*Coll.*, n. 1095.

[77] Litt. ap., 14 iun. 1907, art. XIV—*AAS*, XLI (1908), 7.

[78] Duskie (*op. cit.*, p. 95, footnote 28) states, on information from the ordinary of the Greek-Ruthenians from Galicia in the United States, that the prohibition of the *"Easemper"* was revoked by the Holy See. It is no longer mentioned in the decree *"Cum data fuerit"*—*AAS*, XXI (1929), 152-159.

[79] Canon 881, § 1.

[80] Canons 1248-1249; cf. *"Cum data fuerit,"* art. 29—*AAS*, XXI (1929), 157.

[81] Canon 866; cf. canons 851; 462, 2° and 3°.

[82] Benedictus XIV, ep. encycl. *"Allatae sunt,"* 20 iul. 1755, § 33—*Fontes*, n. 434. The Ruthenians further have the privilege of using the Latin vestments and chalice, which is likewise granted to the Latin priests celebrating Mass in Ruthenian churches. It was originally granted by Clement VIII (1602) and was confirmed by Benedict XIV in the const. *"Imposito nobis,"* 29 mart. 1751,

priests are required to have a celebret from the Sacred Oriental Congregation if they are from abroad, and from their own ordinary if they reside in the United States.[83] Latin priests may also celebrate Mass in churches of the Oriental rite, but only on the proper altar, unless they have the privilege of the *antimension* of the Greeks.[84] Orientals, even if they use leavened bread in their rite, may not serve as deacons or subdeacons at solemn masses of the Latin rite,[85] nor are Orientals permitted to celebrate three masses on Christmas and All Souls Day unless they have an apostolic indult, or a special permission from the local ordinary if they are under his jurisdiction.[86]

The kind of bread used by the different rites for consecration and communion is as follows: (a) *leavened bread* in the Coptic, Ethiopian, Syrian, Chaldean and the various Byzantine rites; (b) *unleavened bread* (azymus), besides the Latin, also in the Armenian, Maronite, and Malabarese rites.

Holy Communion is administered under one or both species as follows: (a) under *one species*, in the Armenian, Maronite and Malabarese rites; (b) under *both species*, in the Syrian, Chaldean and Byzantine rites; (c) the Copts and Ethiopians receive under both species during Mass, but only under the species of bread at other times.

Extreme Unction. Only a priest can validly administer this sacrament,[87] and though any priest can validly administer it in cases of necessity, it is the mind of the Church that, if the Orientals have

§§ 7-8—*Fontes*, n. 410. Cf. Hannan, "Mass and Communion according to the Oriental Rite in a Church of Latin Rite"—*The Jurist*, I (1941), 149-152; Gulovich, "Mass and Communion according to the Oriental Rite in a Church of the Latin Rite"—*The Jurist*, II (1942), 47-52.

[83] Canon 804. Note particularly the special provisions to be observed by priests of the Oriental rite who come for the purpose of begging alms and mass stipends. These will be taken up in the next article.

[84] Canon 823, § 2. Cf. Petrani, *op. cit.*, p. 78.

[85] S. C. de Prop. Fide (C. G.), 30 apr 1866—*Fontes*, n. 4864—*Coll.*, n. 1288.

[86] Canon 806, 1; Benedictus XIV, ep. *"In superiori,"* 29 dec. 1755—*Fontes*, n. 437; S. C. de Prop. Fide pro Neg., R. O., 22 mart. 1916—*AAS*, VIII (1916), 104-105; also in *AER*, LXXX (1929), 384, n. 5.

[87] Canon 938, § 1.

a church and priest of their own rite, their pastor should administer it to them, because it is also a parochial function in the Oriental Church.[88] Priests of the Byzantine rite have the privilege of blessing all the oils except chrism, from an ancient custom that had been approved,[89] and they may not be deprived of it by the Latin ordinary.[90] Latin priests must use the oils consecrated by their own ordinaries.[91]

Matrimony. It is practically impossible to consider in detail the various and complicated aspects of marriages among Orientals themselves, and between Latins and Orientals. That would require a separate work. But few observations may be made concerning these rites in addition to what has been said already regarding the obligation of Greek-Ruthenians in this regard.[92]

In general Orientals marrying among themselves are not bound by the juridical form prescribed by the Code,[93] but are required to follow the laws and customs of their particular disciplines, unless there is a special provision made for them.[94] Orientals contracting marriages with Latins who are bound by the form, must also conform to it,[95] but in marriages of mixed Oriental rites, they must

[88] Cf. canons 733; 462, 2°; 866, § 3.

[89] Benedictus XIV, const. *"Etsi pastoralis,"* IV, n. 1—*Fontes,* n. 328; cf. Petrani, *op. cit.*, p. 90.

[90] Maronites should not exercise this faculty unless the ordinary supply of oil which the bishop had blessed is exhausted. Cf. Synod of Mt. Lebanon, Pars II, cap. VIII, n. 2—*Coll. Lac.* II, 150.

[91] Canon 945. In case of necessity they may validly and licitly use the oils blessed by an Oriental Bishop. Cf. S. C. S. Off., 16 iun. 1831—*Coll.*, n. 822—*Fontes,* n. 870. Oils blessed by a priest of the Oriental rite cannot validly be used outside of cases of necessity. Cf. Cappello, *Tractatus Canonico-Moralis de Sacramentis, De Extrema Unctione* (Taurinorum Augustae: Marietti), II, n. 300.

[92] Cf. Gulovich, "Matrimonial Laws of the Catholic Eastern Churches"—*The Jurist,* IV (1944), 212-239.

[93] Canons 1; 1094-1097. Many of them are held by the provisions of the *"Tametsi"* and the *"Ne temere."*

[94] Cf. Duskie, *op. cit.*, p. 168.

[95] Canon 1099, § 1, n. 3. This is to be observed even if the bride chooses to change her rite at the time of the marriage.—C. P. I., 29 apr. 1940—*AAS,* XXXII (1940), 212.

celebrate the marriage in the rite of the groom and before his pastor, unless there is a particular law to the contrary.[96]

Since some require marriage before the pastor of the groom for validity, and others before any priest of their rite (Armenians), and still others the *benedictio sacerdotalis* of the priest of that rite (Melchites), a general rule must be adopted, namely, that in marriages contracted between persons of different rites, and governed by separate laws, the marriage is valid if contracted according to the law of one of the contracting parties.[97] In places where Orientals are under the jurisdiction of a Latin ordinary and pastor, the problem can be solved practically by following the prescriptions of canon 1094.[98]

The impediments of mixed religion and of disparity of cult are also established in the Oriental Church, the latter as a diriment impediment.[99] Latin ordinaries in the United States do not have general faculties to dispense Orientals from these impediments reserved to the Holy Office, but by virtue of the quinquennial faculties granted by the Holy Office they can also dispense Orientals

[96] Canon 1097, § 2. In the United States the Ruthenians follow the *"Ne temere"*; Italo-Greeks according to the provision of Benedict XIV (const. *"Etsi pastoralis,"* 26 maii 1742, cap. VIII, nn. 11-12—*Fontes,* n. 328), may be married in the Latin rite if they choose, even if the groom is of the Greek rite; the Maronites (Synod of Mt. Lebanon, pars II, cap. XI, n. 12), and the Italo-Greeks living outside of their own dioceses (Clemens VIII, *instr. "Sanctissimus,"* 31 aug. 1595, 5—*Fontes,* n. 179) are ruled by the *"Tametsi,"* and others have particular laws. Cf. Cappello, *De Matrimonio,* n. 925. Gulovich holds the opinion that the Maronites and Italo-Greeks are not ruled by the *"Tametsi."* Cf. "Matrimonial Laws of the Catholic Eastern Churches"—*The Jurist,* IV (1944), 200-245. Certain replies of the Sacred Oriental Congregation concerning the Maronites may be found in the *AER,* LXXX (1929), 384.

[97] Herman, "Quibus Normis Matrimonium Regatur quod inter Fideles Diversi Ritus Contrahitur"—*Miscellanea,* A. Vermeersch (Romae, 1935), p. 254. In this article the author reasons that one and the same marriage in the Church cannot be considered as valid for one party and invalid for the other, and in some cases conflicting prescriptions of different rites cannot be observed. This would happen, for example, in the marriage of a Maronite man and a Melchite woman. Cf. *AER,* LXXX (1929), 384.

[98] Cf. Duskie, *op. cit.,* p. 170; S. C. de Prop. Fide, decr. 6 oct. 1863, C, c—*Coll.,* n. 1243—*Fontes,* n. 4859.

[99] Cappello, *De Matrimonio,* n. 906.

under their jurisdiction. Concerning the other impediments, the Sacred Oriental Congregation has not expressly stated that Latin ordinaries may dispense their Oriental subjects by virtue of the faculties granted them by the other Sacred Congregations, and consequently until such time as it declares such a practice acceptable, it can safely be said that the ordinaries should have recourse to the Sacred Oriental Congregation.[100]

ARTICLE IV. IMMIGRANT ORIENTAL CLERGY

The first concerted efforts to obtain priests for the immigrant population of the Oriental Church in the United States were those of the Ruthenians.[101] These priests seem to have come to the United States with the approval of their own ordinaries and of the Sacred Congregation for the Propagation of the Faith.[102] A decree of this Congregation subsequently required that priests going to the United States be celibates, that they be able to indicate the definite locality to which they were going, and that they receive faculties from the bishop *ad quem* as well as be subject to him upon their arrival.[103]

In 1894, because of the abuses and scandal that had been caused,[104] the Sacred Congregation in a letter to the bishops of the Oriental rites renewed these instructions, insisting particularly that no priest leave without the previous consent of the ordinary *ad quem;* that he be single; that he first declare in writing to the Sacred Congregation the diocese in which he intended to establish his domicile; and that he receive permission from the said Congregation in

[100] Gulovich is of the opinion that the Latin ordinaries may make use of their quinquennial faculties in favor of Orientals without further recourse to the Holy See, but does not cite any express statement of the Sacred Oriental Congregation approving the practice. Cf. "Matrimonial Laws of the Catholic Eastern Churches"—*The Jurist,* IV (1944), 243.

[101] Shipman, "Greek Catholics in America"—*The Catholic Encyclopedia* (17 vols., New York, 1907-1922), VI, 744.

[102] Heuser, "Greek Catholics and Latin Priests"—*AER,* IV (1890), 198.

[103] Cf. letter to Archbishop Gibbons of Baltimore, dated May 10, 1890—*AER,* VII (1892), 66.

[104] Cf. Attwater, *The Catholic Eastern Churches,* p. 87.

each individual case. Having arrived at his destination he was required to present himself to the ordinary under whose jurisdiction he would be. Then only, after showing the permission of the Sacred Congregation, and after presenting the discessorial letters from his bishop, signed by the Apostolic delegate, could he receive the necessary faculties.[105] These same dispositions were subsequently followed in the case of other immigrant clergy from countries of the Oriental rites.[106]

Since abuses continued, the Sacred Oriental Congregation made special regulations concerning emigrant Oriental clerics, both secular and religious, going to America and Australia to care for the faithful of their rite.[107] Fundamentally the former laws and decrees were not changed, but were applied to make them more effective. The Latin ordinaries or Oriental bishops or Patriarchs were to notify the Holy See of the needs of particular communities, and the Sacred Congregation alone granted the necessary permission to the designated and approved priest, sending him the necessary testimonial letters (*celebret*), and the rescript of permission to both ordinaries. Having arrived at his destination he was to present his testimonial letters and the discessorial letters to the local ordinary, and could then receive the faculties, being in the future subject to that ordinary's jurisdiction. He could visit the faithful of his own rite in another diocese, or even change his diocese with only the permission of both ordinaries, but in the latter case the change was to be made known to the Sacred Oriental Congregation. The bishops therefore were not to admit any priest of the Oriental rite to say Mass or exercise the sacred ministry, unless they themselves first received the rescript from the Sacred Oriental Congregation, even if the priest presented letters and documents purporting to have come from the said Congregation. These were severe measures, but they plainly indicated the intention of the Holy See to prevent harm

[105] S. C. de Prop. Fide, litt. encycl., 12 apr. 1894—*Coll.*, n. 1866.

[106] S. C. de Prop. Fide, pro Neg. R. O., decr. *"Cum sat numerosiores,"* 27 mart. 1916—*AAS*, VIII (1916), 105.

[107] Decr. *"Qua sollerti,"* 23 dec. 1929—*AAS*, XXII (1930), 99. This decree became effective April 1, 1930, and did not refer to the Ruthenians who were to be guided by the decree of March 1, 1929—*AAS*, XXI (1929), 152.

and scandal coming to the faithful from unscrupulous clerics and laymen.

Similar provisions were made for Oriental clerics who went to other countries to collect money or for other purposes than the care of souls.[108] In 1928 the Sacred Oriental Congregation issued a warning concerning impostors, who under the guise of Oriental clerics collected money and Mass stipends.[109] For clerics going to America and Australia for other reasons, or simply for a visit, the purpose was to be indicated to the Sacred Congregation through the ordinary or the Apostolic Delegate, and the bishop of the place to which the cleric intended to go was to be notified; if he received no such notification, he could not permit such a priest to celebrate Mass. He was to notify the Sacred Congregation if the Oriental priest without just cause stayed longer than the time allotted for the purpose.[110]

Regarding the collection of money and of Mass stipends by Oriental clerics in Latin dioceses, the Sacred Oriental Congregation does not make it a practice to grant such permissions. If for particular reasons such a permission is granted, the places where the collection is to be made, with the consent of the proper ordinary, will be designated by name, and the local ordinary will be first notified. Neither the ordinary nor the rectors of churches may assist such priests financially, or supply them with Mass stipends under the responsibility of saying the Masses themselves, even if the person has letters of recommendation and documents from other ordinaries, ecclesiastical dignitaries, or even from the Sacred Oriental Congregation itself.[111]

Another instruction concerning Oriental priests in countries or dioceses outside of their own was issued in 1932. It reiterated the previous insistence upon recent discessorial and commendatory letters,[112] the subjection to the jurisdiction of the local ordinary with-

[108] Cf. canon 622, § 4.

[109] S. C. Or., 2 apr. 1928—*AAS*, XX (1928), 107. Previously a circular letter to this effect had been sent out by the Sacred Congregation for the Propagation of the Faith, January 1, 1912—*AAS*, IV (1922), 532.

[110] S. C. Or., decr. *"Saepenumero,"* 7 ian. 1930—*AAS*, XXII (1930), 106.

[111] *AAS*, XXII (1930), 108.

[112] Cf. canon 804, § 1.

out prejudice to the bond with the cleric's own bishop or Patriarch, the report in writing to the Holy See if he is in charge of souls, and the necessity of notifying the Sacred Congregation of any abuse of the permission granted. The priests already in such foreign countries who did not have a rescript were to apply for one.[113] The ordinaries were again urgently reminded of these regulations and decrees in 1937, when the Sacred Congregation admonished them that they would be expressly notified of any authorized collections in the diocese, and would themselves be responsible, therefore, for the celebration of Masses, if Mass stipends were supplied the priests taking up the collection, and in proportion to their guilt, would be accountable for the aid supplied in money and Mass stipends collected by Oriental clerics not duly authorized.[114]

These provisions were made by the Holy See not only to preclude all occasion to fraud, but also to protect properly the good name and reputation of Oriental priests, as well as to provide for the spiritual care of the faithful of the Oriental rite in this country effectively. Many times the work of zealous and excellent priests has been seriously handicapped through the exploitation of charitable persons by impostors and unscrupulous clerics. In making these strict regulations the Church sought to prevent such abuses.

[113] S. C. Or., decr. "*Quo facilior,*" 26 sept. 1932—*AAS,* XXIV (1932), 344.
[114] S. C. Or., 20 iul. 1937—*AAS,* XXIX (1937), 342.

CONCLUSIONS

From the preceding survey of the canonical status of national parishes and personal parishes in general, the following conclusions have been reached:

1. No legislation concerning parishes based on distinct language or rite can be found until the thirteenth century, when it first appears in the IV Lateran Council (1215).

2. Though territorial parishes were the norm established in the Council of Trent, the decrees of the Council, according to the words *"aut alio utiliori modo,"* must be interpreted as permitting the establishment of personal parishes under certain conditions.

3. An act of a competent ecclesiastical authority is necessary and sufficient for the canonical erection of a parish, and a formal decree is not of inherent necessity.

4. If they are duly erected, national parishes are to be considered as canonical parishes, and therefore benefices, and their pastors are obliged to apply the official Mass for the people.

5. Pastors of national parishes can validly assist at all marriages within the territory held cumulatively with other parishes.

6. An apostolic indult is necessary for the lawful erection of a national parish, but not for its valid erection; and any change prior to the consultation with the Holy See, though it be illicit, can not necessarily be considered to be invalid.

7. An apostolic indult is not required for the erection of parishes of a distinct rite.

BIBLIOGRAPHY

Sources

Acta Apostolicae Sedis, Commentarium Officiale, Romae, 1909—

Acta et Decreta Concilii Plenarii Baltimorensis Tertii, A. D. MDCCCLXXXIV, Baltimorae; John Murphy, 1886.

Acta et Decreta Sacrorum Conciliorum Recentiorum Collectio Lacensis, 7 vols., Friburgi Brisgoviae: Herder, 1870-1890.

Acta Sanctae Sedis, 41 vols., Romae, 1865-1908.

Bouscaren, T. L., *The Canon Law Digest,* 2 vols., Milwaukee: Bruce, 1934-1943.

Bullarium Romanum, 25 vols., Augustae Taurinorum, 1857-1872.

Bullarii Romani Continuatio, 14 vols., Prati, 1845-1856.

Bullarium Pontificium Sacrae Congregationis de Propaganda Fide, 7 vols., et index, Romae, 1839-1858.

Codex Iuris Canonici Pii X Pontificis Maximi iussu digestus Benedicti XV auctoritate promulgatus, Romae: Typis Polyglottis Vaticanis, 1917. Reimpressio 1934.

Codicis Iuris Canonici Fontes cura Emi Petri Card Gasparri Editi, 9 vols., Romae: Typis Polyglottis Vaticanis, 1923-1939. (Vols. VII, VIII, IX ed. cura et studio Emi Iustiniano Card. Serédi.

Codificazione Canonica Orientale—Fonti, Fasc. VIII, Romae: Tipographia Poliglotta Vaticana, 1932.

Collectanea S. Congregationis de Propaganda Fide, 2 vols., Romae: Typographia Polyglotta S. C. de Propaganda Fide, 1907.

Concilii Plenarii Baltimorensis II Acta et Decreta, Baltimorae: Joannes Murphy et Soc., 1868.

Concilium Plenarium Totius Americae Septentrionalis Foederatae, Baltimori: Joannes Murphy et Soc., 1853.

Concilia Provincialia Baltimorensia habita ab anno 1829 usque ad annum 1849, Baltimori: Joannes Murphy et Soc., 1851.

Corpus Iuris Canonici, ed. Lipsiensis secunda post Aemilii Ludovici Richteri curas instruxit Aemilius Friedberg, 2 vols., 1879-1881. Editio anastatice repetita, Lipsiae: Tauchnitz, 1922.

Corpus Iuris Civilis, 3 vols., Berolini, 1928-1929. *Institutiones,* quas recognovit P. Krueger; *Digesta,* quae recognovit T. Mommsen et retractavit P. Krueger; *Codex Iustinianus,* quem recognovit et retractavit P. Krueger; *Novellae,* quas recognovit R. Schoell et absolvit G. Kroll.

Decisiones S. Rotae Romanae coram Ansaldo de Ansaldis, 8 vols., Romae, 1711-1777.

Decisiones S. Rotae Romanae coram Marcello Crescentio, 5 vols., Romae, 1758-1763.

Decretum Gratiani Emendatum et Notationibus Illustratum una cum Glossis, Romae, 1582.

Decretales D. Gregorii Papae IX, una cum glossis, Romae, 1582.

Denziger-Bannwart-Umberg, *Enchiridion Symbolorum,* 22-23. ed., Friburgi Brisgoviae: Herder, 1937.

Hardouin, Jean, *Acta Conciliorum et Epistolae Decretales ac Constitutiones Summorum Pontificum,* 12 vols., Parisiis, 1715.

Jaffé, Philippus, *Regesta Pontificum Romanorum ab condita Ecclesia ad annum post Christum natum MCXCVIII,* 2. ed., (Kaltenbrunner, Ewald, Loewenfeld), 2 vols., Lipsiae, 1885-1888.

Kirch, Conradus, *Enchiridion Fontium Historiae Ecclesiae Antiquae,* 2. ed., Friburgi Brisgoviae: Herder, 1914.

Mansi, J. D., *Sacrorum Conciliorum Nova et Amplissima Collectio,* 53 vols. in 59, Paris, Arnhem, Leipzig, 1901-1927.

Monumenta Germaniae Historica, Legum Sectio I, Leges Nationum Germanicarum, Tom. I, ed Heinricus Pertz, Hannoverae et Lipsiae, 1925.

Mühlbauer, W.—Gardellini, A., *Decreta Authentica Cong. S. Rituum et Instructio Clementina,* 4 vols., Monachi: Libreria Lenteriana, 1863-1867.

Official Catholic Directory, The, New York: P. J. Kenedy and Co., 1943.

Pallottini, S., *Collectio Omnium Conclusionum et Resolutionum quae in causis propositis apud Sacram Congregationem Cardinalium S. Concilii Tridentini Interpretum prodierunt ab eius institutione anno MDLXIV ad MDCCCLX, distinctis titulis alphabetico ordine per materias digestas,* 18 vols., Romae, 1868-1895.

Potthast, A., *Regesta Pontificum,* 2 vols., Berolini, 1874-1875.

Quinque Compilationes Antiquae necnon Collectio Canonum Lipsiensis, ad librorum manu scriptorum fidem recognovit et adnotatione critica instruxit Aemilius Friedberg, Lipsiae: ex officina Bernhardi Tauchnitz, 1882.

Rouet, de Journel, M. J., *Enchiridion Patristicum: Loci SS. Patrum, Doctorum, Scriptorum Ecclesiasticorum,* 10.-11. ed., Friburgi Brisgoviae: Herder, 1937.

Sacrae Romanae Rotae Decisiones seu Sententiae, Romae: Typis Polyglottis Vaticanis, 1912—

Sacrosancti et Oecumenici Concilii Tridentini Canones et Decreta, Parisiis, 1832.

Statuta Provincialia et Dioecesana (Philadelphiensia), Philadelphiae: Catholic Standard and Times Print, sine anno.

Statistica con Cenni Storici della Gerarchia e dei Fedeli di Rito Orientale, Sacra Cong. Orientale, Romae: Tipografia Poliglotta Vaticana, 1932.

Thesaurus Resolutionum Sacrae Congregationis Concilii, 167 vols., Romae, 1718-1908.

Reference Works

American Jurisprudence, 48 vols., Rochester, N Y.: The Lawyers Co-operative Co., 1936—

André-Condis-Wagner, *Dictionnaire de Droit Canonique,* 3. ed., 4 vols., Paris, 1901.

Attwater, Donald, *The Catholic Eastern Churches*, Milwaukee: Bruce, 1935.

Ayrinhac, H. A., *Legislation on the Sacraments*, New York: Longmans, Green and Co., 1928.

———, *Constitution of the Church in the New Code of Canon Law*, New York: Longmans, Green and Co., 1930.

(Bachofen), Charles Augustine, *A Commentary on the New Code of Canon Law*, 8 vols., St. Louis: Herder, 1921-1938; Vol. II, 5. ed., 1928; Vol. VI, 2. ed., 1923.

———, *The Canonical and Civil Status of Catholic Parishes in the United States*, St. Louis: Herder, 1926.

Barbosa, Augustinus, *Collectanea Doctorum in varia Concilii Trindentini Decreta et Canones*, Lugduni, 1657.

———, *De Officio et Potestate Parochi*, Lugduni, 1665.

———, *De Officio et Potestate Parochi*, Animadversiones et Additamenta Ubaldo Giraldi, Romae, 1831.

———, *Collectanea Decretorum*, tam Veterum quam Recentiorum in Ius Pontificium Universum, 6 vols., Lugduni, 1716.

———, *Iuris Ecclesiastici Universi Libri Tres*, 3 vols., Lugduni, 1650.

Bargillat, M., *Praelectiones Juris Canonici*, 37. ed., 2 vols., Paris, 1923.

Baronius, Caesar, *Annales Ecclesiastici*, 37 vols.; Vols. I-XXVIII, Barri-Ducis, 1864-1875; Vols. XXIX-XXXVII, Parisiis, 1876-1883.

Bastnagel, Clement, *The Appointment of Parochial Adjutants and Assistants*, The Catholic University of America Canon Law Studies, n. 58, Washington, D. C.: The Catholic University of America, 1930.

Beste, Udalricus, *Introductio in Codicem*, Collegeville, Minn.: St. John's Abbey Press, 1938.

Blat, Albertus, *Commentarium Textus Codicis Iuris Canonici*, 6 vols.; Vol. II, *Ius de Religiosis et Laicis iuxta Codicis Ordinem*, Romae, 1921.

Bluntschli, Johann K., *The Theory of the State*, Oxford, 1892.

Boehmer, I. H., *Ius Parochiale*, Halae, 1760.

Bouix, Dominicus, *Tractatus de Parocho*, 3. ed., Parisiis, 1880.

Bouuaert, F. Claeys—Simenon, G., *Manuale Juris Canonici*, 3 vols ; Vol. I, 3. ed., 1930; Vol. II, 1931, Gandae et Leodii: Dessain.

Cappello, Felix M., *Tractatus Canonico-Moralis de Sacramentis*, 3 vols. in 6; Vol. II, *De Extrema Unctione*, Taurinorum Augustae: Marietti, 1933; Vol. III, *De Matrimonio*, 3. ed., Taurinorum Augustae, 1933.

———, *Summa Iuris Canonici in Usum Scholarum Concinnata*, 3 vol.; Vol. II, Romae: apud Aedes Universitatis Gregorianae, 1930.

Catholic Encyclopedia, The, 17 vols., New York, 1907-1922.

Chelodi, Ioannes, *Ius de Personis iuxta Codicem Iuris Canonici*, 2. ed. ab Ernesto Bertagnolli, Tridenti: Libr. Edit. Tridentum, 1927.

Cicognani, Amleto, *Canon Law*, 2nd revised edition, authorized English version by Joseph O'Hara and Francis Brennan, Philadelphia: The Dolphin Press, 1935.

Coady, John J., *The Appointment of Pastors,* The Catholic University of America Canon Law Studies, n. 52, Washington, D. C.: The Catholic University of America, 1929.

Cocchi, Guidus, *Commentarium in Codicem Iuris Canonici,* 8 vols., Taurinorum Augustae: Marietti, 1931-1940; Vol. I, 5. ed., 1938; Vol. II, 4. ed., 1937.

Connolly, N. P., *The Canonical Erection of Parishes,* The Catholic University of America Canon Law Studies, n. 114, Washington, D. C.: The Catholic University of America, 1938.

Coronata, Matthaeus Conte A., *Institutiones Iuris Canonici,* 5 vols., Taurini: Marietti, 1933-1939; Vol. I, ed. altera, 1939.

D'Angelo, Sosio, *Parroco e Parrocchia nel Codice di Diritto Canonico,* 3. ed., Giarre, 1921.

Dausend, Hugo, *Das interrituelle Recht in Codex Juris Canonici,* 79 Heft, Paderborn: Görres Gesellschaft, Veröffentlichungen der Sektion für Rechts— und Staatwissenschaft, 1939.

De Clavasio, Angelo, *Summa de Casibus Conscientialibus,* 2 vols., Venetiis, 1525.

De Luca, Ioannes Card., *Theatrum Veritatis et Iustitiae,* 16 vols., Coloniae Agrippinae, 1706.

De Smet, Aloysius, *Tractatus Theologico-Canonicus de Sponsalibus et Matrimonio,* 4. ed., Brugis: Car. Beyaert, 1927.

Donnellan, Thomas A., *The Obligation of the Missa pro Populo,* The Catholic University of America Canon Law Studies, n. 155, Washington, D. C.: The Catholic University of America Press, 1942.

Duskie, John, *The Canonical Status of Orientals in the United States,* The Catholic University of America Canon Law Studies, n. 48, Washington, D. C.: The Catholic University of America, 1928.

Eppstein, John, *The Catholic Tradition of the Law of Nations,* London, 1935.

Fagnanus, Prosper, *Commentaria in Libros Decretalium,* 4 vols., Venetiis, 1697.

Fanfani, P. Ludovicus, *De Iure Parochorum* ad Normam Codicis Iuris Canonici, Romae: Marietti, 1924.

Ferraris, F. Lucius, *Bibliotheca Canonica Iuridica Moralis Theologica nec non Ascetica Polemica Rubristica Historica,* 9 vols., Romae, 1885-1899.

Ferreres, Joannes B., *Institutiones Canonicae,* 2. ed., 2 vols., Barcinone, 1920.

Ferry, William A., *Stole Fees,* The Catholic University of America Canon Law Studies, n. 59, Washington, D. C.: The Catholic University of America, 1930.

Florez, Henrique, *España Sagrada,* 52 vols., Vol. III, Madrid, 1748.

Fournier, Paul et Le Bras, Gabriel, *Histoire des Collections Canoniques en Occident* depuis les Fausses Décrétales jusqu'au Décret de Gratien, Tom. I: *De la Réforme Carolingienne à la Réforme Grégorienne,* Paris: Recueil Sirey, 1931.

Gillard, John, *Colored Catholics in the United States,* Baltimore: The Josephite Press, 1941.

Gonzalez-Tellez, Emmanuel, *Commentaria Perpetua in Singulos Textus Quinque Librorum Decretalium Gregorii IX*, 5 vols., Maceratae, 1761.

Grentrup, Theodor, *Religion und Muttersprache*, Heft 47-49, Münster in Westfallen, 1932.

———, *Nationale Minderheiten und Katholische Kirche*, Münster, 1934.

Guilday, Peter, *A History of the Councils of Baltimore*, New York: The Macmillan Company, 1932.

Guiniven, John J., *The Precept of Hearing Mass*, The Catholic University of America Canon Law Studies, n. 158, Washington, D. C.: The Catholic University of America Press, 1942.

Halich, Wasyl, *Ukrainians in the United States*, Chicago: The University of Chicago Press, 1937.

Hefele, Carolus-Leclercq, Henricus, *Histoire des Conciles*, 10 vols., in 19, Paris: Letouzey et Ané, 1907-1938.

Hilling, Nikolaus, *Das Personenrecht des Codex Iuris Canonici*, Paderborn, 1924.

Hilling, P., *Procedure of the Roman Curia*, New York, 1907.

Hinschius, Paulus, *Das Kirchenrecht der Katholiken und Protestanten in Deutschland*, 6 vols., Berlin, 1869-1897. Vols. I-IV, *System des Katholischen Kirchenrechts*, Berlin, 1869-1888.

Hostiensis, Cardinalis (Henricus de Segusia), *In Quinque Decretalium Commentaria*, 5 vols., in 3, Venetiis, 1581.

———, *Summa Aurea*, Venetiis, 1570.

Ioannes, Andreae, *In Decretalium Libros Novella Commentaria*, 5 vols., Venetiis, 1581.

Kremer, M. N., *Church Support in the United States*, The Catholic University of America Canon Law Studies, n. 61, Washington, D. C.: The Catholic University of America, 1930.

Kruszka, Waclaw, *Historya Polska w Ameryce*, 7 vols., Milwaukee: Kuryer, 1905-1908.

Leurenius, Petrus, *Forum Beneficiale*, 2 vols., Venetiis, 1752.

Maroto, Philippus, *Institutiones Iuris Canonici*, 3. ed., 2 vols., Romae, 1921.

Michiels, Gommarus, *Normae Generales Iuris Canonici*, 2 vols., Lublin (Polonia): Universitas Catholica, 1929.

———, *Principia Generalia de Personis in Ecclesia*, Lublin: Universitas Catholica, 1932.

Migne, P. J., *Patrologiae Cursus Completus*, Series Latina, 221 vols. (MPL), Parisiis, 1844-1855; Series Graeca (MPG), 161 vols., Parisiis, 1857-1866.

National Catholic Almanac, The, Paterson, N. J.: St. Anthony Guild, 1943.

Nau, Louis J., *Manual of the Marriage Laws of the Code of Canon Law*, Cincinnati: Pustet, 1934.

O'Brien, *A Hidden Phase of American History*, New York: 1919.

O'Neill, William H., *Papal Rescripts of Favor*, The Catholic University of America Canon Law Studies, n. 57, Washington, D. C.: The Catholic University of America, 1930.

Panormitanus, Abbas (Nicholaus de Tudeschis), *Commentaria in Quinque Libros Decretalium*, 8 vols., Venetiis, 1588.

Petra, Vincentius, *Commentaria ad Constitutiones Apostolicas*, 5 vols., in 2, Venetiis, 1729.

Petrani, Alexius, *De Relatione Iuridica inter Diversos Ritus in Ecclesia Catholica*, Taurini: Marietti, 1930.

Reiffenstuel, Anacletus, *Ius Canonicum Universum*, 7 vols., Venetiis, 1735.

Riganti, Ioannes Baptista, *Commentaria in Regulas Cancelleriae Apostolicae*, 2 vols., Coloniae Allobrogum, 1751.

Rossi, Iosephus, *De Paroecia*, Romae: Pustet, 1932.

Rufinus, *Summa Decretorum*, ed. H. Singer, Paderborn, 1902.

Sabetti, A.-Barrett, T., *Compendium Theologiae Moralis*, 27. ed., New York, 1919.

Salzbacher, *Meine Reise nach Nord-Amerika im Jahre 1842*, Vienna, 1855.

Schäfer, T., *Pfarrer und Pfarrvikare*, Münster, 1922.

Schaff, Philip, *History of the Christian Church*, 7 vols., New York, 1904-1910.

Schmalzgrueber, Franciscus, *Ius Ecclesiasticum Universum*, 5 vols., in 12, Romae, 1843-1845.

Schmidlin, Joseph, *Catholic Mission History*, Techny: Mission Press, 1933.

Shaughnessy, Gerald, *Has the Immigrant Kept the Faith?* New York, 1925.

Shea, John G., *History of the Catholic Church in the United States*, 4 vols., Akron, 1886-1892.

Sipos, Stephanus, *Enchiridion Iuris Canonici*, 3. ed., Pécs: Typografia Haladas R. T., 1936.

Sebastianelli, G., *Praelectiones Iuris Canonici, De Rebus*, Romae: Pustet, 1905.

Smith, S. B., *Elements of Ecclesiastical Law*, 9. ed., 3 vols., New York, 1887.

———, *Counter-points in Canon Law*, Newark, 1879.

Suarez, Franciscus, *Opera Omnia*, ed. nova, 26 vols.; Toms. I-IV a D. M. André; Toms. V-XXVI a Carolo Berton, Parisiis, 1856-1878.

Thomassinus, Ludovicus, *Vetus et Nova Ecclesiae Disciplina*, 10 vols., Parisiis, 1724.

Toso, A., *Ad Codicem Iuris Canonici Commentaria Minora*, Vol. II, Romae, 1922.

Ursaya, Dominicus, *Disceptationes Ecclesiasticae*, 8 vols., Venetiis, 1724.

Van Hove, A., *Commentarium Lovaniense in Codicem Iuris Canonici*, Vol. I, Tom. II, *De Legibus Ecclesiasticis*, *Mechlinae*: Dessain, 1930.

Vermeersch, A.-Creusen, J., *Epitome Iuris Canonici*, 5. ed., 3 vols., Mechlinae: Dessain, 1934-1936.

Waldron, Joseph F., *The Minister of Baptism*, The Catholic University of America Canon Law Studies, n. 170, Washington, D. C.: The Catholic University of America Press, 1942.

Wernz, Franciscus, *Ius Decretalium*, 2. ed., 6 vols., Romae, 1908-1913.

Wernz, F.-Vidal, P., *Ius Canonicum ad Codicis Normam Exactum*, 7 toms. in 8 vols., Romae: Apud Aedes Universitatis Gregorianae, 1923-1938; Tom. II, *De Personis*, 2. ed., 1928; Tom. V, *Ius Matrimoniale*, 2. ed., 1928.

Woywod, Stanislaus, *A Practical Commentary on the Code of Canon Law*, 5. ed., 2 vols., New York: Joseph Wagner, 1939.

Zitelli-Natali, Zephyrinus, *Apparatus Iuris Ecclesiastici*, Romae, 1886.

Zollman, Carl, *American Church Law*, St. Paul: West Publ. Co., 1933.

Periodicals

American Ecclesiastical Review, The, Philadelphia, 1889-1943; Baltimore, 1944—

Analecta Ecclesiastica, Romae, 1893-1911.

Apollinaris, Romae, 1928—

Archiv für Katholisches Kirchenrechts, Innsbruck, 1857-1861; Mainz, 1862—

Archivum Latinitatis Medii Aevi, Paris, 1924—

Canoniste Contemporain, Le, 45 vols., Paris, 1878-1922; *Le Canoniste*, Vols. 46-48, Paris, 1924-1926.

Catholic Historical Review, The, Washington, D. C.: The Catholic University of America, 1915—

Ephemerides Theologicae Lovanienses, Lovanii-Brugis, 1924—

Homiletic and Pastoral Review, The, New York, 1900—

Jurist, The, Washington, D. C.: The Catholic University of America, 1941—

Jus Pontificium, Romae, 1921—

Kirchenrechtliche Abhandlungen, Stuttgart, 1902-1935.

Monitore Ecclesiastico, Il, Romae, 1876—

Nouvelle Revue Théologique, Tournai, 1869 —

Periodica de Re Canonica et Morali utili praesertim Religiosis et Missionariis, Brugis, 1905—; ab anno 1927: *Periodica de Re Canonica, Morali, Liturgica.*

Orientalia Christiana, Romae, 1923—; ab anno 1935: *Orientalia Christiana Analecta.*

Theologisch-praktische Quartalschrift, Linz, 1832—

Theologische Quartalschrift, Tubingen, 1819—

Articles

Bastnagel, C., "Is a Parish for Colored People a 'National' Parish?"—*AER*, CVIII (1943), 382-384.

Braun, M., "Missionary Problems in the Thirteenth Century: A Study in Missionary Preparation"—*The Catholic Historical Review*, XXV (1939), 146-159.

Creusen, J., "L'Eglise Catholique aux Etats-Unis"—*Nouvelle Revue Theologique*, LIV (1927), 655-682.

Gillard, J., "A Significant Jubilee for Negro Catholics"—*AER,* XCII (1935), 235-251.

———, "The Catholic Clergy and the American Negro"—*AER,* XCIV (1936), 144-158.

Gulovich, S., *"Matrimonial Laws of the Catholic Eastern Churches"—The Jurist,* IV (1943), 200-245.

———, "Mass and Communion according to the Oriental Rite in a Church of the Latin Rite"—*The Jurist,* II (1942), 47-52.

Hannan, J., "The Obligation of Church Support"—*The Jurist,* I (1941), 343.

———, "Mass and Communion according to the Oriental Rite in a Church of the Latin Rite"—*The Jurist,* I (1941), 149-152.

Herman, A., "De Conceptu 'Ritus' "—*The Jurist,* II (1942), 333-345.

Heuser, "Greek Catholics and Latin Priests"—*AER,* IV (1890), 194-204.

Lot, F., "A quelle époque a-t-on cessé de parler latin?"—*Archivum Latinitatis Medii Aevi,* VI (1931), 97-152.

Martin, C., "The American Judiciary and Religious Liberty"—*The Catholic Historical Review,* VIII (1928), 13-37.

McNicholas, J., "Difficulties of the New Marriage Legislation"—*AER,* XXXIX (1908), 24-28.

Moroney, T., "Catholic Activity in behalf of the Negro"—*AER,* LXII (1920), 45-56.

Murphy, E., "The Colored Harvest"—*AER,* LXXIX (1928), 496-508.

Ploechl, W., "Two Hundred Years—'Etsi Pastoralis' "—*The Jurist,* II (1942), 211-213.

Roelker, E., "The Interpretation of Invalidating Laws"—*The Jurist,* III (1943), 364-403.

Tennelly, J., "Catholic Negro Missions"—*The National Catholic Almanac* (1943), 403-405.

Walsh, W., "Nigra Sum sed Formosa"—*AER,* CV (1941), 493-498.

Vromant, G., "De Actibus Personae Moralis Collegialis ac Superioris"—*Ephemerides Theologicae Lovanienses,* VII (1930), 681-688.

Zwierlein, F., "New Netherlands Intolerance"—*The Catholic Historical Review,* IV (1918), 186-216.

ABBREVIATIONS

AAS—*Acta Apostolicae Sedis.*
AER—*The American Ecclesiastical Review.*
ASS—*Acta Sanctae Sedis.*
Bull. Rom.—*Bullarium Romanum.*
Bull. Rom. Cont.—*Bullarii Romani Continuatio.*
C.—Codex (Iustinianus).
CHR—*The Catholic Historical Review.*
Coll.—*Collectanea S. C. de Propaganda Fide.*
Coll. Lac.—*Collectio Lacensis.*
C. P. I.—Commissio Pontificia Interpretationis Codicis.
Fontes—*Codicis Iuris Canonici Fontes . . . cura Gasparri editi.*
Hardouin—*Acta Conciliorum,* etc.
Mansi—*Sacrorum Conciliorum Nova et Amplissima Collectio.*
ME—*Il Monitore Ecclesiastico.*
NRT—*Nouvelle Revue Theologique*
Periodica—*Periodica de Re Canonica et Morali.*
R. J.—Regula Juris.
S. C. C.—Sacra Congregatio Concilii.
S. C. Consist.—Sacra Congregatio Consistorialis.
S. C. Or.—Sacra Congregatio pro Ecclesia Orientali.

ALPHABETICAL INDEX

BIOGRAPHICAL NOTE

JOSEPH EDWARD CIESLUK was born March 6, 1910, in Versailles, Connecticut. Having completed his elementary studies in St. Adalbert's School, Grand Rapids, Michigan, he entered St. Joseph's Seminary in the fall of 1925. He was ordained to the priesthood in Rome, March 27, 1937, while completing his theological studies at the Collegio Urbano de Propaganda Fide. He entered the Catholic University of America in September, 1941 to pursue a graduate course of studies in the School of Canon Law, and received the degrees of Baccalaureate in Canon Law in May, 1942, and of the Licentiate in Canon Law in May, 1943.

CANON LAW STUDIES *

1. FRERIKS, REV. CELESTINE A., C.PP.S., J.C.D., Religious Congregations in Their External Relations, 121 pp., 1916.
2. GALLIHER, REV. DANIEL M., O.P., J.C.D., Canonical Elections, 117 pp., 1917.
3. BORKOWSKI, REV. AURELIUS L., O.F.M., J.C.D., De Confraternitatibus Ecclesiasticis, 136 pp., 1918.
4. CASTILLO, REV. CAYO, J.C.D., Disertacion Historico-Canonica sobre la Potestad del Cabildo en Sede Vacante o Impedida del Vicario Capitular, 99 pp., 1919 (1918).
5. KUBELBECK, REV. WILLIAM J., S.T.B., J.C.D., The Sacred Penitentiaria and Its Relation to Faculties of Ordinaries and Priests, 129 pp., 1918.
6. PETROVITS, REV. JOSEPH, J.C., S.T.D., J.C.D., The New Church Law on Matrimony, X-461 pp., 1919.
7. HICKEY, REV. JOHN J., S.T.B., J.C.D., Irregularities and Simple Impediments in the New Code of Canon Law, 100 pp., 1920.
8. KLEKOTKA, REV. PETER J., S.T.B., J.C.D., Diocesan Consultors, 179 pp., 1920.
9. WANENMACHER, REV. FRANCIS, J.C.D., The Evidence in Ecclesiastical Procedure Affecting the Marriage Bond, 1920 (Printed 1935).
10. GOLDEN, REV. HENRY FRANCIS, J.C.D., Parochial Benefices in the New Code, IV-119 pp., 1921 (Printed 1925).
11. KOUDELKA, REV. CHARLES J., J.C.D., Pastors, Their Rights and Duties According to the New Code of Canon Law, 211 pp., 1921.
12. MELO, REV. ANTONIUS, O.F.M., J.C.D., De Exemptione Regularium, X-188 pp., 1921.
13. SCHAAF, REV. VALENTINE THEODORE, O.F.M., S.T.B., J.C.D., The Cloister. X-180 pp., 1921.
14. BURKE, REV. THOMAS JOSEPH, S.T.D., J.C.D., Competence in Ecclesiastical Tribunals, IV-117 pp., 1922.
15. LEECH, REV. GEORGE LEO, J.C.D., A Comparative Study of the Constitution "Apostolicae Sedis" and the "Codex Juris Canonici," 179 pp., 1922.
16. MOTRY, REV. HUBERT LOUIS, S.T.D., J.C.D., Diocesan Faculties According to the Code of Canon Law, II-167 pp., 1922.
17. MURPHY, REV. GEORGE LAWRENCE, J.C.D., Delinquencies and Penalties in the Administration and the Reception of the Sacraments, IV-121 pp., 1923.
18. O'REILLY, REV. JOHN ANTHONY, S.T.B., J.C.D., Ecclesiastical Sepulture in the New Code of Canon Law, II-129 pp., 1923.

* From nn. 1-100 inclusive only nn. 25 and 57 are still obtainable.
From n. 101 onward all numbers are available except the following: nn. 101-118 inclusive, and also n. 122.

19. MICHALICKA, REV. WENCESLAS CYRILL, O.S.B., J.C.D., Judicial Procedure in Dismissal of Clerical Exempt Religious, 107 pp., 1923.
20. DARGIN, REV. EDWARD VINCENT, S.T.B., J.C.D., Reserved Cases According to the Code of Canon Law, IV-103 pp., 1924.
21. GODFREY, REV. JOHN A., S.T.B., J.C.D., The Right of Patronage According to the Code of Canon Law, 153 pp., 1924.
22. HAGEDORN, REV. FRANCIS EDWARD, J.C.D., General Legislation on Indulgences, II-154 pp., 1924.
23. KING, REV. JAMES IGNATIUS, J.C.D., The Administration of the Sacraments to Dying Non-Catholics, V-141 pp., 1924.
24. WINSLOW, REV. FRANCIS JOSEPH, O.F.M., J.C.D., Vicars and Prefects Apostolic, IV-149 pp., 1924.
25. CORREA, REV. JOSE SERVELION, S.T.L., J.C.D., La Potestad Legislativa de la Iglesia Catolica, IV-127 pp., 1925.
26. DUGAN, REV. HENRY FRANCIS, A.M., J.C.D., The Judiciary Department of the Diocesan Curia, 87 pp., 1925.
27. KELLER, REV. CHARLES FREDERICK, S.T.B., J.C.D., Mass Stipends, 167 pp., 1925.
28. PASCHANG, REV. JOHN LINUS, J.C.D., The Sacramentals According to the Code of Canon Law, 129 pp., 1925.
29. PIONTEK, REV. CYRILLUS, O.F.M., S.T.B., J.C.D., De Indulto Exclaustrationis necnon Saecularizationis, XIII-289 pp., 1925.
30. KEARNEY, REV. RICHARD JOSEPH, S.T.B., J.C.D., Sponsors at Baptism According to the Code of Canon Law, IV-127 pp., 1925.
31. BARTLETT, REV. CHESTER JOSEPH, A.M., LL.B., J.C.D., The Tenure of Parochial Property in the United States of America, V-108 pp., 1926.
32. KILKER, REV. ADRIAN JEROME, J.C.D., Extreme Unction, V-425 pp., 1926.
33. MCCORMICK, REV. ROBERT EMMETT, J.C.D., Confessors of Religious, VIII-266 pp., 1926.
34. MILLER, REV. NEWTON THOMAS, J.C.D., Founded Masses According to the Code of Canon Law, VII-93 pp., 1926.
35. ROELKER, REV. EDWARD G., S.T.D., J.C.D., Principles of Privilege According to the Code of Canon Law, XI-166 pp., 1926.
36. BAKALARCZYK, REV. RICHARDUS, M.I.C., J.U.D., De Novitiatu, VIII-208 pp., 1927.
37. PIZZUTI, REV. LAWRENCE, O.F.M., J.U.L., De Parochis Religiosis, 1927. (Not Printed.)
38. BLILEY, REV. NICHOLAS MARTIN, O.S.B., J.C.D., Altars According to the Code of Canon Law, XIX-132 pp., 1927.
39. BROWN, MR. BRENDAN FRANCIS, A.B., LL.M., J.U.D., The Canonical Juristic Personality with Special Reference to its Status in the United States of America, V-212 pp., 1927.
40. CAVANAUGH, REV. WILLIAM THOMAS, C.P., J.U.D., The Reservation of the Blessed Sacrament, VIII-101 pp., 1927.

41. DOHENY, REV. WILLIAM J., C.S.C., A.B., J.U.D., Church Property: Modes of Acquisition, X-118 pp., 1927.
42. FELDHAUS, REV. ALOYSIUS H., C.PP.S., J.C.D., Oratories, IX-141 pp., 1927.
43. KELLY, REV. JAMES PATRICK, A.B., J.C.D., The Jurisdiction of the Simple Confessor, X-208 pp., 1927.
44. NEUBERGER, REV. NICHOLAS J., J.C.D., Canon 6 or the Relation of the Codex Juris Canonici to the Preceding Legislation, V-95 pp., 1927.
45. O'KEEFE, REV. GERALD MICHAEL, J.C.D., Matrimonial Dispensations, Powers of Bishops, Priests, and Confessors, VIII-232 pp., 1927.
46. QUIGLEY, REV. JOSEPH A. M., A.B., J.C.D., Condemned Societies, 139 pp., 1927.
47. ZAPLOTNIK, REV. JOHANNES LEO, J.C.D., De Vicariis Foraneis, X-142 pp., 1927.
48. DUSKIE, REV. JOHN ALOYSIUS, A.B., J.C.D., The Canonical Status of the Orientals in the United States, VIII-196 pp., 1928.
49. HYLAND, REV. FRANCIS EDWARD, J.C.D., Excommunication, Its Nature, Historical Development and Effects, VIII-181 pp., 1928.
50. REINMANN, REV. GERALD JOSEPH, O.M.C., J.C.D., The Third Order Secular of Saint Francis, 201 pp., 1928.
51. SCHENK, REV. FRANCIS J., J.C.D., The Matrimonial Impediments of Mixed Religion and Disparity of Cult, XVI-318 pp., 1929.
52. COADY, REV. JOHN JOSEPH, S.T.D., J.U.D., A.M., The Appointment of Pastors, VIII-150 pp., 1929.
53. KAY, REV. THOMAS HENRY, J.C.D., Competence in Matrimonial Procedure, VIII-164 pp., 1929.
54. TURNER, REV. SIDNEY JOSEPH, C.P., J.U.D., The Vow of Poverty, XLIX-217 pp., 1929.
55. KEARNEY, REV. RAYMOND A., A.B., S.T.D., J.C.D., The Principles of Delegation, VII-149 pp., 1929.
56. CONRAN, REV. EDWARD JAMES, A.B., J.C.D., The Interdict, V-163 pp., 1930.
57. O'NEILL, REV. WILLIAM H., J.C.D., Papal Rescripts of Favor, VII-218 pp., 1930.
58. BASTNAGEL, REV. CLEMENT VINCENT, J.U.D., The Appointment of Parochial Adjutants and Assistants, XV-257 pp., 1930.
59. FERRY, REV. WILLIAM A., A.B., J.C.D., Stole Fees, V-136 pp., 1930.
60. COSTELLO, REV. JOHN MICHAEL, A.B., J.C.D., Domicile and Quasi-Domicile, VII-201 pp., 1930.
61. KREMER, REV. MICHAEL NICHOLAS, A.B., S.T.B., J.C.D., Church Support in the United States, VI-136 pp., 1930.
62. ANGULO, REV. LUIS, C.M., J.C.D., Legislation de la Iglesia sobre la intencion en la application de la Santa Misa, VII-104 pp., 1931.
63. FREY, REV. WOLFGANG NORBERT, O.S.B., A.B., J.C.D., The Act of Religious Profession, VIII-174 pp., 1931.

64. Roberts, Rev. James Brendan, A.B., J.C.D., The Banns of Marriage, XIV-140 pp., 1931.
65. Ryder, Rev. Raymond Aloysius, A.B., J.C.D., Simony, IX-151 pp., 1931.
66. Campagna, Rev. Angelo, Ph.D., J.U.D., Il Vicario Generale del Vescovo, VII-205 pp., 1931.
67. Cox, Rev. Joseph Godfrey, A.B., J.C.D., The Administration of Seminaries, VI-124 pp., 1931.
68. Gregory, Rev. Donald J., J.U.D., The Pauline Privilege, XV-165 pp., 1931.
69. Donohue, Rev. John F., J.C.D., The Impediment of Crime, VII-110 pp., 1931.
70. Dooley, Rev. Eugene A., O.M.I., J.C.D., Church Law on Sacred Relics, IX-143 pp., 1931.
71. Orth, Rev. Clement Raymond, O.M.C., J.C.D., The Approbation of Religious Institutes, 171 pp., 1931.
72. Pernicone, Rev. Joseph M., A.B., J.C.D., The Ecclesiastical Prohibition of Books, XII-267 pp., 1932.
73. Clinton, Rev. Connell, A.B., J.C.D., The Paschal Precept, IX-108 pp., 1932.
74. Donnelly, Rev. Francis B., A.M., S.T.L., J.C.D., The Diocesan Synod, VIII-125 pp., 1932.
75. Torrente, Rev. Camilo, C.M.F., J.C.D., Las Procesiones Sagradas, V-145 pp., 1932.
76. Murphy, Rev. Edwin J., C.PP.S., J.C.D., Suspension Ex Informata Conscientia, XI-122 pp., 1932.
77. MacKenzie, Rev. Eric F., A.M., S.T.L., J.C.D., The Delict of Heresy in its Commission, Penalization, Absolution, VII-124 pp., 1932.
78. Lyons, Rev. Avitus E., S.T.B., J.C.D., The Collegiate Tribunal of First Instance, XI-147 pp., 1932.
79. Connolly, Rev. Thomas A., J.C.D., Appeals, XI-195, pp., 1932.
80. Sangmeister, Rev. Joseph V., A.B., J.C.D., Force and Fear as Precluding Matrimonial Consent, V-211 pp., 1932.
81. Jaeger, Rev. Leo A., A.B., J.C.D., The Administration of Vacant and Quasi-Vacant Episcopal Sees in the United States, IX-229 pp., 1932.
32. Rimlinger, Rev. Herbert T., J.C.D., Error Invalidating Matrimonial Consent, VII-79 pp., 1932.
83. Barrett, Rev. John D. M., S.S., J.C.D., A Comparative Study of the Third Plenary Council of Baltimore and the Code, IX-221 pp., 1932.
84. Carberry, Rev. John J., Ph.D., S.T.D., J.C.D., The Juridical Form of Marriage, X-177 pp., 1934.
85. Dolan, Rev. John L., A.B., J.C.D., The Defensor Vinculi, XII-157 pp., 1934.
86. Hannan, Rev. Jerome D., A.M., S.T.D., LL.B., J.C.D., The Canon Law of Wills, IX-517 pp., 1934.

87. LEMIEUX, REV. DELISE A., A.M., J.C.D., The Sentence in Ecclesiastical Procedure, IX-131 pp., 1934.
88. O'ROURKE, REV. JAMES J., A.B., J.C.D., Parish Registers, VII-109 pp., 1934.
89. TIMLIN, REV. BARTHOLOMEW, O.F.M., A.M., J.C.D., Conditional Matrimonial Consent, X-381 pp., 1934.
90. WAHL, REV. FRANCIS X., A.B., J.C.D., The Matrimonial Impediments of Consanguinity and Affinity, VI-125 pp., 1934.
91. WHITE, REV. ROBERT J., A.B., LL.B., S.T.B., J.C.D., Canonical Ante-Nuptial Promises and the Civil Law, VI-152 pp., 1934.
92. HERRERA, REV. ANTONIO PARRA, O.C.D., J.C.D., Legislacion Ecclesiastica sobra el Ayuno y la Abstinencia, XI-191 pp., 1935.
93. KENNEDY, REV. EDWIN J., J.C.D., The Special Matrimonial Process in Cases of Evident Nullity, X-165 pp., 1935.
94. MANNING, REV. JOHN J., A.B., J.C.D., Presumption of Law in Matrimonial Procedure, XI-111 pp., 1935.
95. MOEDER, REV. JOHN M., J.C.D., The Proper Bishop for Ordination and Dismissorial Letters, VII-135 pp., 1935.
96. O'MARA, REV. WILLIAM A., A.B., J.C.D., Canonical Causes for Matrimonial Dispensations, IX-155 pp., 1935.
97. REILLY, REV. PETER, J.C.D., Residence of Pastors, IX-81 pp., 1935.
98. SMITH, REV. MARINER T., O.P., S.T.Lr., J.C.D., The Penal Law for Religious, VIII-169 pp., 1935.
99. WHALEN, REV. DONALD W., A.M., J.C.D., The Value of Testimonial Evidence in Matrimonial Procedure, XIII-297 pp., 1935.
100. CLEARY, REV. JOSEPH F., J.C.D., Canonical Limitations on the Alienation of Church Property, VIII-141 pp., 1936.
101. GLYNN, REV. JOHN C., J.C.D., The Promoter of Justice, XX-337 pp., 1936.
102. BRENNAN, REV. JAMES H., S.S., M.A., S.T.B., J.C.D., The Simple Convalidation of Marriage, VI-135 pp., 1937.
103. BRUNINI, REV. JOSEPH BERNARD, J.C.D., The Clerical Obligations of Canons 139 and 142, X-121 pp., 1937.
104. CONNOR, REV. MAURICE, A.B., J.C.D., The Administrative Removal of Pastors, VIII-159 pp., 1937.
105. GUILFOYLE, REV. MERLIN JOSEPH, J.C.D., Custom, XI-144 pp., 1937.
106. HUGHES, REV. JAMES AUSTIN, A.B., A.M., J.C.D., Witnesses in Criminal Trials of Clerics, IX-140 pp., 1937.
107. JANSEN, REV. RAYMOND J., A.B., S.T.L., J.C.D., Canonical Provisions for Catechetical Instruction, VII-153 pp., 1937.
108. KEALY, REV. JOHN JAMES, A.B., J.C.D., The Introductory Libellus in Church Court Procedure, XI-121 pp., 1937.
109. MCMANUS, REV. JAMES EDWARD, C.SS.R., J.C.D., The Administration of Temporal Goods in Religious Institutes, XVI-196 pp., 1937.

110. MORIARTY, REV. EUGENE JAMES, J.C.D., Oaths in Ecclesiastical Courts, X-115 pp., 1937.
111. RAINER, REV. ELIGIUS GEORGE, C.SS.R., J.C.D., Suspension of Clerics, XVII-249 pp., 1937.
112. REILLY, REV. THOMAS F., C.SS.R., J.C.D., Visitation of Religious, VI-195 pp., 1938.
113. MORIARTY, REV. FRANCIS E., C.SS.R., J.C.D., The Extraordinary Absolution from Censures, XV-334 pp., 1938.
114. CONNOLLY, REV. NICHOLAS P., J.C.D., The Canonical Erection of Parishes, X-132 pp., 1938.
115. DONOVAN, REV. JAMES JOSEPH, J.C.D., The Pastor's Obligation in Prenuptial Investigation, XII-322 pp., 1938.
116. HARRIGAN, REV. ROBERT J., M.A., S.T.B., J.C.D., The Radical Sanation of Invalid Marriages, VIII-208 pp., 1938.
117. BOFFA, REV. CONRAD HUMBERT, J.C.D., Canonical Provisions for Catholic Schools, VII-211 pp., 1939.
118. PARSONS, REV. ANSCAR JOHN, O.M.Cap., J.C.D., Canonical Elections, XII-236 pp., 1939.
119. REILLY, REV. EDWARD MICHAEL, A.B., J.C.D., The General Norms of Dispensation, XII-156 pp., 1939.
120. RYAN, REV. GERALD ALOYSIUS, A.B., J.C.D., Principles of Episcopal Jurisdiction, XII-172 pp., 1939.
121. BURTON, REV. FRANCIS JAMES, C.S.C., A.B., J.C.D., A Commentary on Canon 1125, X-222 pp., 1940.
122. MIASKIEWICZ, REV. FRANCIS SIGISMUND, J.C.D., Supplied Jurisdiction According to Canon 209, XII-340 pp., 1940.
123. RICE, REV. PATRICK WILLIAM, A.B., J.C.D., Proof of Death in Prenuptial Investigation, VIII-156 pp., 1940.
124. ANGLIN, REV. THOMAS FRANCIS, M.S., J.C.D., The Eucharistic Fast, VIII-183 pp., 1941.
125. COLEMAN, REV. JOHN JEROME, J.C.D., The Minister of Confirmation, VI-153 pp., 1941.
126. DOWNS, REV. JOHN EMMANUEL, A.B., J.C.D., The Concept of Clerical Immunity, XI-163 pp., 1941.
127. ESSWEIN, REV. ANTHONY ALBERT, J.C.D., Extrajudicial Penal Powers of Ecclesiastical Superiors, X-144 pp., 1941.
128. FARRELL, REV. BENJAMIN FRANCIS, M.A., S.T.L., J.C.D., The Rights and Duties of the Local Ordinary Regarding Congregations of Women Religious of Pontifical Approval, V-195 pp., 1941.
129. FEENEY, REV. THOMAS JOHN, A.B., S.T.L., J.C.D., Restitutio in Integrum, VI-169 pp., 1941.
130. FINDLAY, REV. STEPHEN WILLIAM, O.S.B., A.B., J.C.D., Canonical Norms Governing the Deposition and Degradation of Clerics, XVII-279 pp., 1941.

131. Goodwine, Rev. John, A.B., S.T.L., J.C.D., The Right of the Church to Acquire Property, VIII-119 pp., 1941.
132. Heston, Rev. Edward Louis, C.S.C., Ph.D., S.T.D., J.C.D., The Alienation of Church Property in the United States, XII-222 pp., 1941.
133. Hogan, Rev. James John, A.B., S.T.L., J.C.D., Judicial Advocates and Procurators, XIII-200 pp., 1941.
134. Kealy, Rev. Thomas M., A.B., Litt.B., J.C.D., Dowry of Women Religious, IX-152 pp., 1941.
135. Keene, Rev. Michael James, O.S.B., J.C.D., Religious Ordinaries and Canon 198, V-164 pp., 1942.
136. Kerin, Rev. Charles A., S.S., M.A., S.T.B., J.C.D., The Privation of Christian Burial, XVI-279 pp., 1941.
137. Louis, Rev. William Francis, M.A., J.C.D., Diocesan Archives, X-101 pp., 1941.
138. McDevitt, Rev. Gilbert Joseph, A.B., J.C.D., Legitimacy and Legitimation, X-247 pp., 1941.
139. McDonough, Rev. Thomas Joseph, A.B., J.C.D., Apostolic Administrators, X-217 pp., 1941.
140. Meier, Rev. Carl Anthony, A.B., J.C.D., Penal Administrative Procedure Against Negligent Pastors, XI-240 pp., 1941.
141. Schmidt, Rev. John Rogg, A.B., J.C.D., The Principles of Authentic Interpretation in Canon 17 of the Code of Canon Law, XII-331 pp., 1941.
142. Slafkosky, Rev. Andrew Leonard, A.B., J.C.D., The Canonical Episcopal Visitation of the Diocese, X-197 pp., 1941.
143. Swoboda, Rev. Innocent Robert, O.F.M., J.C.D., Ignorance in Relation to the Imputability of Delicts, IX-271 pp., 1941.
144. Dubé, Rev. Arthur Joseph, A.B., J.C.D., The General Principles for the Reckoning of Time in Canon Law, VIII-299 pp., 1941.
145. McBride, Rev. James T., A.B., J.C.D., Incardination and Excardination of Seculars, XX-585 pp., 1941.
146. Król, Rev. John T., J.C.D., The Defendant in Ecclesiastical Trials, XII-207 pp., 1942.
147. Comyns, Rev. Joseph J., C.SS.R., A.B., J.C.D., Papal and Episcopal Administration of Church Property, XIV-155 pp., 1942.
148. Barry, Rev. Garrett Francis, O.M.I., J.C.D., Violation of the Cloister, XII-260 pp., 1942.
149. Bolduc, Rev. Gatien, C.S.V., A.B., S.T.L., J.C.D., Les Études dans les Religions Cléricales, VIII-155 pp., 1942.
150. Boyle, Rev. David John, M.A., J.C.D., The Juridic Effects of Moral Certitude on Pre-Nuptial Guarantees, XII-188 pp., 1942.
151. Canavan, Rev. Walter Joseph, M.A., Litt.D., J.C.D., The Profession of Faith, XII-143 pp., 1942.
152. Desrochers, Rev. Bruno, A.B., Ph.L., S.T.B., J.C.D., Le Premier Concile Plénier de Québec et le Code de Droit Canonique, XIV-186 pp., 1942.

153. Dillon, Rev. Robert Edward, A.B., J.C.D., Common Law Marriage, X-148 pp., 1942.
154. Dodwell, Rev. Edward John, Ph.D., S.T.B., J.C.D., The Time and Place for the Celebration of Marriage, X-156 pp., 1942.
155. Donnellan, Rev. Thomas Andrew, A.B., J.C.D., The Obligation of the Missa pro Populo, VII-131 pp., 1942.
156. Eltz, Rev. Louis Anthony, A.B., J.C.D., Cooperation in Crime, XII-208 pp., 1942.
157. Gass, Rev. Sylvester Francis, M.A., J.C.D., Ecclesiastical Pensions, XI-206 pp., 1942.
158. Guiniven, Rev. John Joseph, C.SS.R., J.C.D., The Precept of Hearing Mass, XIV-188 pp., 1942.
159. Gulczynski, Rev. John Theophilus, J.C.D., The Desecration and Violation of Churches, X-126 pp., 1942.
160. Hammill, Rev. John Leo, M.A., J.C.D., The Obligations of the Traveler According to Canon 14, VIII-204 pp., 1942.
161. Haydt, Rev. John Joseph, A.B., J.C.D., Reserved Benefices, XI-148 pp., 1942.
162. Huser, Rev. Roger John, O.F.M., A.B., J.C.D., The Crime of Abortion in Canon Law, XII-187 pp., 1942.
163. Kearney, Rev. Francis Patrick, A.B., S.T.L., J.C.D., The Principles of Canon 1127, X-162 pp., 1942.
164. Linahen, Rev. Leo James, S.T.L., J.C.D., De Absolutione Complicis in Peccato Turpi, V-114 pp., 1942.
165. McCloskey, Rev. Joseph Aloysius, A.B., J.C.D., The Subject of Ecclesiastical Law According to Canon 12, XVII-246 pp., 1942.
166. O'Neill, Rev. Francis Joseph, C.SS.R., J.C.D., The Dismissal of Religious in Temporary Vows, XIII-220 pp., 1942.
167. Prince, Rev. John Edward, A.B., S.T.B., J.C.D., The Diocesan Chancellor, X-136 pp., 1942.
168. Riesner, Rev. Albert Joseph, C.SS.R., J.C.D., Apostates and Fugitives from Religious Institutes, IX-168 pp., 1942.
169. Stenger, Rev. Joseph Bernard, J.C.D., The Mortgaging of Church Property, 186 pp., 1942.
170. Waldron, Rev. Joseph Francis, A.B., J.C.D., The Minister of Baptism, XII-197 pp., 1942.
171. Willett, Rev. Robert Albert, J.C.D., The Probative Value of Documents in Ecclesiastical Trials, X-124 pp., 1942.
172. Woeber, Rev. Edward Martin, M.A., J.C.D., The Interpellations, XII-161 pp., 1942.
173. Benko, Rev. Matthew Aloysius, O.S.B., M.A., J.C.D., The Abbot *Nullius*, XVI-148 pp., 1943.
174. Christ, Rev. Joseph James, M.A., S.T.L., J.C.D., Dispensation from Vindicative Penalties, XIV-285 pp., 1943.

175. Clancy, Rev. Patrick M. J., O.P., A.B., S.T.Lr., J.C.D., The Local Religious Superior, X-229 pp., 1943.
176. Clarke, Rev. Thomas James, J.C.D., Parish Societies, XII-147 pp., 1943.
177. Connolly, Rev. John Patrick, S.T.L., J.C.D., Synodal Examiners and Parish Priest Consultors, X-223 pp., 1943.
178. Drumm, Rev. William Martin, A.B., J.C.D., Hospital Chaplains, XII-175 pp., 1943.
179. Flanagan, Rev. Bernard Joseph, A.B., S.T.L., J.C.D., The Canonical Erection of Religious Houses, X-147 pp., 1943.
180. Kelleher, Rev. Stephen Joseph, A.B., S.T.B., J.C.D., Discussions with Non-Catholics: Canonical Legislation, X-93 pp., 1943.
181. Lewis, Rev. Gordian, C.P., J.C.D., Chapters in Religious Institutes, XII-169 pp., 1943.
182. Marx, Rev. Adolph, J.C.D., The Declaration of Nullity of Marriages Contracted Outside the Church, X-151 pp., 1943.
183. Matulenas, Rev. Raymond Anthony, O.S.B., A.B., J.C.D., Communication, a Source of Privileges, XII-225 pp., 1943.
184. O'Leary, Rev. Charles Gerard, C.SS.R., J.C.D., Religious Dismissed After Perpetual Profession, X-213 pp., 1943.
185. Power, Rev. Cornelius Michael, J.C.D., The Blessing of Cemeteries, XII-231 pp., 1943.
186. Shuhler, Rev. Ralph Vincent, O.S.A., J.C.D., Privileges of Religious to Absolve and Dispense, XII-195 pp., 1943.
187. Ziolkowski, Rev. Thaddeus Stanislaus, A.B., J.C.D., The Consecration and Blessing of Churches, XII-151 pp., 1943.
188. Heneghan, Rev. John Joseph, S.T.D., J.C.D., The Marriages of Unworthy Catholics: Canons 1065 and 1066, XVI-213 pp., 1944.
189. Carroll, Rev. Coleman Francis, M.A., S.T.L., J.C.L., Charitable Institutions.
190. Ciesluk, Rev. Joseph Edward, Ph.B., S.T.L., J.C.L., National Parishes in the United States.
191. Coburn, Rev. Vincent Paul, A.B., J.C.D., Marriages of Conscience, XII-172 pp., 1944.
192. Connors, Rev. Charles Paul, C.S.Sp., A.B., J.C.D., Extra-Judicial Procurators in the Code of Canon Law, X-94 pp., 1944.
193. Coyle, Rev. Paul Raymond, A.B., J.C.D., Judicial Exceptions, X-142 pp., 1944.
194. Fair, Rev. Bartholomew Francis, A.B., S.T.L., J.C.D., The Impediment of Abduction, XII-122 pp., 1944.
195. Gallagher, Rev. Thomas Raphael, O.P., A.B., S.T.Lr., J.C.D., The Examination of the Qualities of the Ordinand, X-166 pp., 1944.
196. Gannon, Rev. John Mark, S.T.L., J.C.D., The Interstices Required for the Promotion to Orders, XII-100 pp., 1944.

197. Goldsmith, Rev. J. William, B.C.S., S.T.L., J.C.D., The Competence of Church and State Over Marriages—Disputed Points, X-128 pp., 1944.
198. Goodwine, Rev. Joseph Gerard, A.B., S.T.B., J.C.D., The Reception of Converts, XIV-326 pp., 1944.
199. Kowalski, Rev. Romuald Eugene, O.F.M., A.B., J.C.D., Sustenance of Religious Houses of Regulars, X-174 pp., 1944.
200. McCoy, Rev. Alan Edward, O.F.M., J.C.D., Force and Fear in Relation to Delictual Imputability and Penal Responsibility, XII-160 pp., 1944.
201. McDevitt, Rev. Vincent John, Ph.B., S.T.L., J.C.L., Perjury.
202. Martin, Rev. Thomas Owen, Ph.D., S.T.D., J.C.D., Adverse Possession, Prescription and Limitation of Actions: The Canonical "Praescriptio," XX-208 pp., 1944.
203. Miklosovic, Rev. Paul John, A.B., J.C.L., Attempted Marriages and Their Consequent Juridic Effects.
204. Mundy, Rev. Thomas Maurice, A.B., S.T.L., J.C.D., The Union of Parishes, X-164 pp., 1944.
205. O'Dea, Rev. John Coyle, A.B., J.C.D., The Matrimonial Impediment of Nonage, VIII-126 pp., 1944.
206. Olalia, Rev. Alexander Ayson, S.T.L., J.C.D., A Comparative Study of the Christian Constitution of States and the Constitution of the Philippine Commonwealth, XII-136 pp., 1944.
207. Poisson, Rev. Pierre-Marie, C.S.C., A.B., Ph.L., Th.L., J.C.L., Droits Patrimoniaux des Maisons et des Eglises Religieuses.
208. Stadalnikas, Rev. Casimir Joseph, M.I.C., J.C.D., Reservation of Censures, X-141 pp., 1944.
209. Sullivan, Rev. Eugene Henry, S.T.L., J.C.D., Proof of the Reception of the Sacraments, X-165 pp., 1944.
210. Vaughan, Rev. William Edward, J.C.D., Constitutions for Diocesan Courts, X-210 pp., 1944.
211. Paro, Rev. Gino, S.T.D., J.C.L., The Right of Apostolic Legation.
212. Balzer, Rev. Ralph Francis, C.P., J.C.D., The Computation of Time in a Canonical Novitiate, X-227 pp., 1945.
213. Dougherty, Rev. John Whelan, A.B., S.T.L., J.C.L., De Inquisitione Speciali.
214. Dziob, Rev. Michael Walter, J.C.L., The Sacred Congregation for the Oriental Church.
215. Eidenschink, Rev. John Albert, O.S.B., B.A., J.C.D., The Election of Bishops in the Letters of Pope Gregory the Great, VIII-200 pp., 1945.
216. Gill, Rev. Nicholas, C.P., J.C.L., The Spiritual Prefect in Clerical Religious Houses of Study.
217. Hynes, Rev. Harry Gerard, S.T.L., J.C.D., The Privileges of Cardinals, XII-183 pp., 1945.
218. McDevitt, Rev. Gerald Vincent, S.T.L., J.C.D., The Renunciation of an Ecclesiastical Office, XIV-179 pp., 1945.

219. Manning, Rev. Joseph Leroy, J.C.D., The Free Conferral of Offices, VII-116 pp., 1945.
220. Meyer, Rev. Louis G., O.S.B., A.B., S.T.B., J.C.D., Alms-gathering by Religious, XII-163 pp., 1945.
221. O'Donnell, Rev. Cletus Francis, M.A., J.C.L., The Marriage of Minors.
222. Prunskis, Rev. Joseph, J.C.D., Comparative Law, Ecclesiastical and Civil, in Lithuanian Concordat, X-161 pp., 1945.
223. Sweeney, Rev. Francis Patrick, C.SS.R., J.C.D., The Reduction of Clerics to the Lay State, X-199 pp., 1945.
224. Vogelpohl, Rev. Henry John, J.C.L., The Simple Impediments to Holy Orders.
225. Brockhaus, Rev. Thomas Aquinas, O.S.B., J.C.L., Religious who are known as *Conversi.*
226. Griese, Rev. Orville Nicholas, S.T.D., J.C.L., Marriage and the Procreation of Offspring.
227. Boudreaux, Rev. Warren Louis, J.C.L., The *"ab acatholicis nati"* of Canon 1099, § 2.
228. Bowe, Rev. Thomas Joseph, A.B., J.C.L., Religious Superioresses.
229. Diederichs, Rev. Michael Ferdinand, S.C.J., J.C.L., The Jurisdiction of the Latin Ordinaries over their Oriental Subjects.
230. Dingman, Rev. Maurice John, A.B., S.T.L., J.C.L., The Plaintiff in Contentious Trials.
231. Frison, Rev. Basil, C.M.F., M.Mus., J.C.L., The Retroactivity of Law.
232. Galvin, Rev. William Anthony, M.A., J.C.L., The Administrative Transfer of Pastors.
233. Goracy, Rev. Joseph C., J.C.L., The Diriment Matrimonial Impediment of Major Orders.
234. Hale, Rev. Joseph Francis, M.A., S.T.L., J.C.L., The Pastor of Burial.
235. Henry, Rev. Joseph Arthur, A.B., J.C.L., The Mass and Holy Communion: Interritual Law.
236. Linenberger, Rev. Herbert, C.PP.S., J.C.L., The False Denunciation of an Innocent Confessor.
237. Lowry, Rev. James Martin, A.B., J.C.L., Dispensation from Private Vows.
238. Lynch, Rev. George Edward, A.B., S.T.L., J.C.L., Coadjutors and Auxiliaries of Bishops.
239. Lynch, Rev. Timothy, M.S.SS.T., J.C.L., Contracts between Bishops and Religious Congregations.
240. McClunn, Rev. Justin David, A.B., S.T.L., J.C.L., Administrative Recourse.
241. McGarvey, Rev. Thomas Joseph, A.B., S.T.L., J.C.L., Bination.
242. McGrath, Rev. James, A.B., J.C.L., The Privilege of the Canon.
243. Marbach, Rev. Joseph Francis, A.B., J.C.L., Marriage Legislation for the Catholics of the Oriental Rites in the United States and Canada.

244. SHIMKUS, REV. BERNARD ALOYSIUS, A.B., J.C.L., The Determination and Transfer of Rite.

245. SMITH, REV. VINCENT MICHAEL, A.B., S.T.L., J.C.L., Ignorance Affecting Matrimonial Consent.

246. WACHTRLE, REV. PAUL ANTHONY, A.B., J.C.L., The Baptism of the Children of Non-Catholics.

www.ingramcontent.com/pod-product-compliance
Lightning Source LLC
LaVergne TN
LVHW050231080826
844660LV00012B/516

* 9 7 8 0 8 1 3 2 2 3 7 7 3 *